50 Ways to Win at Chess

Steve Giddins

First published in the UK by Gambit Publications Ltd 2007

ISBN-13: 978-1-904600-85-5
ISBN-10: 1-904600-85-9

DISTRIBUTION:
Worldwide (except USA): Central Books Ltd, 99 Wallis Rd, London E9 5LN, England.
Tel +44 (0)20 8986 4854 Fax +44 (0)20 8533 5821. E-mail: orders@Centralbooks.com

Gambit Publications Ltd, 99 Wallis Rd, London E9 5LN, England.
E-mail: info@gambitbooks.com
Website (regularly updated): www.gambitbooks.com

Edited by Graham Burgess
Typeset by John Nunn
Cover image by Wolff Morrow
Printed in Great Britain by The Cromwell Press, Trowbridge, Wilts.

10 9 8 7 6 5 4 3 2 1

Gambit Publications Ltd
Managing Director: Murray Chandler GM
Chess Director: Dr John Nunn GM
Editorial Director: Graham Burgess FM
German Editor: Petra Nunn WFM
Webmaster: Dr Helen Milligan WFM

Contents

Symbols 5
Preface 6

1 Attack and Defence 7

1: **Hodgson – Hebden**, *London 1986*   Trompowsky 8
2: **Gheorghiu – W. Watson**, *London 1980*   King's Indian 11
3: **Vasiukov – Van Wely**, *Moscow 2002*   Sicilian, 4 ♕xd4 14
4: **Adams – Topalov**, *Wijk aan Zee 2006*   Sicilian, Scheveningen 17
5: **Wells – Emms**, *Southend 2000*   English 20
6: **Topalov – Kasparov**, *Amsterdam 1995*   Sicilian, English Attack 23
7: **Gelfand – Short**, *Brussels Ct. (8) 1991*   QGD, Exchange 26
8: **Lilienthal – V. Ragozin**, *Moscow 1935*   Nimzo-Indian 31

2 Opening Play 35

9: **Salov – M. Gurevich**, *Leningrad 1987*   Nimzo-Indian 36
10: **Aronian – I. Sokolov**, *Wijk aan Zee 2006* Slav 39
11: **Ribli – Pomar**, *Buenos Aires Ol. 1978*   Réti 43
12: **J. Littlewood – Horner**, *Manchester 1980* King's Indian Attack 45

3 Structures 48

13: **I. Watson – Nunn**, *British Ch 1980*   Modern Benoni 49
14: **Penrose – Tal**, *Leipzig Ol. 1960*   Modern Benoni 52
15: **G. Kuzmin – T. Georgadze**, *Odessa 1972*   Benko 55
16: **Browne – Alburt**, *USA Ch 1983*   Benko 59
17: **R. O'Kelly – Penrose**, *England 1978*   Czech Benoni 62
18: **Summerscale – Snape**, *Coulsdon 2002*   King's Indian 64
19: **Cheparinov – Stellwagen**, *Amsterdam 2005* King's Indian 67
20: **Timman – Tal**, *Tallinn 1973*   King's Indian/Benoni 70
21: **Ehlvest – Novik**, *St Petersburg 1994*   King's Indian 73
22: **Pilnik – Geller**, *Interzonal, Gothenburg 1955* Sicilian, Boleslavsky 76
23: **Sokolsky – N.P. Andreev**, *USSR corr. Ch 1960-3* Sokolsky 79
24: **Stanec – Beliavsky**, *Graz 1996*   Nimzo-Indian 82
25: **I. Sokolov – Khalifman**, *Pardubice 1994* Semi-Slav 84
26: **Chernin – Van der Sterren**, *Amsterdam 1980* English 87
27: **Andersson – Seirawan**, *London 1982*   English 90
28: **Nikolić – Paunović**, *Yugoslav Ch 1983*   Semi-Slav 94

4 Thematic Endings 97

29: **Ribli – Karpov**, *Amsterdam 1980*   Catalan 98
30: **Uhlmann – Gligorić**, *Hastings 1970/1*   King's Indian 101

31: **D. Howell – Kramnik**, *London 2002*   Ruy Lopez   104
32: **Kosteniuk – P.H. Nielsen**, *Hastings 2002/3*   Caro-Kann   108
33: **Sveshnikov – Novikov**, *USSR Rapid Cup 1988*   Sicilian, 2 c3   112

5 Other Aspects of Strategy   **115**

34: **Fischer – Uhlmann**, *Buenos Aires 1960*   French   116
35: **Dorfman – Bronstein**, *USSR Ch 1975*   Old Indian   120
36: **Mamedyarov – Brodsky**, *Russian Clubs Ch 2006*   Queen's Pawn   123
37: **T. Bennett – Keene**, *England 1970*   Modern   126
38: **Kramnik – Vaganian**, *Horgen 1995*   Queen's Indian   128
39: **Lilienthal – Botvinnik**, *USSR Ch 1940*   Queen's Indian   131
40: **P. Johansson – Giddins**, *Gausdal 1995*   Bogo-Indian   134
41: **Petrosian – Gheorghiu**, *Moscow 1967*   English Opening   137
42: **Carlsen – Vescovi**, *Wijk aan Zee 2006*   Sicilian, Taimanov   140
43: **Stein – Spassky**, *USSR Ch 1962*   Ruy Lopez   143

6 Endgame Themes   **146**

44: **Miles – Larsen**, *Tilburg 1978*   Queen's Indian   147
45: **L'Ami – Mamedyarov**, *World Junior Ch 2005*   Ruy Lopez   150
46: **Kramnik – Leko**, *Dortmund 2006*   Nimzo-Indian   155
47: **Djurhuus – Sargissian**, *Turin Ol. 2006*   Ruy Lopez   158
48: **Bronstein – Alexander**, *Hastings 1953/4*   Dutch   161

7 Psychology in Action   **166**

49: **M. Gurevich – Short**, *Interzonal, Manila 1990*   French   167
50: **Kasparov – Karpov**, *Seville World Ch (24) 1987*   Réti   170

Index of Players   174
Index of Openings   175

Symbols

+	check
++	double check
#	checkmate
!!	brilliant move
!	good move
!?	interesting move
?!	dubious move
?	bad move
??	blunder
Ch	championship
corr.	correspondence game
1-0	the game ends in a win for White
½-½	the game ends in a draw
0-1	the game ends in a win for Black
(D)	see next diagram

Preface

My book *50 Essential Chess Lessons* (henceforth referred to as '*50ECL*') was published by Gambit Publications in January 2006. As the Preface to that book explains, it was modelled on Irving Chernev's old classic *The Most Instructive Games of Chess Ever Played*, and aimed to present a more modern selection of highly instructive positional games, annotated primarily with words, rather than variations. I felt that such a book would appeal to the average club player, and prove a useful positional handbook.

The overall reaction to *50ECL* was very positive, and the present volume is effectively a follow-up. As with its predecessor volume, this book presents 50 highly instructive games, illustrating various aspects of positional play. Once again, the games are grouped in chapters dealing with specific subjects, which I hope will make it easier for readers who wish to study a specific aspect of the game to do so.

The subjects covered are in some cases the same as those in *50ECL*, such as attack and defence, pawn-structures, etc. However, in this volume, I have in most cases concentrated on different aspects of each of those subjects, so that the two books will complement each other, rather than covering the same ground. In the Pawn Structure chapter, for example, *50ECL* gave three examples of the King's Indian Defence, each covering a different type of pawn-structure reached from that opening. The present volume includes another half-dozen examples, each of which shows a slightly different structure. I hope that the reader who goes in detail through all of the King's Indian games from the two books, should by the end have a good grasp of the basics of King's Indian pawn-structures.

This book also deals with some subjects which were not covered in *50ECL*, such as opening play, and the psychological issues involved in playing games where a specific result is important. Inevitably, there is only sufficient space to scratch the surface of such topics, but I hope that the material presented will nonetheless prove useful and instructive.

Finally, just as with *50ECL*, I have again tried to avoid presenting too many very well known games, so I hope that the reader will find many highly interesting and unfamiliar masterpieces in this book.

Steve Giddins
Rochester
September 2007

Acknowledgements

As always, thanks are due to Graham Burgess and the Gambit team, for their excellent production work. This book is dedicated to John B, for 20 years of beer, curry, music, and loyal friendship.

1 Attack and Defence

Attacking the king is the most obvious and fundamental way to win a game of chess. In *50ECL*, we looked at three examples of kingside attacks, one with the defending king in the centre, one with same-side castling, and one with opposite-side castling. In the present volume, we look at six more successful kingside attacks.

As emphasized in *50ECL*, the essential element in any successful attack is to bring more firepower to the relevant sector of the board, so as to overwhelm the defences. Frequently, this involves the attacker exploiting an advantage in development, as we see in Games 1 and 2 here. Having caught the defender napping as it were, it is vital to maintain the initiative, operating the whole time with new threats, so as to deprive the defender of chances to bring more pieces into the defence.

Where the kings have castled on opposite sides, speed is also of the essence. The game typically develops into a race between the opposing attacks, so it is vital to prosecute one's own attack with maximum speed, although this does not mean totally ignoring essential defensive steps on the other flank. The ability to blend attack and defence in the correct measure is frequently what makes the difference between success and failure in such positions.

The corollary to attack is defence. The latter tends to receive much less attention, chiefly because most players understandably prefer to attack than defend. Nonetheless, good defence is an essential part of being a strong player, and all of the great players have been fine defenders. In the two examples of successful defence presented here, we see Black survive positions which are objectively inferior, even demonstrably lost. In such cases, the defender must just concentrate on making his opponent's task as difficult as possible, in the hope that the pressure of finding the best way to finish the game off will eventually induce an error.

Game 1
Julian Hodgson – Mark Hebden
Lloyds Bank Masters, London 1986
Trompowsky Attack

This is an illustration of the dangers involved in getting one's king trapped in the centre of the board. Having gained the bishop-pair early on, Black seeks to open the position, but neglects his development in the process. As a result, White is able to sacrifice material to trap the enemy king in the centre, where it falls victim to a withering attack.

1 d4 ♘f6 2 ♗g5

This move characterizes the Trompowsky Attack, named after a minor Brazilian master who played and analysed it. Until the 1980s, it was firmly a theoretical backwater, very rarely seen in master chess, but then it was taken up by various Spanish and English players, most notably Julian Hodgson. He moulded the 'Tromp' into a very dangerous weapon, as the present game illustrates, and won numerous games with it. Eventually, the theory developed and reliable defensive methods were found for Black, and nowadays the Tromp remains a useful way to avoid main lines, but not especially dangerous.

2...♘e4

This is possibly Black's most principled reply, avoiding White's threat to capture on f6, doubling Black's pawns. Other approaches for Black include 2...e6, when White usually takes the centre at the cost of the bishop-pair by 3 e4 h6 4 ♗xf6, and 2...d5, which argues that taking on f6 is not really much of a threat anyway. There is no widespread consensus which defence is best, although one Trompowsky author, GM Joe Gallagher, has written that he would employ the opening more often as White if fewer opponents replied 2...d5.

3 h4?! *(D)*

This is an extravagant but rather dubious move, which became a Hodgson speciality for a while. White invites his opponent to capture on g5, hoping that the open h-file will prove a sufficient attacking weapon to counterbalance the bishop-pair and White's damaged pawn-structure. The more usual moves are 3 ♗h4 and 3 ♗f4, with the latter being accepted by almost all authorities as the best.

3...d5

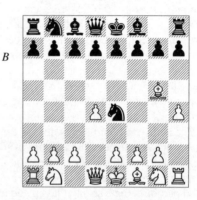

Since this position has not been widely tested at top GM level, it is hard to know which line is best for Black, but in this game, things go wrong for him very quickly. The move 3...c5 looks respectable, when White should probably go in for a speculative pawn sacrifice by 4 d5 ♕b6 5 ♘d2 ♘xg5 6 hxg5 ♕xb2 7 e4. White has some compensation for the pawn, but it is not clear if it is really enough.

4 ♘d2 ♘xg5 5 hxg5 e5?!

This looks rather too optimistic. Black hopes that opening the game will favour his bishop-pair, but the result is that his queen loses too much time, and he soon falls fatally behind in development. 5...♗f5 is a solid move, which has the added benefit that the bishop defends the g6- and h7-squares, thereby removing the possible threat of White playing g6, and freeing his rook from the obligation to defend the pawn on h7.

6 dxe5 ♕xg5 7 ♘gf3 ♕d8 8 e4! *(D)*

An excellent move. White has a lead in development, which in itself is a transitory thing. White needs to capitalize on it before Black can catch up, after which he could stand better because of his two bishops and better pawn-structure. Consequently, White strikes immediately in the centre, notwithstanding the fact that

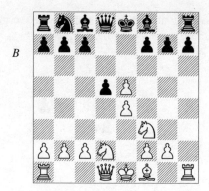

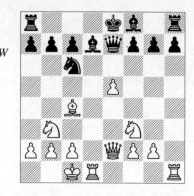

opening the position may itself favour the bishops. This dilemma is one which American IM John Watson has written about instructively. Since gaining the bishop-pair frequently comes at the cost of some lag in development, the opening phase often sees the player with the bishops trying to keep the position closed, whilst his opponent tries to open it, to exploit his superior development.

8...♘c6

After 8...dxe4 9 ♘xe4 ♕xd1+ 10 ♖xd1, White's large lead in development would count for more than his weak e-pawn and Black's bishop-pair. Similarly, trying to keep the position closed by 8...d4 also gives White a strong initiative, after 9 ♘b3 c5 10 ♕d2 followed by 11 0-0-0.

9 exd5 ♕xd5 10 ♗c4

Just as at move 7, White develops with tempo, thanks to the exposed black queen.

10...♕c5 11 ♕e2!

This is the key to White's plan. He intends to trap the black king in the centre. It is clear that castling kingside is hardly feasible for Black in view of the open h-file, so his aim must be to castle queenside. However, the weakness of the f7-pawn prevents him from doing so in time, since in due course, White will castle queenside himself, after which his rook on the open d-file will prevent Black from castling.

11...♗f5

If Black tries to block the d-file by 11...♗d7, the reply 12 ♘g5 is extremely strong. Black therefore places the bishop on f5, so that a later ♘g5 can be met by ...♗g6, defending f7.

12 ♘b3 ♕e7 13 0-0-0 ♗d7 *(D)*

The critical moment. White has mobilized all of his pieces (the open h-file means that the rook on h1 can certainly be considered to be

developed), whilst Black is still uncastled, and his kingside pieces are undeveloped. However, with his last move, he prepares 14...0-0-0, after which he would be able to untangle his kingside. If he is allowed to do this, he might even stand better, because of his bishop-pair. It is therefore imperative that White strike while the iron is hot, so as to exploit his temporary lead in development.

14 e6! fxe6 *(D)*

If 14...♗xe6, 15 ♖he1 would leave Black terribly tied up (15...♗xc4?? 16 ♕xc4 costs him his queen).

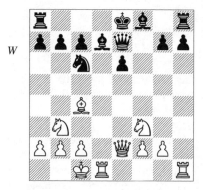

15 ♖xd7!

The key follow-up to his previous move. Now the black king is forced into the centre, where it comes under the combined fire of White's remaining pieces.

15...♔xd7 *(D)*

15...♔xd7 16 ♗xe6 ♕e7 17 ♖e1 leaves Black defenceless, because the natural 17...♕d6 loses in spectacular fashion to 18 ♗f7++! ♔xf7 (18...♔d8 19 ♕e8#) 19 ♕c4+ ♔f6 20 ♘c5!, when the threats of ♘e4+ and ♖e6+ are lethal, since 20...♕xc5 21 ♕e6# is mate. It should not be thought that such variations are just luck on

White's part. On the contrary, they arise very logically from the position. Although nominally Black is an exchange ahead, his two rooks and bishop are all out of the game, so that in the area of the board where it matters, White has far more firepower in action than does Black. Add to that the open central lines towards the black king, and it is no surprise that he has no adequate defence.

16 ♗b5!

16 ♖d1+ is also very strong, but the text-move is better still. White now threatens 17 ♘e5+.

16...♚e8

16...a6 17 ♘e5+ is hopeless for Black, as also is 16...♚c8 17 ♗xc6 bxc6 18 ♕a6+.

17 ♘bd4

Another white piece joins the attack. The way in which White's initiative flows is typical of such positions.

17...♖d8

This is despair, giving back the exchange, without in any real way diminishing the force of White's attack. However, it is impossible to suggest anything better. Both c6 and e6 hang, and if the king tries to run with 17...♚f7, White has the hammer-blow 18 ♘xe6!. Then 18...♕xe6 loses to 19 ♘g5+, whilst in the meantime, White has threats of ♘fg5+, etc. There is simply no defence.

18 ♗xc6+ bxc6 19 ♘xc6 ♕f6 20 ♘xd8 ♚xd8

Giving back the sacrificed material has not eased Black's plight. His kingside remains undeveloped, his pawns are broken, and his monarch is wandering around in the midst of the storm, like Shakespeare's King Lear.

21 ♕b5 (D)

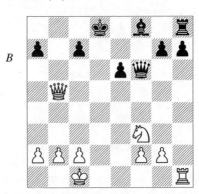

Hodgson continues to maintain his initiative. This move has the point of preventing Black from developing his kingside, since if 21...♗d6, White wins a rook after 22 ♕b8+. Meanwhile, 22 ♖d1+ is the chief threat.

21...♕f4+ 22 ♚b1 ♕d6 23 ♘g5

Relentless. New threats appear from all sides, exactly the way in which an initiative flows. Now ♘f7+ is threatened, whilst 23...♚e7 walks into the firing line again after 24 ♖e1.

23...♕d7 24 ♕b8+ ♚e7 25 ♕xa7

Now White even has a material advantage to go with everything else.

25...h6 26 ♕a3+ ♚f6 27 ♘e4+ ♚f7 28 ♕f3+ ♚g8 29 ♖d1 ♕e8 30 ♕g3

White keeps up the never-ending threats. Now both ♘f6+ and ♕xc7 are threatened.

30...♕f7 31 ♖d7! ♕f5

If 31...♗e7, finally developing the bishop, it is lost to a pin after 32 ♕xc7.

32 f3

Rather sadistically inviting Black to find a move that doesn't lose instantly.

32...c5 33 a4 h5 34 ♘d6 ♕d5 35 ♘e8! ♕e5?

Dropping the queen, but 35...♕xd7 36 ♘f6+ does likewise, and other moves do not defend g7.

36 ♕xe5 1-0

Note that in the final position, Black's king's rook and king's bishop still remain undeveloped!

Game 2

Florin Gheorghiu – William Watson

Lloyds Bank Masters, London 1980

King's Indian Defence, Sämisch Variation

This is another case where a king finds itself trapped in the centre of the board, and subjected to a ferocious assault. It is all the more striking for the fact that the white player was at the time a world-class grandmaster, whilst his opponent was a relatively unknown junior. As the notes below reveal, the game was responsible for Watson acquiring a memorable nickname.

1 d4 ♘f6 2 c4 g6 3 ♘c3 ♗g7 4 e4 0-0

A slightly unusual and provocative move-order. Instead of the standard 4...d6, Black castles immediately, tempting his opponent to push on in the centre by 5 e5. However, this is probably not a good idea, especially when followed by further space-grabbing; the white centre is liable to become overstretched after 5...♘e8 6 f4 d6. The classic game Letelier-Fischer, Leipzig Olympiad 1960 is an example of this. If White does not take up the challenge, the play usually transposes back into normal King's Indian variations, but there are also some cases where Black can try to benefit from not having played ...d6.

5 ♗e3

Gheorghiu was always a fan of the Sämisch Variation, which usually arises via 4...d6 5 f3. In the present move-order, 4...0-0 5 f3 gives Black an extra option of the immediate 5...c5, when 6 dxc5 b6 offers interesting compensation on the dark squares. Gheorghiu attempts to avoid this, hoping now for 5...d6 6 f3, transposing back into normal Sämisch lines, but Watson continues to seek more original paths.

5...♘c6!? (D)

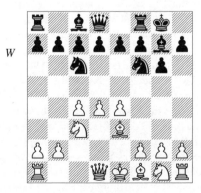

6 f3?!

Gheorghiu is adamant about achieving his beloved Sämisch, but this runs into a dynamic riposte. One attempt to exploit Black's move-order was 6 d5 ♘e5 7 h3, planning f4. If White can consolidate his space advantage and catch up in development, he will stand very well, and so Black would need to seek active play at an early stage. The position is rather unclear, but I suspect White should stand better, with accurate play.

6...e5 7 d5 ♘d4!

A thematic tactical idea in King's Indian positions. White cannot win a pawn by 8 ♗xd4 exd4 9 ♕xd4, in view of the reply 9...♘xe4! (10 ♕xe4? ♖e8).

8 ♘ge2 c5! (D)

Black continues to play with dynamism. Instead, exchanging on e2 would simply leave White standing better after 8...♘xe2 9 ♗xe2.

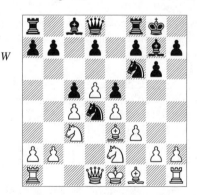

9 dxc6

Accepting the pawn sacrifice runs into a thunderbolt, so White should instead settle for quiet development. However, with his excellently-placed knight on d4, Black would clearly have won the opening battle, something Gheorghiu is reluctant to acknowledge. There is almost certainly a psychological factor at work here. At the time of this game, Gheorghiu was a grandmaster, not far from world class, whereas his opponent was a relatively unknown 18-year-old, rated over 300 points below him. As a result, it is to be expected that Gheorghiu's sense of danger would have been somewhat diminished. Had he been facing another 2600-rated GM, he would probably have taken Black's adventurous plan a little more seriously, and may not have walked into the full force of the attack.

9...dxc6 10 ♘xd4 exd4 11 ♗xd4 *(D)*

If instead 11 ♕xd4, Black would have excellent compensation after 11...♘d5! 12 ♕d2 ♘xe3 13 ♕xe3 f5. The dark squares in White's camp are seriously weakened, in the absence of his dark-squared bishop, whilst his development is still lagging.

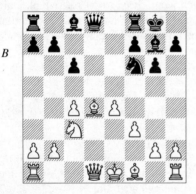

11...♘xe4!!

This is the real point of Black's play. The white king will be caught in the centre and subject to a furious attack.

12 ♗xg7

White has little choice, since 12 ♘xe4 ♗xd4 leaves him positionally busted, without any material investment by Black.

12...♕h4+ 13 g3

13 ♔e2? allows mate in two by 13...♕f2+ 14 ♔d3 ♘c5#, so the text-move is again forced.

13...♘xg3 *(D)*

The critical moment of the attack. White's last few moves have been forced, but now he has to take stock and try to find a way out. Materially, White has a piece extra, for just one pawn.

Taking on f8 is impossible, since 14 ♗xf8 ♘xh1+ 15 ♔d2 ♔xf8 regains the piece and

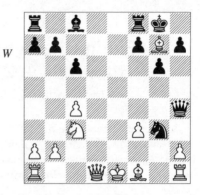

leaves Black with an extra pawn and a raging attack. Likewise, 14 hxg3 loses to 14...♕xg3+! 15 ♔d2 ♖d8+ 16 ♘d5 (16 ♗d3 ♗f5 is no better) 16...♔xg7, when the best White can manage is an ending two pawns down after 17 ♕e1 ♕xe1+ 18 ♖xe1 cxd5.

Another try is 14 ♕d4, but this also goes down in flames. Black continues 14...♖e8+ 15 ♗e2 (15 ♔d1 ♖d8 16 ♘d5 ♕xd4+ 17 ♗xd4 ♘xh1 and Black regains the material with interest) 15...♘e4+ 16 ♔d1 ♘xc3+ 17 ♕xc3 ♗f5!, threatening 18...♖ad8+. White cannot stop this by 18 ♗f6, since Black carries on regardless: 18...♖ad8+! 19 ♗xd8 ♖xd8+ 20 ♔c1 ♕f4+ and mate next move.

Faced with this Hobson's Choice, Gheorghiu tries a tactic of his own, but it is insufficient.

14 ♗f6!?

Trying to deflect the queen from the discovered check.

14...♖e8+ 15 ♘e4 *(D)*

Once again, the alternatives are no better, but are worth examining, since the variations illustrate the way the attack flows. After 15 ♔d2, 15...♕f4+ followed by 16...♘xh1 is good enough, but 15...♕xf6 is also decisive; e.g., 16 hxg3 ♗f5! 17 ♗d3 ♖ad8 18 ♘e4 ♕xb2+, and the attack is too strong. 15 ♘e2 is met by 15...♕xf6 16 hxg3 ♕xf3 17 ♖h2 ♕xg3+ 18 ♖f2 ♗g4, when there is no defence to the threat of 19...♖xe2+ and 20...♖e8. Finally, 15 ♗e2 can be met most simply by 15...♘xe2+ 16 ♗xh4 ♘xc3+ 17 ♔d2 ♘xd1 18 ♖axd1 ♗e6, when Black has regained his piece and has an extra pawn in the ending. The presence of opposite-coloured bishops gives White some hope of survival, although the fact that both pairs of rooks remain on the board gives Black excellent winning chances. Nonetheless, this line probably represents White's best chance of survival.

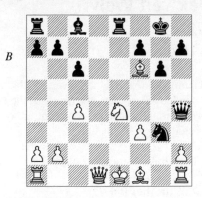

B

15...♖xe4+!

Watson continues to attack with savage fury. One can understand why Boris Spassky, after seeing this game, paid Watson the double-edged compliment of describing him as "very dangerous – like a drunken machine-gunner"!

16 fxe4 ♕xe4+ 17 ♔f2

17 ♔d2 ♘xh1 leaves Black two pawns up, with an overwhelming position. The text-move tempts Black with a whole rook with check, but in fact 17...♘xh1+?? would be a blunder; after 18 ♔g1, the threats of 19 ♕d8+, mating, and 19 ♗g2 would leave the tables having turned, and White with the advantage.

17...♗g4 18 ♕d3 ♘xh1+ 19 ♔g1 *(D)*

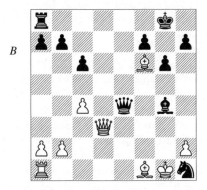

B

19...♘f2!!

The final trick, which Black needed to have foreseen some time ago. Now 20 ♔xf2 ♕f4+ regains the bishop on f6, with a winning advantage.

20 ♕g3 ♘d1 21 h3 ♗h5 22 b3 ♖e8 23 ♖c1 ♕e3+ 24 ♕xe3 ♘xe3

The outcome of Black's brilliant assault is an endgame where he has two extra pawns. White could already resign, but doubtless shell-shocked, Gheorghiu plays on for some time. The remainder requires little comment, other than to say that in such situations, Black should be ready to adjust his focus to the changed circumstances. One sometimes sees such endgames mishandled, because the player gets carried away by the excitement of the attack, and does not adjust in time to the fact that he is now playing an ending. Just as with all endings, the focus now should be on careful, methodical play, taking one's time, etc. Providing the player does this, there should be few problems winning such positions.

25 ♗d3 ♖e6 26 ♗g5 f6 27 ♗f4 ♔f7 28 b4 a6 29 b5 g5 30 ♗b8 ♗g6 31 bxa6 bxa6 32 ♗e2 ♘c2 33 ♔f2 ♘d4 34 ♗f1 ♗h5 35 ♖c3 c5 36 ♗a7 ♖e5 *(D)*

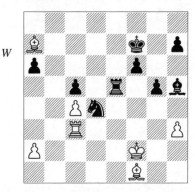

W

Black keeps his pieces active and gradually prepares the advance of his kingside pawns.

37 ♖a3 ♗e2

Simplification usually favours the stronger side in such endings. Rather than exchange bishops, Gheorghiu jettisons a whole piece, but the position is quite hopeless, and he could certainly have spared his opponent the remaining moves.

38 ♖xa6 ♖f5+ 39 ♔e3 ♗xf1 40 ♖a5 ♘e6 41 ♗b8 ♗xh3 42 a4 ♗g4 43 ♖a7+ ♔g6 44 a5 ♖f3+ 45 ♔d2 ♖a3 46 ♗d6 ♗f5 47 ♔c1 ♖c3+ 48 ♔b2 ♖xc4 49 ♗e7 ♗e4 50 ♖a6 ♔f5 0-1

Game 3
Evgeny Vasiukov – Loek van Wely
Moscow 2002
Sicilian Defence, 4 ♕xd4

In *50ECL*, we examined the game Averbakh-Sarvarov (Game 1), in which the players castled on opposite sides. In such positions, the standard technique is to launch a pawn-storm against the enemy king. The present game is another example, and sees a veteran Russian grandmaster pull off a brilliant sacrificial attack against a world-class opponent, some 40 years his junior.

1 e4 c5 2 ♘f3 d6 3 d4 cxd4 4 ♕xd4 *(D)*

This early queen capture has never been regarded as a major threat to Black, but it is a useful surprise weapon, to avoid the heavily-analysed main lines after 4 ♘xd4. The white queen takes up an active position in the centre, but in order to maintain it, White must be prepared to surrender the bishop-pair.

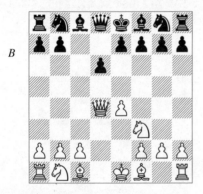

4...♘c6

This is the most principled response. However, Black can insist on removing the enemy queen from its powerful post, by first playing 4...a6 (or 4...♗d7), after which 5...♘c6 will follow. In that case, White will usually make use of the tempo to play 5 c4, establishing a Maróczy Bind formation.

5 ♗b5 ♗d7 6 ♗xc6 ♗xc6

The alternative recapture 6...bxc6 strengthens Black's pawn-centre, but after 7 c4, White is generally considered to retain a small advantage.

7 ♘c3 ♘f6 8 ♗g5 e6 9 0-0-0

Having surrendered the bishop-pair, White must play energetically to utilize his superior development. A slower plan, such as establishing the Maróczy formation by 7 c4, or castling

kingside in this position, would not be sufficiently challenging to Black.

9...♗e7 10 ♖he1 0-0 *(D)*

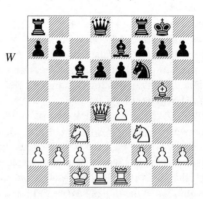

Once again, we have a position with opposite-side castling. Each side will advance his pawns against the enemy king, in the hope of opening lines for attack. Speed is a key factor in such positions.

11 ♔b1

This move looks a little slow, in the light of the preceding note, but once Black plays ...♕a5, the move will usually be forced sooner or later, to defend the a2-pawn. Back in the 1960s, some attention was devoted to the immediate attacking try 11 e5 dxe5 12 ♕h4, by which White transfers his queen to the kingside as rapidly as possible. However, adequate defences were found for Black, and a pawn advance on the kingside is nowadays considered more testing.

11...♕a5!? 12 ♕d2

This move has a double purpose. On the one hand, White prepares to bring his knight to d4, which will free the f-pawn to start the intended kingside pawn-storm. At the same time, White sets up the tactical threat of 13 ♘d5, a typical idea to exploit the undefended black queen.

Since 13...♕xd2? would lose a piece to the *zwischenzug* 14 ♘xe7+, Black would be forced to accept the loss of a pawn after 13...♕d8 14 ♘xe7+ ♕xe7 15 ♕xd6. This explains Black's next move, but putting the queen on a6 is a trifle unnatural. It may be that the plan beginning 11...♕a5 is not the best, and it is perhaps no coincidence that Garry Kasparov preferred 11...h6 12 ♗h4 ♖e8 against Svidler at Linares 1999.

12...♕a6 13 ♘d4 ♖fc8 14 f4 *(D)*

White commences his storm. Another way of so doing, and indeed one which Vasiukov had previously employed with success, is 14 f3 followed by 15 g4. This is similar to the English Attack seen in Game 6.

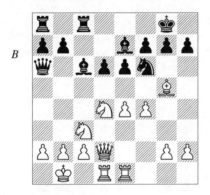

14...h6 15 h4!?

A sign of White's aggressive intentions, and a typical sacrificial idea in positions where White has a rook on h1, or can get one there quickly. To a considerable extent, the sacrifice is a natural consequence of White's last move, since 15 ♗h4? would lose a pawn to the typical tactic 15...♘xe4!, whilst taking on f6 would not be terribly effective in this position.

15...♕e4

There is no immediate mate after 15...hxg5, but after the simple continuation 16 hxg5 ♘d7 17 ♖h1, White would threaten to bring his queen to h3, against which it is hard to find an adequate defence. The black king cannot run away because of 17...♔f8? 18 ♖h8#, whilst the attempt to build a fianchetto fortress by 17...♗f8 18 ♕e3 g6 19 ♕h3 ♗g7 fails to 20 ♘xe6!, with a winning attack. Black therefore decides that there is no necessity to take the bishop immediately, since it is not really threatening to go anywhere, and so he brings his queen into a more active position.

16 g4 ♔f8 *(D)*

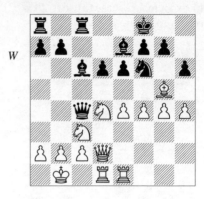

17 f5!

White pushes on energetically, and he is now committed to the attack 100%. One point of Black's 15th move is that White cannot play 17 ♗xf6 ♗xf6 18 g5, since Black can exchange queens on d4, when the endgame would be no more than equal.

17...hxg5

Black finally decides to accept the offered piece. By now he has little choice, since 17...e5 18 ♗xf6! ♗xf6 19 ♘f3, followed by 20 g5, gives White a powerful attack for no material investment.

18 hxg5 ♘d7 19 fxe6 *(D)*

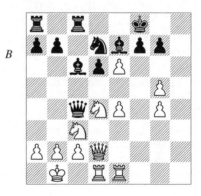

19...♘e5

A typical defensive device. Rather than recapture on e6, Black gives a pawn back, hoping to keep lines closed. Thus, after 20 exf7, White would not easily be able to open the f-file, and the black king could hide behind the f7-pawn. By contrast, 19...fxe6 would be met very strongly by 20 b3!, when the black queen can no longer defend the e6-pawn.

20 ♖h1! *(D)*

White has sacrificed a whole piece to open the h-file, so it makes sense to use it. 20 ♕h2! is another way to do so.

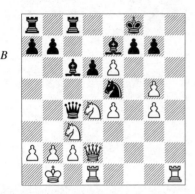

B

This is one of the critical positions of the game. 21 ♖h8# is the threat. Some beautiful variations follow after 20...♔e8. Vasiukov gives 21 ♖h8+ ♗f8 22 e7! ♔xe7 23 ♘f5+, and now either 23...♔e8 24 ♕xd6 ♘g6 25 ♘xg7#, or the even nicer 23...♔e6 24 ♕xd6+! ♗xd6 25 ♖xd6#.

Seeing these variations, the move 20...g6 suggests itself, giving the black king a flight-square on g7, and also depriving White's knight of the f5-square, where it was so effective in the previous lines. However, as Vasiukov points out, this loses to 21 ♖h8+ ♔g7 22 ♖h7+! ♔xh7 23 ♕h2+ ♔g8 24 ♖h1, when the only way for Black to avoid immediate mate is to sacrifice the queen for inadequate compensation by 24...♕f1+.

Black's third defensive try is 20...♘g6, which again results in a beautiful finish. Vasiukov gives 21 ♖df1 ♔e8 22 ♘d5, when the most attractive variation is 22...♗xg5 23 ♕xg5 ♕xd4 and now a lovely mate in 3: 24 ♕e7+! ♘xe7 25 ♖h8+ ♘g8 26 e7#.

In view of all these lines, Van Wely chose a fourth option.

20...fxe6 21 b3!

We have already seen this idea in the note to Black's 19th move. The black queen is driven away from the defence of e6.

21...♕b4 22 ♖h8+!

Stronger than 22 ♘xe6+.

22...♔f7 23 ♕f4+ ♗f6 *(D)*

Only after 23...♔g6 does White capture on e6: 24 ♘xe6, when the threat of 25 ♕f5# is decisive.

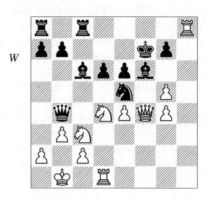

W

24 ♖h7!!

The crowning glory of a fabulous attack. Now 25 ♕xf6+ is threatened, and 24...♘xg4 loses to 25 g6+ (even stronger than Vasiukov's 25 gxf6, which also wins) 25...♔e8 (25...♔e7 26 ♖xg7+! mates in 7) 26 ♕xg4, with a decisive attack on e6, since 26...♗d7 27 ♖h8+ is mate in 4.

24...♔g8 25 gxf6! ♔xh7 *(D)*

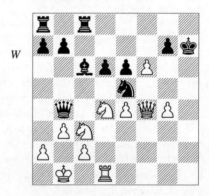

W

26 ♕g5!! ♖c7 27 ♘xe6

27 ♖h1+ ♔g8 28 ♕h5+ forces a speedy mate according to my silicon friend, but Vasiukov's choice is more than adequate.

27...♖ac8 28 fxg7 ♔g8 29 ♖h1 ♗xe4 30 ♖h8+ ♔f7 31 ♘xc7

31 g8♕+ also wins.

31...♕xc3 32 g8♕+ 1-0

A dazzling attacking display by the veteran Russian GM, who was 69 years old when this game was played.

Game 4
Michael Adams – Veselin Topalov
Wijk aan Zee 2006
Sicilian Defence, Classical Scheveningen

The present game shows a kingside attack in conditions where both players have castled kingside. In such a case, a pawn-storm is much less likely to be effective, since the attacker would risk exposing his own king as much as the opponent's. Instead, the attack is usually carried out by pieces, as here.

1 e4 c5 2 ♘f3 d6 3 d4 cxd4 4 ♘xd4 ♘f6 5 ♘c3 a6 6 ♗e2

With this move, White eschews the sharper lines of the Najdorf, beginning with such moves as 6 ♗g5 and 6 ♗e3. Instead, he concentrates on sound development, postponing the weight of the struggle to the middlegame. In the immediate future, he will play 0-0, ♗e3 and f4.

6...e6

Black chooses to go into a Scheveningen-style set-up, with his two central pawns on d6 and e6. The pure Najdorf interpretation is 6...e5, accepting the backward d-pawn in return for control of the squares d4 and f4. We saw a classic example of a similar strategy working for Black in the game Matulović-Fischer, examined in *50ECL* (Game 30). Although 6...e5 is theoretically perfectly sound after 6 ♗e2, in recent years, the more flexible 6...e6 has become more popular at GM level, largely due to the influence of Garry Kasparov.

7 0-0 ♗e7 8 a4

This is a sign of White's relatively restrained plan. Rather than launching a violent attack on Black's king with g4-g5, as he would do if he had castled queenside, he intends to build up his attack in more patient fashion. As part of that approach, he prefers to limit Black's counterplay on the queenside, by holding back the advance ...b5.

8...♘c6 9 ♗e3 0-0 10 f4 ♕c7 11 ♔h1 ♖e8 (D)

This is the modern way to play the black position, following the example of Kasparov. Black intends to drop his bishop back to f8, defending his king. In the longer term, he hopes one day to break out with the central pawn-thrust ...d5, which will release the energy of his pieces. In this case, the rook on e8 is likely to prove

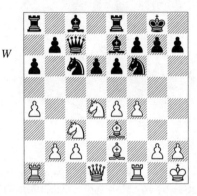

effective on the e-file. Black's position is very similar to the Hedgehog formation that we examined in Uhlmann-Bönsch, in *50ECL* (Game 41). As that game demonstrated so clearly, Black's 'coiled spring' position contains the seeds of a devastating counterattack if White over-extends himself in the search for attacking chances on the kingside.

Nonetheless, the move 11...♖e8 does have its drawbacks. In particular, Black leaves the f7-square undefended, and as we shall see later in the game, this becomes a factor when White breaks with e5.

12 ♗f3 ♗f8 13 ♕d2 ♘a5

13...♖b8 has also been played here, and may even be more accurate. In the present game, Black plays a number of very natural and normal-looking moves in the early middlegame, but emerges with a difficult position.

14 b3 ♖b8

The purpose of this move is to prepare 15...b6, and then develop his bishop to b7 (of course, the immediate 14...b6? would lose material after 15 e5). The bishop could just go to d7 immediately, but it would be less active on that square. From b7, it puts pressure on White's e4-pawn, and it also allows the f6-knight to retreat to d7, if attacked by a later g4-g5 thrust. However, the drawback to Black's plan is that his development takes longer to complete, and Adams later suggested that he should perhaps settle for 14...♗d7 and 15...♖ac8, completing his mobilization.

15 ♖ad1 *(D)*

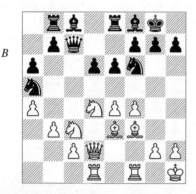

15...♘c6

The consistent move here is 15...b6, but this allows White to break in the centre in energetic style by 16 e5!. A typical variation, given by Adams, would be 16...dxe5 17 fxe5 ♘d7 (17...♕xe5? 18 ♗f4 costs Black the exchange) 18 ♗h5 ♘xe5 (or 18...g6 19 ♕f2) 19 ♗f4 g6 20 ♘e4, with dangerous threats for the pawn. Note how in this variation, White is able to bring pressure to bear down the f-file, against the f7-square, thereby illustrating the point made in the note to 11...♖e8.

In view of these lines, Topalov felt that 15...b6 was too risky, but in this case, his plan of 14...♖b8 must be considered to have been inaccurate, since its whole point was to allow 15...b6 and 16...♗b7. This is a good example of how apparently small tactical points can influence strategy. In principle, placing Black's bishop on b7 is strategically a good idea, but since it proves tactically impossible to carry out, the whole plan beginning 14...♖b8 is called into question.

16 ♗f2

Adams pointed out that 16 ♕f2! would have been stronger here, once again utilizing Black's weaknesses on the f-file. The threat of 17 e5 would then have been awkward to meet. However, the move chosen is also quite good. White intends to bring his bishop to h4, after which the threat of e5 gains in strength. Black's next move is designed to prevent this.

16...♘d7 17 ♗g3 ♘xd4 18 ♕xd4 b5 19 axb5 axb5 20 b4

This move is unusual in such positions, since it creates weaknesses down the c-file. However, in this particular position, it is more important to secure the position of White's knight on c3. White is ready to break with e5, after which the c-file weaknesses will become secondary.

20...g6?!

This turns out to be just about the decisive mistake. Black was already in trouble, and in Adams's view, he had no choice but to go into an inferior ending with 20...♕c4. White retains the better chances after 21 ♕xc4 bxc4 22 b5, but his advantage is significantly less than in the game.

21 e5 d5 *(D)*

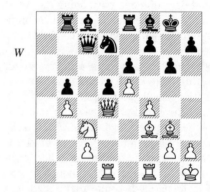

22 f5!

Setting in motion what proves to be a winning attack. Black has little choice but to capture, since it is already too late for 22...♕c4, which loses to 23 fxe6 fxe6 24 ♘xd5! ♕xd4 (24...exd5? 25 ♗xd5+ costs Black his queen) 25 ♖xd4 exd5 26 ♗xd5+ ♔h8 27 ♗f7 ♖e7 28 e6.

22...gxf5 23 ♘xd5! ♕c4

Capturing by 23...exd5? loses at once to 24 e6; e.g., 24...♕b6 25 exf7+ ♔xf7 26 ♗h5+, with a winning attack.

24 ♕d2

In the middle of an attack, it is natural to keep the queens on the board, but the computer points out that 24 ♘f6+ is also very strong. After 24...♘xf6 25 exf6, the b8-rook is very short of squares, and after the further moves 25...♕xd4 26 ♖xd4 ♖b6 27 ♖e1, Black is terribly tied up. Nonetheless, Adams's move is more thematic and pursues the attack on the black king. The main point is that 24...exd5 loses to 25 ♕g5+

♔h8 26 ♗xd5 ♕g4 27 ♕xg4 fxg4 28 ♗xf7.
This explains Black's next move, which prevents the check on g5.

24...h6 (D)

25 h3!
A very surprising quiet move in the middle
of a raging attack, and also a nice echo of
Black's previous move. White simply takes the
g4-square away from Black's queen, as well as
making *luft* for his own king. Usually, the attacker would not have time for such luxuries in
the middle of an attack, as maintaining the initiative and keeping the defender off-balance
with continual threats is usually the order of the
day. Here, however, Adams has appreciated
that Black does not have any obvious defensive
moves.

25...exd5
There is nothing else. 25...♗g7 26 ♘f6+
♘xf6 (or 26...♗xf6 27 exf6, when both b8 and
h6 are hanging) 27 exf6 attacks both b8 and g7,
whilst 25...♔h8 26 ♘f6 ♘xf6 27 exf6 e5 28
♗d5 ♕c7 (28...♕xb4 29 ♗xf7 traps the rook)
29 ♕e2 gives White a devastating attack, for no
material investment. Topalov decides he may as
well have a piece to suffer for.

26 ♗xd5 ♕xb4 27 c3 ♕c5
Giving back the piece by 27...♕e7 28 ♖xf5
♘xe5! 29 ♖xe5 ♗e6 was a slightly tougher defence, although White is still winning with accurate play. Adams then gives 30 ♗xe6 fxe6 31
♕e2 as the strongest, when the exposed black
king and weakness on e6 will cost him the game.

28 ♖xf5 ♖e6 (D)
A desperate attempt to block the a2-g8 diagonal, at the cost of the exchange. Instead,
28...♖e7 29 e6 is decisive, since the b8-rook is
once again *en prise*.

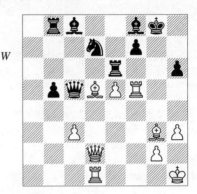

29 ♖xf7!
Crashing through decisively, and much better
than the routine capture of the exchange on e6.

29...♘b6
29...♔xf7 30 ♕f4+ ♔e8 (or 30...♔e7 31
♗h4+ winning) 31 ♗xe6 is crushing.

30 ♖df1
Good enough, but Adams points out that
30 ♕f4! was even better, with the point that
30...♘xd5 loses to 31 ♖xd5!.

30...♘xd5
30...♗g7 31 ♕f4 ♘xd5 32 ♕g4 mates.

31 ♖xf8+ ♕xf8 32 ♖xf8+ ♔xf8 33 ♕xd5
The attack has triumphed. Not only does
White have a material advantage of ♕+2♙ vs
2♖, but he also has an ongoing attack against
the highly exposed black king. The rest is just a
mopping-up exercise.

33...♔e8 34 ♗h4 ♗d7 35 ♗f6 b4 36 ♕e4
Adams himself pointed out that 36 ♕d3!
wins even more quickly, but in some time-
trouble, he preferred simply to annex another
black pawn, since 36...bxc3? 37 ♕g6+ leads to
mate.

**36...♗c8 37 cxb4 ♖b7 38 ♕g6+ ♔d7 39
♕xh6 ♔c7 40 ♕f4 ♔b8 41 h4 ♖c7 42 h5 1-0**
A fine kingside attack, conducted in conditions of same-side castling.

Game 5

Peter Wells – John Emms
Redbus Knockout, Southend 2000
English Opening

This game also features an attack in conditions of same-side castling. The key feature of the game is Wells's long-term exchange sacrifice, played primarily to maintain his bind on the dark squares. The result is a brilliant game, not only in terms of the attack itself, but perhaps even more impressively, the underlying positional build-up in the early middlegame.

1 ♘f3 c5 2 c4 ♘c6 3 ♘c3 g6 4 e3 ♘f6

After 4...♗g7 5 d4 d6 6 d5, White is rather better, so Black prefers the text-move, which enables him to achieve a quick ...d5.

5 d4 cxd4 6 exd4 d5 *(D)*

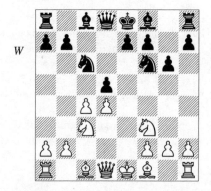

We have now reached a position that can also arise from the Caro-Kann, Panov Attack.

7 cxd5

For many years, this was considered to give White the advantage, but as this game shows, the situation is not so clear. The alternative way to fight for an advantage is 7 ♗g5, when 7...♘e4 8 cxd5 ♘xc3 9 bxc3 ♕xd5 10 ♕b3!? may be somewhat better for White. The text-move leads to a type of IQP structure.

7...♘xd5 8 ♕b3 ♘xc3

8...♘b6 is met by 9 d5, with advantage.

9 ♗c4!

This *zwischenzug* has been known since the early 1960s, and has been the basis for assessing the position as better for White. The pawn on f7 is threatened, and Black cannot retain his extra piece by 9...♘e4? because of 10 ♗xf7+ ♔d7 11 ♕e6+. Consequently, he is forced to weaken his position by playing ...e6, leaving weaknesses around f6 and d6.

9...♘d5!?

Black himself uses a tactic to force White to accept an IQP. Instead, the immediate 9...e6 10 bxc3 would give White a hanging pawn pair on c3 and d4, which is generally regarded as stronger than the IQP, although this is not entirely clear in the present position.

10 ♗xd5 e6 11 ♗xc6+ bxc6 12 0-0 ♕d5! *(D)*

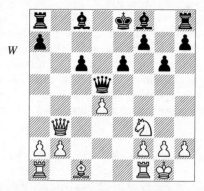

This is the key defensive idea that revived interest in Black's position, after years of neglect. Although Black has his weaknesses on the dark squares, and the pawn on c6, he also has two bishops and the long-term plan of liberating his position and eliminating his weakness by playing ...c5. If he can achieve this, his bishop-pair will come into their own. The position is therefore one of dynamic imbalance, and each side must make the best of his own pluses.

I had the privilege of witnessing this game as it was played, and took a specially strong interest in it, because some six months earlier, I had myself reached the white side of the position against John Emms. On that occasion, I had failed to understand the essence of the position, and had been instructively outplayed. It was therefore doubly interesting and instructive to see Peter Wells give such a splendid demonstration of how the white position should be handled.

13 ♗f4!

Already an improvement over my play. Of course, the very last thing White wants to do is exchange queens on d5, which would leave Black with the better pawn-structure and no kingside worries after 13...cxd5. That much even I understood, but my choice of 13 ♕c2?! was too passive. It will be useful to show the next few moves of Giddins-Emms, Port Erin 1999, because they illustrate what Black is aiming for: 13...♗g7 14 ♗f4 0-0 15 ♗e5? f6 16 ♗g3 ♗b7 17 ♖fe1 ♖fe8 18 ♖e3 ♖ac8 19 ♖c3 ♗f8 20 a3 c5 21 dxc5 ♖xc5 22 ♖xc5 ♕xc5 23 ♕xc5 ♗xc5. Despite trying to do so, White was unable to prevent the ...c5 advance, and the endgame reached after move 23 is very favourable for Black, who went on to win easily. Wells's move, which was actually suggested to me by Emms after our game, is based on the view that the exchange 13...♕xb3 14 axb3 is not very good for Black. Although White's queenside pawns are damaged, Black is well behind in development, and the absence of his queen means that the c6-pawn is very weak. For example, 14...♗e7 15 ♖fc1 ♗b7 16 ♘e5 is already winning a pawn, whilst 14...c5 is bad in view of 15 ♗e5 ♖g8 16 ♘g5.

13...♗e7

Another point of Wells's last move is that the natural 13...♗g7 is met by the irritating 14 ♕a3.

14 ♖fc1 f6! *(D)*

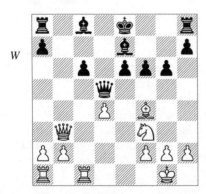

This move is an important part of Black's defensive set-up, covering the weak dark squares on the kingside, and even threatening a later

...g5 is many variations. The obvious drawback to the move is that it weakens the light squares, notably e6, but since Black has a light-squared bishop, and White does not, it proves nigh-on impossible for White to exploit this apparent weakness. This is one of the key points I failed to understand in my own game against Emms. The alert reader will notice that I even invested a tempo in playing ♗e5, to provoke the 'weakening move' ...f6, in the mistaken belief that I was improving my position.

15 h4!

Another link in White's chain. This move prevents Black's potential ...g5 advance, and also prepares to push on to h5, to attack Black's king, once it castles kingside.

15...♗d7 16 ♕e3 ♖c8 17 ♖c3 0-0 18 ♗h6 ♖fe8 19 ♖ac1! *(D)*

As the game Giddins-Emms showed, White must try at all costs to keep a lid on Black's ...c5 break. Since 19 b3 would allow an immediate 19...c5, Wells sacrifices the a-pawn, to prevent the crucial freeing advance.

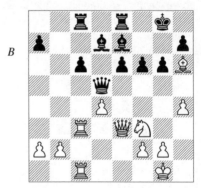

19...♕xa2

This puts the queen offside, but other moves would be answered by 20 b3, when White has achieved his aim of stopping ...c5, free of charge.

20 h5

White continues with his kingside play.

20...♕d5

Snatching a second pawn by 20...♕xb2 is immediately fatal: 21 hxg6 hxg6 22 ♘e5! fxe5 23 ♕e4 ♔h7 24 ♖h3 winning.

21 hxg6 hxg6 *(D)*

White has a strong initiative for his pawn, but no clear forcing line is apparent. How should he continue?

22 ♖c5!!

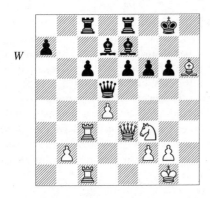

A brilliant solution, worthy of the High Priest of positional exchange sacrifices, Tigran Petrosian himself. Black's dark squares are the key weakness in his position, so White invests an exchange in order to deprive Black of the bishop that defends those squares.

22...♗xc5

Black's only other option is to decline the Greek gift by 22...♕a2 (22...♕d6? is impossible because of 23 ♗f4). However, it would be amazing if such a decentralization of the queen should prove tenable, and indeed, after 23 ♕e4 ♔f7 24 ♕f4 ♔g8 25 ♖g5! fxg5 26 ♕e4 ♔h7 27 ♗xg5, White has a strong attack.

23 ♖xc5 ♕d6 24 ♕d3! *(D)*

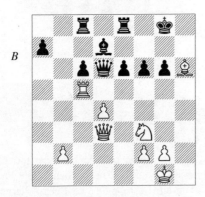

This quiet follow-up to the sacrifice is the key to White's idea. Black has enormous trouble defending g6.

24...♔f7?

This loses by force, as does 24...♔h7? 25 ♖h5. The only defence was the positionally vile

move 24...f5. After 25 ♘e5, White has over-whelming-looking positional compensation, with such threats as ♕g3 in the air, but Black does have an exchange and a pawn more, so his position cannot be written off – whenever the defender has such a large material advantage, there is always the possibility of giving back material to break the attack.

25 ♘e5+!

A further sacrifice, which tears apart the black king's defences. An important point to note about this final attack is how most of it is on the dark squares, and that the presence of opposite-coloured bishops actually helps the attacker, rather than being a drawing factor, as they usually are in the endgame. This is because in an attacking situation, such as here, the attacker effectively has an extra piece, since his bishop can attack squares that the defender's bishop cannot defend.

25...fxe5 26 ♕f3+ ♔g8

26...♔e7 27 ♗g5# is mate.

27 ♕f6 *(D)*

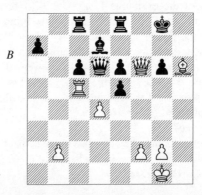

27...♖e7

27...♕e7 28 ♕xg6+ ♔h8 29 ♗g5 wins for White. Again, all the action is taking place on dark squares, whilst the prelate on d7 sits idly by, only able to spectate.

28 ♕xg6+ ♔h8 29 ♕f6+

This is totally decisive, although the computer points out that 29 ♖c3 forces mate.

29...♔h7 30 ♗f8 ♖xf8 31 ♕xf8 ♗e8 32 ♖c3 exd4 33 ♖h3+ ♔g6 34 ♖h6+ 1-0

Game 6
Veselin Topalov – Garry Kasparov
Euwe Memorial, Amsterdam 1995
Sicilian Defence, English Attack

Here, we see another opposite-castling situation, with each side attacking the other's king. However, unlike such games as Vasiukov-Van Wely (Game 3), here it is Black's counterattack which proves the faster, and he crashes through while White's kingside demonstration is barely off the ground.

1 e4 c5 2 ②f3 ②c6 3 d4 cxd4 4 ②xd4 e6 5 ②c3 d6 6 ♗e3 ②f6 7 f3 ♗e7 8 g4 0-0 9 ♕d2 a6 10 0-0-0 *(D)*

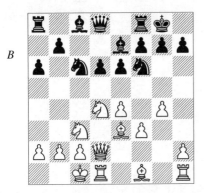

Via a Taimanov move-order, we have transposed into a typical Najdorf/Scheveningen Sicilian position. White's set-up, with ♗e3, ♕d2, 0-0-0 and f3, is known as the English Attack, having been developed by the English GMs Nunn, Chandler and Short during the 1980s. It is a very direct and natural plan. White castles queenside, and as is typical of such opposite-castling positions, he throws his kingside pawns up to attack the enemy king. Black, meanwhile, uses his queenside pawns and the half-open c-file to counterattack against White's king. Victory goes to he who manages to prosecute his attack the more vigorously, with great accuracy being demanded of both players.

10...②xd4

Black wishes to play ...b5, which is impossible at once because of the undefended knight on c6, hence this exchange. He could instead defend the knight by 10...♕c7, but it is not yet clear that c7 is the best square for the black queen. Likewise, defending the knight by 10...♗d7?! would be too passive, since the bishop is poorly placed on d7, being both inactive itself, and also depriving Black's king's knight of the retreat-square on d7.

11 ♗xd4 b5! *(D)*

Continuing with his active play on the queenside. Several previous games had seen Black preface this move with 11...②d7, but Kasparov's choice is more energetic. The point of 11...②d7 is that after Kasparov's 11...b5, White could now play 12 ♗xf6. Clearly, it would be bad to play 12...gxf6?, exposing Black's king, and after 12...♗xf6, White can win a pawn by 13 ♕xd6. However, Kasparov appreciates that Black would then have excellent compensation after 13...♕a5!. This type of pawn sacrifice is a common theme in the Sicilian, and usually offers Black good counterplay. This particular version of it is especially good, as White would have serious problems meeting the threats of 14...♗xc3 and 14...b4, especially as 14 e5 is met by 14...♗g5+ 15 ♔b1 b4, threatening 16...♖d8.

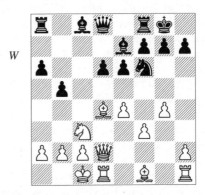

12 ♔b1

As noted above, opposite-castling positions are usually all about a race between the opposing attacks, with time being very much of the essence. For this reason, the text-move may appear a little slow, but it is usually necessary sooner or later. Black will follow up with some combination of ...b4 and ...♛a5, after which the king move will generally be necessary to defend the a-pawn. In addition, once a black rook comes to the c-file, the king will feel uncomfortable on c1.

12...♝b7 13 h4 ♖c8 14 g5 ♘d7 *(D)*

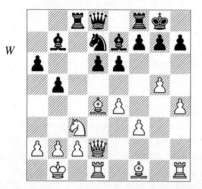

15 ♖g1!?

This is a critical moment. Both sides have deployed their forces logically and started their attacks, and White must now decide how to continue. Clearly, White would like to play 15 h5, but this is impossible because the g5-pawn would hang, and hence the text-move. However, removing the rook from the h-file is not ideal, since in many lines, after a later h5 and g6, the h-file may well be opened. One typical idea for White here is the pawn sacrifice 15 g6, aiming to open lines quickly after 15...hxg6 16 h5, and if then 16...g5, 17 h6 gives White a winning attack. In all likelihood, Black would not have captured on g6, but would have answered 15 g6 with 15...b4 16 gxh7+ ♚h8. Allowing an enemy pawn to stand in front of one's king like this is a standard defensive technique, which makes it relatively difficult for the attacker to get at the black king. Even so, this may have been a better way for White to continue, since after the text-move, he soon loses the initiative.

15...b4!

Kasparov continues to prosecute his queenside play with the utmost vigour. Some earlier games had seen Black play 15...♘e5 followed by 16...♘c4. Kasparov's plan is more straightforward, driving away the defending knight on c3. As well as furthering Black's attack on the white king, this has another point – to weaken White's control of the d5-square. In such Sicilian positions, one of Black's key strategic ideas is to achieve the break ...d5 in favourable circumstances. As we shall see later in this game, such a break can release the potential energy of Black's pieces, such as the bishop on e7, with great effect.

16 ♘e2

16 ♘a4? would be bad because of 16...♝c6! 17 ♕xb4 d5!, when White loses material; e.g., 18 ♘c5 (18 ♕b3 ♖b8 wins a piece) 18...♘xc5 19 ♝xc5 ♝xc5 20 ♕xc5 ♝a4 winning.

16...♘e5 *(D)*

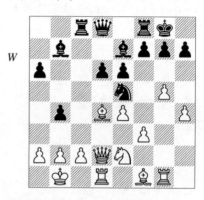

17 ♖g3?!

After this, Black's initiative soon grows to decisive proportions. Probably the best defence was 17 ♝xe5 dxe5 18 ♕xd8 ♖fxd8, although in the resulting endgame, Black would have a clear advantage, with his bishop-pair and control of the dark squares.

17...♘c4 18 ♕c1 e5! *(D)*

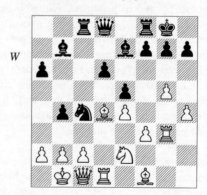

This structural change is very common in Sicilian positions. We saw it in the game Matulović-Fischer, in *50ECL* (Game 30), and it also occurs in the present book, in Game 22,

Pilnik-Geller. In the present example, White's pieces are in no position to exploit the weakened d5-square, and so Black is able to expand his central influence, without any downside.

19 &f2 a5

It is very obvious that White has been outplayed in the race between the two attacks. His pieces are very awkwardly placed on the kingside, whereas Black's position is a model of harmony. With this move, Black prepares to activate his light-squared bishop along the f1-a6 diagonal, as well as setting up ...a4 and ...b3, breaking open White's king position. White's attack on the kingside, meanwhile, is stymied.

20 &g2 &a6 21 &e1

21...&a3+ was a threat.

21...a4 22 &h3 &c6

Now 23...b3 is threatened.

23 &d1 (D)

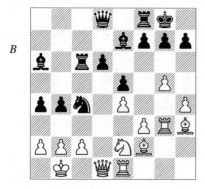

23...d5!

This classic central breakthrough decides matters in short order. Now all Black's pieces spring into action, and White's back rank proves weak. Now 24 &xd5? drops the queen after 24...&d6 25 &c5 &d1+.

24 exd5 &d6 25 f4 (D)

25 &f5 is a logical try, hoping to involve the bishop in the defence, but it loses material after 25...&xd5 26 &c1 (on 26 &d3, the simplest is 26...b3 winning quickly) 26...&xb2!, with the point that 27 &xb2 (or 27 &xb2 &xe2 28 &xe2 &d1+ winning the queen) then loses to 27...&xe2 28 &xe2 &d1 29 &e3 a3+ 30 &b3 &b1+, and the white king is soon hunted to its death in the open.

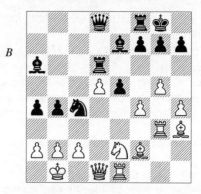

25...&xd5 26 &d3

The pressure down the open d-file is irresistible. 26 &c1 loses to 26...&d2+ 27 &a1 &e4 28 &f3 &xe2.

26...&a3+! (D)

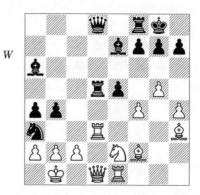

The final blow, demolishing White's resistance.

27 bxa3 &xd3 28 cxd3 &xd3 0-1

The bishop on h3 is lost. A splendid example of how such a position can collapse if White loses the initiative. As Kasparov gleefully pointed out at the time, one unusual feature of the game is that Black's queen never moved from its starting position on d8!

Game 7
Boris Gelfand – Nigel Short
Candidates match (game 8), Brussels 1991
Queen's Gambit Declined, Exchange Variation

The natural corollary to attack is defence, and, although much less glamorous, it is an equally integral part of the game of chess. When things go wrong, as they do for Short in the present game, the defender's task is to make things as difficult as possible for the opponent. Even if the defender's position is objectively lost, he can frequently save the game by determined defence, putting obstacle after obstacle in his opponent's way, until eventually the latter errs.

1 d4 ♘f6 2 c4 e6 3 ♘f3 d5 4 ♘c3 ♘bd7

This is a slightly unusual move-order, 4...♗e7 being more normal. The text-move is most often associated with an intention to answer 5 ♗g5 with 5...c6 6 e3 ♕a5, the so-called Cambridge Springs Variation, whilst 5 ♗f4 can be answered by 5...dxc4 6 e3 ♘b6. In the present game, Gelfand side-steps both possibilities, with a slightly unusual move of his own.

5 ♕c2 *(D)*

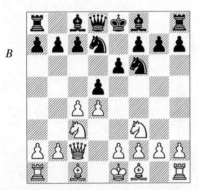

5...♗e7

Now 5...c6 could be met by 6 e4, with interesting play, whilst 6 e3 would transpose into a line of the Semi-Slav. Short prefers more standard QGD paths.

6 cxd5 exd5 7 ♗f4

By various devious means, we have transposed into a line of the Exchange Variation, with White putting his bishop on f4, rather than the more usual g5. We actually saw this set-up in Game 1 in *50ECL* (Averbakh-Sarvarov) where White followed up by castling queenside and launching a pawn-storm against Black's king.

7...c6 8 h3 *(D)*

A useful prophylactic move, very common in similar positions. Once he has played ...c6, Black is threatening to meet 8 e3 by 8...♘h5, exchanging off White's dark-squared bishop, whereas the immediate 7...♘h5? would have been met by 8 ♘xd5. The move 8 h3 looks slow, but as we saw in the Averbakh game, if White is intending to castle queenside, followed by h3 and g4, it fits in with his plans anyway.

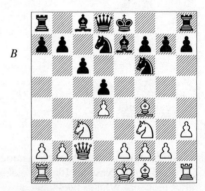

8...♘f8!?

This move initiates a manoeuvre well-known in such positions, although in this particular version, it may not be entirely accurate. 8...0-0 would be normal.

9 e3 ♘g6

Another common follow-up to Black's last move is 9...♘e6 10 ♗h2 g6, with the intention of ...♘g7 and ...♗f5, exchanging off Black's light-squared bishop. In the Orthodox QGD, this piece is frequently difficult to activate, and exchanging it for its opposite number is thus a logical plan. However, the knight manoeuvre to g7 is rather slow, and in this position, White has not yet committed his king to castling kingside.

This means that he is well-placed to meet the ...♘e6, ...g6 and ...♘g7 manoeuvre by a timely g4, preventing the move ...♗f5. For this reason, Short puts his knight on g6 immediately, but this also has its drawbacks, as the knight could easily become a target if White were to castle queenside and push his kingside pawns.

10 ♗h2 0-0 11 ♗d3 ♖e8?!

Gelfand criticized this move, and recommended 11...♗d6, preventing White's next move.

12 ♘e5 ♗d6 13 f4! *(D)*

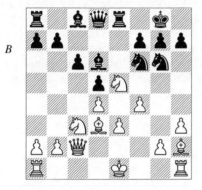

This is the problem. Now White has been able to reinforce the position of the knight on e5. White's central pawn-formation d4-e3-f4 is similar to a Stonewall Dutch, but whereas in the Stonewall proper, White's dark-squared bishop would usually be buried at c1, here it is already developed outside the pawn-chain. If White is given enough time, the Stonewall can often be the prelude to a powerful kingside attack, so Black needs to react immediately, and start counterplay. In the long run, his dream would be to evict the knight from e5, and then exploit the backward pawn on e3 and the hole on e4, but in the present position, that is unlikely to be possible for a long time to come.

13...c5! 14 0-0

Black's last move already reaps some reward. 14 0-0-0 would be more consistent with White's plans to attack on the kingside, but Gelfand was afraid of Black's counterplay after 14...c4 15 ♗e2 b5!, a typical pawn sacrifice to open lines on the queenside. After the further moves 16 ♘xb5 ♘e4, followed by ...♕a5 and ...♖b8, Black would have excellent counter-chances against the white king.

14...c4 15 ♗e2 ♗b4

This is a typical manoeuvre in such positions. Since the e4-square is White's major weakness in such Stonewall formations, Black seeks to trade off the knight at c3, which defends that square. If he can do so, he will more easily be able to occupy e4 with his own knight. Conceding the bishop-pair is rarely so important in Stonewall formations, since the nature of the pawn-structure means that bishops do not have so much scope, whereas the availability of outposts on squares such as e4 and e5 suits the knights.

16 f5 ♘f8

This retreat is rather passive, but is unfortunately almost forced. The immediate capture 16...♗xc3?? loses at once to 17 fxg6, whilst the thematic idea of placing his knight on e4 by means of 16...♘xe5 17 dxe5 ♗xc3 18 ♕xc3 ♘e4 still leaves Black with serious problems after 19 ♕d4. The d5-pawn is weak and difficult to defend after 20 ♖ad1, and White also has the immediate tactical threat of 20 ♗xc4.

17 ♗f3 ♗xc3 18 bxc3 ♗d7 *(D)*

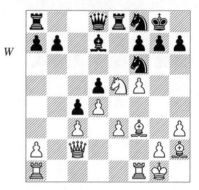

19 g4!

Initiating a pawn-storm on the kingside. As we have discussed previously, both in this book and in *50ECL*, when the kings have castled on the same side, it is relatively rare to see a pawn-storm, since White risks exposing his own king as much as the enemy's. However, it is sometimes possible, especially when the centre is blocked or otherwise fairly secure, and White is not vulnerable to a central counter. In the present position, that is the case. The central pawn-formation is fairly fixed, and Black does not have any pawn-breaks, so White is able to launch the pawns in front of his king without taking much risk.

The results of the opening and early middle-game are very much in White's favour, as he has a strong kingside attack, with Black having no counterplay. In such positions, the defender must recognize his inferiority and set about putting up the toughest resistance he can manage. In particular, he must not waste time or energy berating himself for having got into such a mess in the first place, nor must he worry too much about whether he is already lost. Whether the advantage is already decisive, with best play, is of no consequence – what matters is whether White will actually succeed in winning the game. This will depend on how well he plays, and how well Black plays, from now on. Even if the position is objectively winning for White, there are still numerous defensive resources to be found for Black, and numerous obstacles to be placed in White's path, any one of which may be enough to cause him to trip up and miss the best line of play. The defender's job is therefore to make White's task as difficult as possible.

19...♗c6 20 ♕g2 ♘8d7 21 g5 *(D)*

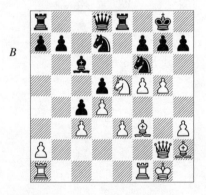

21...♘xe5

This brings White's bishop to a powerful post on e5, but 21...♘e4 also leaves Black with many problems. After 22 ♗xe4 dxe4, Gelfand intended the exchange sacrifice 23 ♘xc4 ♗b5 24 ♘d6 ♗xf1 25 ♖xf1, with strong compensation, although the simple 23 f6 also looks very good.

22 ♗xe5 ♘e4 23 ♗xe4 dxe4 *(D)*

The position now involves bishops of opposite colours. It is well-known that in the endgame, such bishops are often a strong drawing factor, but in the middlegame, the reverse is frequently the case. Opposite-coloured bishops

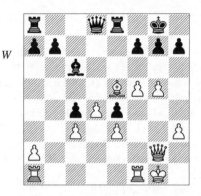

generally favour the side which is attacking the king, since by concentrating his attack on the squares controlled by his bishop, he effectively has an extra piece. We saw this in Wells-Emms above (Game 5), whilst here, for example, in so far as White can attack on the dark squares around Black's king, he will have an extra bishop with which to attack those squares, whilst Black's bishop will be unable to defend them.

24 h4

This move is powerful, but Gelfand later analysed 24 ♕g3! as stronger still. This bears out the preceding note, since White's attack now develops on the dark squares. His intention is 25 ♕h4; for example, 24...♔h8 25 ♕h4, threatening 26 f6 g6 27 ♕h6 ♖g8 27 ♖f4 ♕f8 28 ♕xh7+, and mate. Note how this whole attack develops on the dark squares, with Black's bishop being quite impotent in the defence.

24...♔h8 25 f6! g6 26 h5 ♖g8

Forced, since Black must be able to meet 27 hxg6 by recapturing with a piece.

27 ♔f2 *(D)*

Making way for the rook to come to the h-file. It seems that Black has nothing with which to oppose this simple plan, but Short continues to make things difficult for White. As always, there are two aspects to the defence – meeting the direct threats, and creating counterplay. The two go hand-in-hand, since purely passive defence is rarely good enough – counterplay is essential to distract White from his attacking plans.

27...♕a5

Going for counterplay. Another attempt was 27...gxh5 28 ♖h1 ♕b6, hoping for 29 ♖ae1 (to meet the threat of 29...♕b2+) 29...♗d7, when the bishop gets to f5 to defend the h7-square.

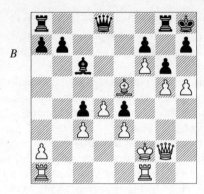

However, the computer points out that White can ignore the apparent threat of 29...♕b2+, and play instead 29 ♖xh5! ♕b2+ 30 ♔g3. Now 30...♕xa1 loses attractively to 31 ♖xh7+ ♔xh7 32 ♕h3+ ♔g6 33 ♔f4! (threatening 34 ♕h6#) 33...♖h8 34 ♕f5+ ♔h5 35 g6+ and mate next move. Black would therefore be forced to enter the endgame after 30...♕xg2+ 31 ♔xg2 ♗d7, followed by ...♗f5, when the opposite-coloured bishops would now offer him some drawing chances, although the position is still bad.

28 ♖h1 ♕xc3 29 ♖ae1 ♗d7! (D)

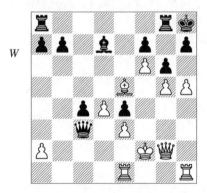

Once again, Black finds his best defensive chance. Indeed, Gelfand even awarded the move two exclamation marks, as the only way to fight on. The bishop needs to head towards f5, to defend h7.

30 hxg6!

Gelfand faced a very tough choice here, but deep analysis after the game suggests that he made the right decision. He himself pointed out two very tempting alternatives, both of which fail to remarkable defences. The first line is 30 ♕xe4 ♗f5 31 hxg6! ♗xg6 (not 31...♖xe4? 32 ♖xh7#) 32 ♖xh7+ ♔xh7 33 ♖h1, when White wins beautifully after 33...♖g6? 34 ♕xg6!!.

However, instead of this, Black has the spectacular defence 33...♕d2+ 34 ♔f3 ♕d1+!!, when White has to allow perpetual check after 35 ♔f2 ♕d2+, etc., since 35 ♔f4 is met by another spectacular deflection: 35...♕f1+! 36 ♖xf1 ♗xe4 37 ♔xe4 ♖xg5, when Black even stands better.

White's other try is the astonishing 30 ♔g3!? (D), simply aiming to put his king on f4, where it is safe from enemy queen checks.

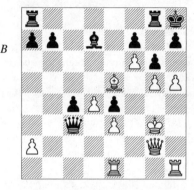

This also appears, at first sight, to win. Thus, after, say, 30...♗f5 31 ♔f4 ♖ae8, with his king now safe, White has simply 32 ♕h2, when Black has no adequate defence to the threat of mate by 33 hxg6 ♗xg6 34 ♕xh7+! ♗xh7 35 ♖xh7+ ♔xh7 36 ♖h1+ ♔g6 37 ♖h6#. However, Black again has a study-like defence. He answers 30 ♔g3 with 30...gxh5 31 ♔f4, and now not the obvious 31...♗g4? (which again loses in spectacular fashion to 32 ♕xg4! hxg4 33 ♖xh7+, forcing mate in two), but 31...♖g6!, when the position is totally unclear.

Apart from their intrinsic beauty, the main reason for quoting these variations is to show the extent of the defensive resources which a chess position can contain. It certainly looks as though White should have any number of ways to win this position, but deep analysis uncovers remarkable tactical resources for Black. It is the defender's task to find as many of these resources as possible, so as to complicate his opponent's job to the maximum. Even if, at a given moment, the attacker finds the best option amongst the various choices (as Gelfand does here), it will take him time on the clock, thus increasing the chances of a mistake later on.

30...♖xg6 (D)

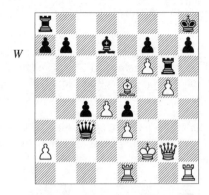

31 ♕xe4

31 ♕h2 is now met by 31...h6. After the text-move, White again threatens the queen sacrifice 32 ♕xg6.

31...♚g8! 32 ♕xb7 ♕c2+ 33 ♖e2 ♕f5+ 34 ♗f4 ♖c8

34...♖e8 35 ♕f3 ♖e4 was recommended by several commentators, but Gelfand points out that 36 ♖b2 is then very strong.

35 ♕f3 c3

Once again, Black makes the most of his chances for counterplay, using the passed c-pawn to distract White from his own plans.

36 e4 ♕a5 37 d5 c2 38 e5 ♖c3 *(D)*

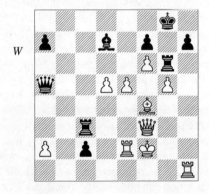

39 ♕h5??

Thus far, Gelfand has navigated his way through some incredible complications in fine style, but now the pressure takes its toll. He had only seconds on his clock at this point, with two moves to make to reach the time-control, and he blunders. He could have won by 39 ♕e4!, when

39...♗g4 loses to 40 e6! fxe6 41 f7+ ♚xf7 42 ♖xh7+, whilst the ending after 39...♕c5+ 40 ♗e3 ♕c4 41 ♕xc4 ♖xc4 42 ♗c1 should be winning for White.

Thus, it turns out that against the most accurate move, all of Short's ingenious defence would not have availed him, and many might consider him to be lucky to have escaped. In reality, though, a player makes his own luck. Gelfand's mistake was by no means an 'unforced error', but resulted from the time-trouble into which he had been driven, trying to overcome Short's tenacious last-line defence. If the defender's position is objectively lost, there is nothing he can do, except put up the best possible defence, and hope for an error from the opponent. That is what has happened here.

39...h6 40 e6 ♗e8

The wheel has now turned full circle, and it is White who is lost. The powerful passed pawn on c2, plus the exposed white king, make his position hopeless.

41 ♗c1

41 gxh6 ♕c5+ 42 ♗e3 ♖xf6+ is no better.

41...♕xd5 42 e7 ♖xg5! 43 ♗xg5 *(D)*

43 ♕xh6 ♖g2+ 44 ♚f1 ♕f3+ mates.

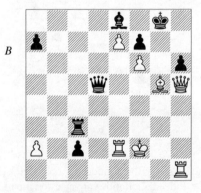

43...♕f5+ 44 ♚e1

44 ♚g1 c1♕+ is equally hopeless.

44...c1♕+ 45 ♗xc1 ♖xc1+ 46 ♚d2 ♖c2+ 47 ♚d1 ♕d3+ 48 ♚e1 ♕g3+ 49 ♚d1 ♕d3+ 50 ♚e1 ♕c3+ 51 ♚f2 ♕d4+ 0-1

52 ♚f1 ♕f4+ 53 ♚g1 ♖c1+ 54 ♚g2 ♗c6+ wraps things up.

Game 8
Andor Lilienthal – Viacheslav Ragozin
Moscow 1935
Nimzo-Indian Defence, Sämisch Variation

The present game is a classic example of defence and counterattack. From the opening, White obtains a central pawn-majority, and for much of the middlegame, Black is forced to defend carefully, so as to prevent the majority from advancing. By extremely clever use of tactical possibilities, he manages to do so, whilst at the same time preparing a counterattack. At the crucial moment, an unexpected exchange sacrifice turns the tables completely, and Black emerges with a decisive pawn-majority of his own.

1 d4 ♘f6 2 c4 e6 3 ♘c3 ♗b4 4 a3

This move, the Sämisch Variation, is the most radical challenge to the Nimzo-Indian Defence. White invites his opponent to carry out his positional threat, by taking on c3 and doubling White's pawns. White hopes that his bishop-pair and the additional support for his pawn-centre will outweigh he weakness of the doubled pawns. The Sämisch has always had its supporters, but most GMs have tended to prefer the black side, and nowadays the line is rarely seen.

4...♗xc3+ 5 bxc3 c5 6 f3 d5 7 e3

The immediate 7 cxd5 is more common, when Black usually recaptures with the knight.

7...0-0 8 cxd5 exd5 9 ♗d3 ♘c6 10 ♘e2 *(D)*

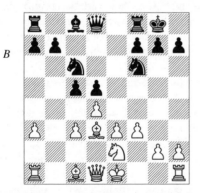

We have reached a structure that we examined in *50ECL*, in the context of the game Furman-Lilienthal (Game 26). White has a central pawn-majority, and his middlegame plan is to try to achieve the advance e4. As the Furman game showed, this can yield White a very strong kingside attack if he can achieve the advance in favourable circumstances. Black's task is to restrain the enemy e-pawn, whilst gradually preparing to utilize his queenside pawn-majority later in the game.

10...♖e8

The start of Black's plan. The rook moves to stop e4.

11 0-0 a6 *(D)*

In Furman-Lilienthal, Black left his queen's knight on b8 and played ...b6 followed by ...♗a6 to exchange off White's king's bishop. This is a logical plan, since the bishop on d3 supports the e4 advance, and may also prove an important piece in any subsequent attack on the black king. In this case, Ragozin's knight is already committed to c6, so the plan of ...b6 and ...♗a6 is not available to him. On the other hand, his c6-knight exerts pressure on the d4-pawn, and thus contributes to hindering White's planned advance e4. In the meantime, Black gets on with mobilizing his own pawn-majority.

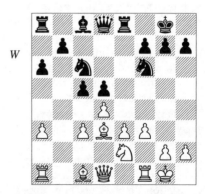

12 ♕e1

White transfers the queen to f2, from where it will defend the d4-pawn, and thus threaten e4. A more common plan in such positions is 12 ♘g3, followed by ♖a2 and ♖e2/f2.

12...b5 13 ♕f2 *(D)*

Note that there is no value in White capturing on c5, since Black can easily regain the pawn (e.g., by 13...♕e7), and White will simply have given up his pawn-centre. The potential weakness of Black's isolated pawn on d5 will be more than compensated by White's weaknesses on c3 and e3.

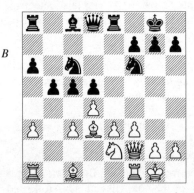

After the text-move, White is threatening 14 e4, since after 14...dxe4 15 fxe4 ♘xe4??, he would have 16 ♕xf7+. Such a transaction would favour White, so Black must attend to the threat of 14 e4.

13...♗e6

An example of tactical restraint. It does not look as though this stops 14 e4 (indeed, by shutting off the influence of Black's rook on e8, it seems positively to encourage the move), but in fact, Black has a tactical defence in mind. Thus, 14 e4 will be met by 14...dxe4 15 fxe4 (15 ♗xe4 is positionally bad, destroying White's pawn-centre) 15...♘g4!, after which White's queen can no longer defend the d4-pawn. However, Black had to see a little further than this, since after 16 ♕g3 cxd4 17 cxd4 ♘xd4, White has the apparently strong move 18 ♗b2. Now the d4-knight is attacked, and after 18...♘xe2+ 19 ♗xe2, the g4-knight is *en prise*, and cannot move away because of the threat to g7. However, Ragozin had seen the sting in the tail: 19...♕d2!, attacks both white bishops, and enables Black to emerge with an extra pawn.

This variation emphasizes how important calculation is in chess. One can have all the positional understanding in the world, but unless one can calculate tactics, it will be to no avail.

Thus, in this case, Ragozin understands that his positional task is to deter the advance 14 e4, but he uses tactics to achieve this.

14 h3

In the light of the previous note, this move is easy to understand. By taking control of the g4-square, White eliminates the defence outlined above, and renews the threat of 15 e4.

14...♖a7! *(D)*

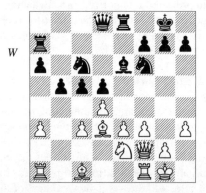

Another tactical defence against White's positional threat. The rook defends f7, so that 15 e4 can now be met by 15...dxe4 16 fxe4 cxd4 17 cxd4 ♗c4!, undermining the support of the e4-pawn. After the forced exchange 18 ♗xc4 bxc4, White has to advance by 19 e5 (else the e4-pawn falls), after which 19...♘d5 followed by 20...f6 will break up White's immobilized pawn-centre. The whole variation is only possible because the f7-pawn is defended in the final position. In addition, Black prepares to bring his queen's rook to e7, setting up further pressure on the e-file.

The above variation also illustrates something about the positional factors in this structure. We have said that White's basic plan is to advance his pawn-majority with e4. So indeed it is, but White wishes to do so in such a way that the pawns do not become fixed and blockaded. In the above variation, White achieves e4, but only ends up with his pawns blockaded on d4 and e5, where they can be broken up by a later ...f6.

15 ♗d2 ♕b6 16 ♖fb1!

White in turn finds a subtle idea. The move 16 e4 would be answered in the same way as the previous note. White's problem is that Black currently has too much pressure against d4 and e4, so by his last move, he plans to play a4, and thus induce Black to advance ...c4. This move will take the pressure off the d4-pawn, whereupon White will return his rook to the kingside, and resume his e4 plan.

16...Rae7 17 a4 c4 18 Bc2 Bc8 *(D)*

Both sides play logically. 19 e4 was now a threat, so Black unmasks his rooks along the e-file. White, in his turn, needs to support the e4-square further, which he does with his next move.

19 Ng3 h5

And Black immediately renews his pressure against e4, by threatening to drive the knight away by a subsequent ...h4.

20 Ne2

Having provoked a weakening of Black's kingside, White regroups the knight. The more aggressive-looking continuation 20 Nf5 would be less effective, thanks again to a tactical defence: 20...Bxf5 21 Bxf5 b4! 22 cxb4 Nxd4!, with the point 23 exd4? Re2 regaining the piece.

20...Nd8 21 Ra2 Bd7 22 axb5 axb5 23 Rba1 Bc8

24 Ra6 was threatened.

24 Rb2 Bd7

Despite all of Black's fine defensive play so far, White retains the advantage, thanks to the power of his central pawn-majority. Black's ingenious defence has only managed to keep White at bay, without putting paid to the long-term strategic dangers Black faces. In this position, White has a draw if he wants it, but Lilienthal is after more, and justifiably so.

25 Qh4! Ne6 26 Kh1?!

Black has provided yet another tactical defence against 26 e4: 26...dxe4 27 fxe4 Nf8 28 Ng3 (28 e5? allows 28...Rxe5!) 28...Ng6 29

Qg5 h4, followed by 30...Nxe4. However, instead of putting the king on h1, Ragozin recommended the slightly odd-looking 26 Kf2!, defending the e3-pawn further. He considered that White would then retain the advantage.

26...Nf8 27 Ng3? *(D)*

But this is a serious mistake, which allows the tables to be radically turned. White should have over-protected e3 by means of 27 Re1.

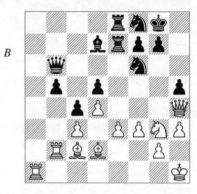

With h5 hanging, and 28 e4 again threatened, Black needs something special to prevent his position from collapsing...

27...Rxe3!!

...and this is it. The exchange sacrifice destroys White's pawn-centre and initiates strong counterplay. Once again, the move required deep and accurate calculation.

28 Bxe3 Rxe3 29 Nxh5 Nxh5 30 Qxh5 Bc6

For the time being, Black does not have any pawns for the exchange, but c3 is attacked, and if it falls, it is clear that Black will have dangerous counterplay thanks to his two connected passed pawns on the queenside. It appears that c3 can be defended by 31 Ra3, but Ragozin had seen that this loses to 31...Re1+ 32 Kh2 Qc7+ 33 g3 Qe7, with the double threat of 34...Qe2# and 34...Qxa3. However, Lilienthal finds a more subtle, indirect defence of the c3-pawn.

31 Qg5!

Now the point is that after 31...Rxc3 32 Qd2, the black rook is trapped.

31...Rxc3!!

Anyway! This second exchange sacrifice is the key to Black's play, and had to be foreseen before the first sacrifice on e3.

32 Qd2 Rxc2

Forced, since 32...b4?? loses to 33 Qxc3.

33 ⃞xc2 ♘e6 *(D)*

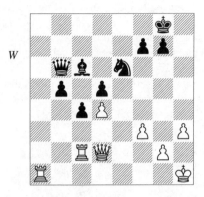

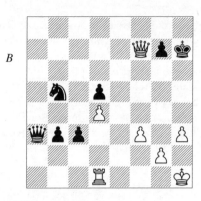

The result of the sacrificial operation begun at move 27 is that White has two extra exchanges, for just one pawn. However, his d4-pawn is weak, and Black has two powerful passed pawns on the queenside. In addition, the black knight on e6 proves an exceptionally effective piece, much more effective than either of White's rooks. The nature of the position is that there are few open files for the rooks to exploit, especially since the c6-bishop controls the squares a8 and e8, thus preventing White's rooks from penetrating on either of the open files.

34 ⃞d1 b4 35 ⃞b2 b3 36 ♕c3 ♘c7

The knight's next task is to break down the blockade of the passed pawns.

37 ⃞e2 ♕a7 38 ♕b4

Ragozin points out that both 38 ⃞e7 and 38 ⃞a1 would be strongly met by 38...♘b5!.

38...♘b5 39 ⃞e7 ♕a3

Despite his material deficit, Black is happy to exchange queens. After 40 ♕xa3 ♘xa3 his passed pawns would soon romp home; e.g., 41 ⃞c7 ♗a4 42 ⃞a7 c3! winning.

40 ♕e1 c3 41 ⃞e8+

Giving back one exchange is White's only hope of drumming up some counterplay.

41...♗xe8 42 ♕xe8+ ♔h7 43 ♕xf7 *(D)*

43 ♕xb5 loses quickly to 43...c2, so White's only chance is to hope for a perpetual check against the exposed black king.

43...♕a8!

Stopping the threat of perpetual by 44 ♕h5+ and 45 ♕e8+.

44 ⃞e1

The checks run out after 44 ♕f5+ ♔h8 45 ♕h5+ ♔g8. After the text-move, the threat is 45 ♕h5+ and 46 ⃞e8+.

44...♘d6

It is a well-known fact of endgame theory that two connected passed pawns on the 6th rank defeat a lone rook. This means that Black can afford to retreat his queen and knight, to stop the perpetual-check threats, and the pawns will win the game by themselves.

45 ♕c7 c2!

Even the knight can be thrown onto the fire.

46 ♕xd6

46 ♕c3 is a trifle more stubborn, but still hopeless. Ragozin gives the line 46...♕c8 (the alternative 46...♕a4 also wins) 47 ♕d3+ ♘f5! 48 ♕xb3 c1♕ winning.

46...b2 47 ♕f4 ♕c6 *(D)*

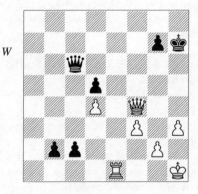

0-1

The two passed pawns on the 7th rank underline the triumph of Black's strategy.

2 Opening Play

The opening is the phase of the game which receives the most attention from amateur players. Unfortunately, the attention it receives is usually disproportionate to its real importance, but nevertheless, there is no doubt that the opening plays a key role in the fate of many games, especially at grandmaster level. The games in this chapter illustrate various aspects of opening play.

In the first two games, we see the effect of a powerful opening innovation. In each case, the winner comes to the board armed with a new idea in a previously well-known position. Taken by surprise, his opponent uses a great deal of time on the clock, and still walks into a dangerous position, succumbing in decisive fashion. Such experiences are always memorable for the winner, but they are somewhat uncommon, even in these days of deep opening preparation.

Another aspect of opening play is exploiting weak play by the opponent, which we see in Game 11. Black's series of small errors is ruthlessly exploited by his opponent. An important point to notice here is that in order to take advantage of such weak play, it is frequently important to react specifically to the opponent's errors, rather than merely continuing to play 'natural' (read: routine) moves. The latter rarely yields the dividends one might expect.

The remaining game in this chapter illustrates a particularly important aspect of opening play, which is understanding the typical middlegame and endgame plans associated with a given opening. Many players make the mistake of thinking that 'knowing' an opening just involves memorizing long sequences of moves, by rote. In reality, it is developing a deep understanding of the types of middlegame and endgame to which the opening leads, which is the key to successful play in any opening. This is strikingly illustrated by Game 12.

Game 9
Valery Salov – Mikhail Gurevich
Leningrad 1987
Nimzo-Indian Defence, Rubinstein System

1 d4 ♘f6 2 c4 e6 3 ♘c3 ♗b4 4 e3

In Game 46, we shall see White answer the Nimzo-Indian with 4 ♕c2, immediately meeting Black's positional threat of ...♗xc3+, doubling White's pawns. In this game, however, Salov adopts the Rubinstein System, simply continuing with his kingside development. Theory considers that the immediate exchange on c3 is not terribly good for Black, since White can follow up with ♗d3, ♘e2, f3 and e4. Black therefore usually postpones the exchange to a more favourable moment, in particular until such time as White expends a tempo on the move a3.

4...c5

This is one of several sound options for Black, the main alternatives being 4...0-0 and 4...b6.

5 ♘e2 *(D)*

The move 5 ♗d3 is also perfectly possible, but the text-move is the pure Rubinstein follow-up. White defends his knight on c3, thereby avoiding the doubled pawns, and prepares to secure the bishop-pair by playing a3 next move. Just as with the move 4 ♕c2, the main drawback to this plan is that White's development is delayed, and Black can generally utilize this circumstance to secure reasonable chances, in return for conceding the two bishops.

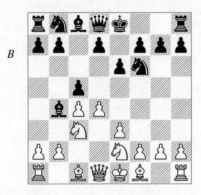

5...cxd4

Again, Black has alternatives here, the main one being the immediate 5...d5. This usually leads to an IQP structure after the further moves 6 a3 ♗xc3+ 7 ♘xc3 cxd4 8 exd4 dxc4 9 ♗xc4. This particular IQP structure is slightly unusual, in that White does not have a knight on f3, and Black does not have a dark-squared bishop. These factors more or less balance each other out, although White is considered to have a slight edge in the resulting position.

6 exd4 d5 7 a3!?

At the time this game was played, this move was very popular, but the defensive idea shown by Black here soon led to a sharp decline in the popularity of the text-move. Nowadays, White more often prefers the immediate 7 c5, which after 7...♘e4 8 ♗d2 ♘xd2 9 ♕xd2 leads to a position with approximately equal chances.

7...♗e7 8 c5 *(D)*

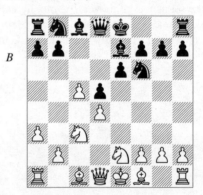

All of these moves were seen in Game 28 of *50ECL*, Gligorić-Szabo. White sets up a queenside pawn-majority, with the aim of continuing b4-b5, and creating a powerful passed pawn on the c-file. In return, Black gets the chance to advance his majority in the centre. In Gligorić-Szabo, Black's strategy triumphed in spectacular style, as he managed to blockade White's queenside pawns and push his own centre pawns right through the heart of White's position. Nonetheless, there is nothing objectively wrong with White's position, and in the 31 years since Gligorić-Szabo had been played (in 1956), White's play had been refined to such an extent that the line was considered to be in White's favour. That is, until the present game!

8...0-0 9 g3 b6 10 b4 bxc5 11 dxc5 a5 12 ♖b1 ♘c6 13 ♗g2 *(D)*

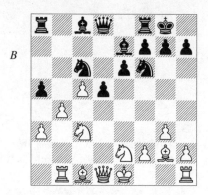

13...♖b8!

This is the start of Gurevich's new plan. In Gligorić-Szabo, and all of the other previous games played in this variation, Black had first exchanged pawns on b4, and only then played 14...♖b8. However, this allows White to defend his b4-pawn by 15 ♗a3. Gurevich's novelty, which he prepared at home together with fellow Russian GM Igor Novikov, was to attack the b-pawn immediately, without the preliminary exchange of pawns on b4. That has the point that the a3-square is no longer available for White's bishop, so he has problems defending the b4-pawn.

14 ♗f4?! *(D)*

Faced with Black's novelty, White immediately goes wrong, albeit with a very natural move. Annotating the game in *Informator 43*, Gurevich suggested 14 ♘d4 as a better try. This was subsequently tested in Marin-Portisch, from the Subotica Interzonal, played a few months later in 1987. However, after the moves 14...♘xd4 15 ♕xd4 ♘d7! 16 0-0 ♗a6 17 ♖d1 ♗f6 18 ♕d2 axb4 19 axb4 ♘e5, Black had good play, and went on to win. Another plausible, but bad, move is 14 b5?, which is met by the piece sacrifice 14...♗xc5! 15 bxc6 ♖xb1 16 ♘xb1 ♕b6!, when the follow-up 17 ♗e3 ♗xe3 18 fxe3 ♘g4! gives Black a very dangerous attack.

White's best try is another Gurevich suggestion, 14 ♕a4 axb4 15 axb4! (but not 15 ♕xc6? ♗d7, with advantage to Black), with an unclear position. However, it is probably not a

coincidence that few top GMs have tried this as White, suggesting that they do not trust White's position. Indeed, so strong is Gurevich's new plan with 13...♖b8, that it has virtually put 7 a3 out of business at top GM level – a strikingly successful piece of opening preparation!

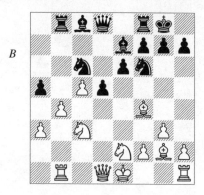

14...axb4!

Refuting White's last move, and undoubtedly all part of Gurevich's home analysis. Note that the superficially strong 14...e5? is bad because of 15 ♘xd5!, when 15...exf4 is met by 16 ♘xf6+ and 17 ♗xc6, regaining the piece. Gurevich instead sacrifices the exchange, obtaining in return a pawn and a powerful initiative. White has little choice but to accept, since 15 axb4 ♖xb4 simply leaves Black a pawn up, with a second pawn on c5 likely to drop off soon as well.

15 ♗xb8 bxc3 *(D)*

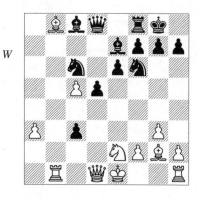

16 ♕a4?!

This is probably also not best, although White is already struggling to equalize. In his *Informator* notes, Gurevich gave 16 ♗d6, although after 16...♗xd6 17 cxd6 ♕a5! 18 0-0 ♕xa3 19 ♕c2 ♕xd6 20 ♘xc3, Black has two pawns for the exchange and stands somewhat better.

16...♘xb8 17 ♖xb8 ♘d7!

This is why 16 ♕a4 was inaccurate. Black's knight reaches d3 with tempi, thanks to the unfortunate position of the white rook and queen.

18 ♖a8 *(D)*

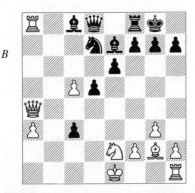

Hoping to use the pin along the back rank to make it harder for Black to play ...♗a6, supporting a knight on d3. However, the rook proves to be in danger on a8, but it is already impossible to hold the white position together.

18...♘xc5 19 ♕b5

Now we see the problem of having the white rook on a8. White would like to play 19 ♕d4, trying to round up the dangerous passed pawn on c3. However, this is met by 19...♕b6!, when 20 ♘xc3 loses the exchange back after 20...♕b7! 21 ♖a5 ♘b3. Likewise, 19 ♕c2 is also bad, since Black can just play 19...d4, defending the c3-pawn, with a crushing position.

19...♕d6! *(D)*

This is the final accurate move. White's last move had set the cunning trap 19...d4 20 0-0 c2? 21 ♖xc8! ♕xc8 22 ♘xd4, when White will eliminate the c2-pawn as well, with equality, since 22...♘d3? is refuted by 23 ♘c6, and it is White who wins. Gurevich's move puts paid to all of the tricks.

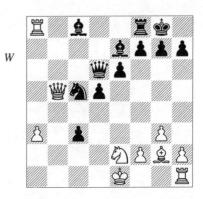

20 ♗f3

The point of Black's last move is that 20 ♘xc3 is refuted by 20...♗a6!. White would then be forced to give back the exchange by 21 ♖xa6, since 21 ♖xf8+ ♗xf8 leaves him defenceless against ...♘d3+. 20 0-0 ♗a6 is also losing material; hence the text-move, defending the knight on e2.

20...♗a6 21 ♖xf8+ ♗xf8 22 ♕a5

This move is forced, since after 22 ♕b1 ♘d3+ 23 ♔f1, Black has 23...♕c5, when the f2-square collapses.

22...♘d3+ 23 ♔f1 ♘e5 *(D)*

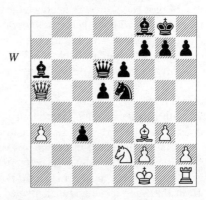

24 ♕xc3

Or 24 ♔g2 ♘xf3 25 ♔xf3 d4, with an overwhelming position.

24...d4 25 ♕b3 ♗c4 0-1

Game 10
Levon Aronian – Ivan Sokolov
Wijk aan Zee 2006
Queen's Gambit, Slav Defence

Here, we see another spectacularly successful piece of opening preparation. Aronian comes to the board armed with a new idea in a popular Slav line, which had already been seen several times in the same tournament. He proceeds to play almost 30(!) moves in just a couple of minutes, and by the time he reaches the end of his home analysis, his advantage is already decisive.

1 d4 d5 2 c4 c6

The Slav Defence, one of Black's most respected defences to 1 d4, and especially popular at the time of writing. A blood-brother of the Caro-Kann against 1 e4, the Slav aims to defend Black's central pawn on d5, without blocking in his c8-bishop, as occurs after 2...e6.

3 ♘f3 ♘f6 4 ♘c3 (D)

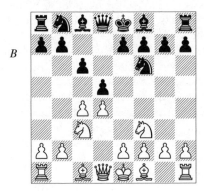

4...dxc4

The immediate 4...♗f5?! leads to problems with the b7-pawn after 5 cxd5 cxd5 6 ♕b3, so Black instead captures on c4 first. This does have the drawback of conceding White a central pawn-majority, but Black hopes that his free development and the enforced weakening of White's queenside will provide compensation.

5 a4

This is what I mean by the enforced weakening of White's queenside. In order to ensure that he can regain his pawn, White is forced to play this move, conceding a hole on b4, which Black can exploit to station a minor piece. Instead, the immediate 5 e4 would involve a gambit after 5...b5, and although it has enjoyed some popularity over the years, most grandmasters do not

consider that White has sufficient compensation for his pawn.

5...♗f5 (D)

White was now threatening 6 e4, taking control of the centre, so Black prevents this and develops his bishop to an active post.

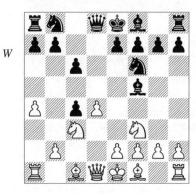

6 ♘e5

This is one of two moves for White in this position. The alternative is quiet development by 6 e3, when play usually continues 6...e6 7 ♗xc4 ♗b4 8 0-0 0-0. White will eventually aim to expand in the centre by e4, whilst Black completes his development with ...♘bd7. Chances are considered more or less equal.

The text-move is more ambitious. White wishes to continue with a rapid f3 and e4, establishing his pawn preponderance in the centre, and trying to shut Black's light-squared bishop out of the game on g6. If he can achieve this, White can expect to obtain some advantage, but the plan involves neglecting his development, and Black can exploit this to create counterplay.

6...♘bd7

Other moves are possible (notably 6...e6), but the text-move has been reestablished as the main line. Black challenges the centralized white knight and prepares to break out with ...e5.

7 ♘xc4 ♛c7

The point of Black's play. He prepares the freeing advance ...e5, which White cannot really prevent, since the hideous 8 f4? can scarcely be contemplated. Instead, White develops in such a way as to cause Black's pieces some tactical embarrassment.

8 g3 e5 9 dxe5 ♘xe5 10 ♗f4! *(D)*

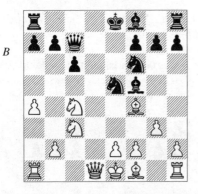

This is White's idea. Although Black has achieved his thematic pawn-break in the centre, he will have to place his pieces a little awkwardly to deal with this pin.

10...♘fd7 11 ♗g2 f6

This weakens the black position, notably the e6-square and the a2-g8 diagonal, but Black wishes to free his d7-knight from the task of defending its colleague on e5. In fact, all of these moves are very well-known, having been tested extensively in the two Alekhine-Euwe world championship matches in the 1930s. In recent years, Black has tried an even more radical way of untangling his position, with the move 11...g5!?, originally an invention of the Russian super-GM, Alexander Morozevich. Play often continues 12 ♘e3 gxf4 13 ♘xf5 0-0-0, with a thoroughly unclear position.

12 0-0 ♘c5 13 ♘e3 ♗g6 14 b4

Having completed his development, White takes the initiative on the queenside, setting up the possibility of a later break with b5. This will exert pressure against the c6-pawn, in conjunction with White's fianchettoed bishop, and also prepare to open the b-file with bxc6. In many ways, it is reminiscent of certain English Opening positions, such as seen in Game 25.

14...♘e6 *(D)*

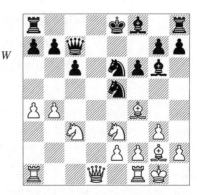

15 ♛b3 *(D)*

Here, it will be useful to set the present game in some context. It was played in the final round of the tournament, and this line of the Slav had been tested in several previous games in the same event. In fact, the position after 14...♘e6 had twice been reached by Boris Gelfand in earlier rounds. Bacrot-Gelfand had seen the thematic 15 b5, but Black achieved good play after 15...♖d8 16 ♛b3 ♘d4 17 ♛b2 ♗c5, and went on to win. Aronian himself had tried 15 a5 against Gelfand, but also achieved nothing. In preparing for the present game, Aronian and his second, Gabriel Sargissian, had anticipated the possibility of Sokolov repeating the same line, and had prepared a new idea, starting with the text-move. As we shall see, their analysis had gone very deeply into the position.

15...♗f7

One of the main points of White's new idea is to prevent Black from developing his f8-bishop actively. As the game Bacrot-Gelfand showed, against an early 15 b5, the bishop can come to c5, whereas now this is not possible.

After a passive development of the bishop, such as 15...♘d4 16 ♕b2 ♗e7, White can continue 17 b5, and by comparison with the Bacrot game, Black's bishop stands less actively.

16 ♕b1 ♘xf4

Here, too, 16...♗e7 17 b5 gives White an improved version of the earlier games, so Sokolov chooses the critical continuation, weakening White's pawn-structure.

17 gxf4 ♘g6 18 b5! *(D)*

White has no good way to defend the pawn on f4, and 18 f5? ♘f4 would leave Black an excellent game. White is therefore forced to play dynamically.

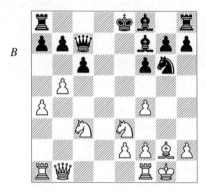

B

18...♕xf4

Played after long thought, as one might expect, whilst Aronian, by contrast, was still moving instantly. The main alternative was 18...♘xf4, whereupon Aronian intended to continue 19 bxc6 ♘xg2 (19...bxc6? loses to 20 ♕e4+ and 21 ♕xc6+) 20 ♕e4+!. Now 20...♗e7 is bad because of 21 cxb7 ♖b8 22 ♘b5!, when 22...♕xb7? is impossible due to 23 ♘d6+. Instead, Black would have to play 20...♕e5, when after 21 ♕xg2, the c-pawn is still immune, and White has excellent compensation after 21...♖c8 22 cxb7 ♖xc3 23 ♕g4. The pawn on b7 is very dangerous, and although the position is by no means 100% clear, one can understand that Sokolov was reluctant to enter such a position against an opponent who was clearly still in his preparation.

Sokolov's choice hopes to develop with tempo by 19...♗d6, but Aronian had prepared another shock for his opponent.

19 ♖d1!

After 19 bxc6? ♗d6, White cannot defend h2, but now 20 bxc6 is a real threat.

19...♗d6 *(D)*

This allows White to demonstrate his idea. There was no time to defend the c6-pawn by 19...♖c8, because of 20 bxc6 bxc6 21 ♗h3, but 19...♗c5 was an important alternative. Understandably, Aronian did not reveal how he intended to meet this move, preferring to save his secrets for another day and another opponent. The natural follow-up is 20 bxc6 0-0 21 cxb7 ♖ae8, and now both 22 ♕d3 and 22 ♘cd5 are possible. Even if Black regains his pawn, the b7-pawn is very strong. In any event, we can be sure that Aronian and Sargissian will have had this position on their board at home before the game, and will have prepared something.

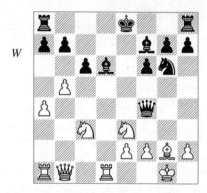

W

20 ♖xd6!

Much stronger than the passive defence 20 ♘f1?, after which 20...0-0 would give Black the advantage. One must not forget that White is temporarily a pawn down in this position, and his kingside has been seriously weakened, so he cannot settle for a normal continuation of the struggle. The whole of his play is predicated on dynamic possibilities, especially establishing a powerful passed pawn on b7, and for this he must be prepared to sacrifice the exchange. In such situations, the player is committed to decisive action, and must continue consistently. Of course, it is easier to do this when you have already analysed the position at home, and Aronian was still moving instantly at this stage.

20...♕xd6 21 bxc6 0-0?!

This is a very natural, practical decision, getting the black king out of the centre and connecting his rooks. However, it allows White to establish a monster passed pawn on b7, and the resulting position offers Black few saving chances. Objectively, therefore, Black should probably prefer 21...bxc6, after which White continues 22 ♘b5! ♕d7 (after 22...cxb5? White would not settle for regaining the exchange – instead, 23 ♕e4+ wins immediately) 23 ♕b4, trapping the enemy king in the centre. The threats of ♖d1 and ♘d6+ are very hard to meet, but Black does have an extra exchange and a pawn, and may be able to find some way to give back the material to break the attack.

22 ♘b5 ♕c5 23 cxb7 ♖ab8 *(D)*

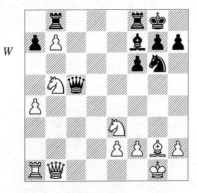

The result of all White's brilliance is a position where he has one pawn for the exchange, that pawn being a huge passed pawn on b7, supported by White's fianchettoed bishop. With his active pieces, he has a definite advantage, but he needs to avoid any counterplay, particularly on the kingside, where White's king is somewhat weak. In addition to his advantages on the board, Aronian also by now had a huge advantage on the clock. He was still moving instantly, whilst Sokolov was down to just a few minutes to reach the time-control at move 40.

24 ♕f5!

A nice move, keeping the black queen away from the kingside. White would be only too happy to exchange queens, after which his king would be secured and he would soon be able to round up Black's a-pawn.

24...♘e5?!

Aronian gives 24...♕b6 as a better defensive try, although White retains the advantage.

25 ♕c2 ♕b6 26 ♕c7 *(D)*

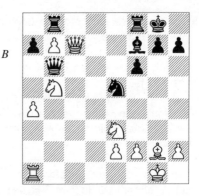

Remarkably, this was the first move of the game that Aronian had to find for himself at the board. He spent 9 minutes on it, treble the amount of time he had spent on his first 25 moves! Add to that the fact that his position is now completely winning, and one can appreciate the full effectiveness of his opening preparation.

26...♖fd8 27 ♖c1

Threatening 28 ♕xb8 followed by 29 ♖c8+.

27...♕a6 28 ♘f5

Now the threat is 29 ♘bd6 followed by 30 f4.

28...♕b6 *(D)*

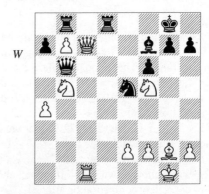

29 ♕xb8!

Decisive.

29...♖xb8 30 ♖c8+ ♕d8 31 ♘xa7 ♗e8 32 ♖xd8 ♖xd8 33 ♗d5+ ♗f7 34 ♘e7+ ♔f8 35 ♘ec6 1-0

A real crush by Aronian, and a brilliant example of deep opening preparation.

Game 11
Zoltan Ribli – Arturo Pomar
Buenos Aires Olympiad 1978
Réti Opening

This game is an example of how to exploit weak opening play. Pomar plays the early moves sloppily, and soon finds himself with problems. Rather than settle for a slightly inferior position, he commits the typical mistake of trying to seek salvation by tactical means. Tactics usually favour the player with the superior mobilization, and Ribli duly punishes him. The key thing to note is that in order to punish Black's inferior play, Ribli adopts concrete, tactical measures. If White had simply continued with routine development, this would in all likelihood have allowed Black to get away with his inaccuracies, but after Ribli's accurate response, Pomar's sins soon catch him up.

1 ♘f3 ♘f6 2 g3 d5 3 ♗g2 e6 4 0-0 ♘bd7?!

Although this develops a piece, and in one sense, 'cannot be bad', it is nevertheless not a good move. The objection is that Black commits himself unnecessarily early. It is not yet clear where this knight will stand best, and much depends on how White develops. If White continues in Réti fashion with d3, the knight may be well-placed on d7, but in other formations, Black may well do better to play ...c5 and ...♘c6. Flexibility is an important element in chess, and one should try to avoid committing oneself any earlier than necessary. Whichever set-up White adopts, it is highly likely that Black's bishop will be best on e7, so he should play 4...♗e7 and 5...0-0 immediately, postponing his queenside development until he sees how White will play.

5 d4! (D)

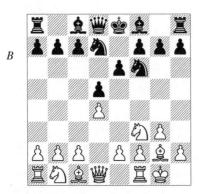

White immediately responds to Black's last move. The pawn on d4 rather 'dominates' the knight, depriving it of the squares c5 and e5.

5...b6?!

Another inaccuracy. The early fianchetto does not fit in well with the moves ...d5 and ...♘bd7. Black should still play 5...♗e7 and 6...0-0, with a line of the Closed Catalan that is satisfactory for Black, if a trifle passive.

6 c4 ♗b7 7 cxd5!

Without his knight on c3, this exchange is particularly effective.

7...♘xd5?!

The most solid recapture is 7...exd5, but then the bishop on b7 would not stand very well, and White would have a small but definite edge. Pomar tries to keep the long diagonal open, but runs into much worse trouble.

8 ♖e1! (D)

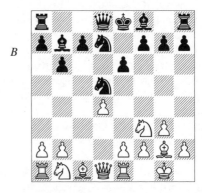

White prepares to advance in the centre. Black should probably settle for 8...♗e7 9 e4 ♘5f6 10 ♘c3, although White would stand better even then. Instead, Pomar again tries to avoid such a simple, inferior position, but once again, he runs into even more trouble. The words 'frying pan' and 'fire' come to mind.

8...♗b4?! 9 ♗g5!

No doubt an unpleasant surprise. Black had presumably counted on 9 ♗d2, but the text-move is much stronger. Now after 9...f6 10 ♗d2, Black has a nasty weakness on e6. Even though the e-file is closed, Pomar prefers to avoid this permanent weakness, and instead re-treats the bishop. The alternative was 9...♘7f6, which Pomar may have rejected for the same reason as many of the commentators at the time, namely 10 e4 ♗xe1 11 exd5 ♗a5? 12 b4! winning material. However, this line fails to 11...♗xf2+!, when both 12 ♔xf2 and 12 ♔f1 are refuted by 12...♘e4(+)!. Instead, White should play 10 ♘bd2!, when the threat of 11 e4 remains unpleasant for Black.

9...♗e7 10 e4! (D)

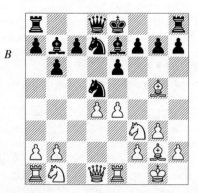

Ribli continues to produce one accurate, concrete move after another, and his play is an excellent example of how one should exploit inaccurate opening play by the opponent. Now 10...♘5f6 11 ♘c3 leaves White with the same comfortable edge that Pomar has been trying so hard to avoid, but he should nonetheless grin and bear it. His chosen cure proves worse than the disease.

10...♗xg5? 11 exd5 ♗xd5 12 ♘xg5 ♗xg2 13 ♘xe6! fxe6 14 ♔xg2 (D)

The upshot of the opening is a clear advan-tage for White, whose weakness on d4 is less important than Black's on e6. Even so, Black's disadvantage would be manageable after simply 14...0-0, when 15 ♖xe6 ♘c5! gives Black some compensation on the light squares. Instead,

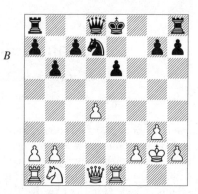

Pomar continues to avoid such simple inferior-ity, in favour of what he evidently considered to be more troubled waters. The result is that he loses in short order.

14...♕f6?! 15 ♕g4 0-0-0

Now he loses the pawn without any compen-sation, but 15...♘f8 16 ♘c3 was also terrible for Black.

16 ♖xe6 ♕f7 17 ♘c3 ♖hf8 18 ♕e2 ♔b8 19 ♖e1

Black's position is lost and the mercifully swift conclusion must have been a relief to Pomar.

19...h5 20 ♘d5 ♘f6 21 ♘b4

Now the denouement ensues on the light squares.

21...♖de8 22 ♘c6+ ♔b7 23 ♕f3 ♔c8 (D)

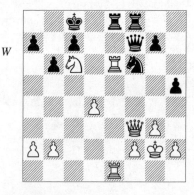

24 ♘e5 1-0

Poor play from Pomar, but Ribli gave an ex-cellent demonstration of how to exploit weak opening play.

Game 12
John Littlewood – Jeff Horner
Manchester 1980
King's Indian Attack

One of the most effective ways to improve one's play is to build up a stock of middlegame positions and plans which one understands in detail and has played and analysed before. This enables the player to orientate himself more quickly and confidently, saving time on the clock and enabling him to devote less time to divining the correct strategy, and more to calculating specific variations. This is a very nice example. The experienced England international John Littlewood is faced with an unusual opening set-up from his opponent. Unluckily for Horner, Littlewood had once faced a similar line with reversed colours against no less an opponent than Smyslov, and the lessons he learned from that game are turned to great effect on the unsuspecting Horner.

1 ♘f3 e6 2 g3 b5 *(D)*

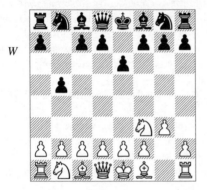

Opening lines featuring this unusual move are sometimes referred to as the Polish Defence. Black meets White's fianchetto with an extended fianchetto of his own, hoping to use the additional queenside space to develop an initiative on that side of the board. The line also has the merit of being relatively rare, with the result that most opponents will not be very familiar with the resulting positions, and it is thus often a good choice for a player who wishes to take his opponent out of the book. Unluckily for Horner, in this game he runs into an exceptionally erudite opponent.

3 ♗g2 ♗b7 4 0-0 ♘f6 5 d3 ♗e7 6 e4 0-0 7 a4

This is White's principal attempt to take advantage of Black's early ...b5. If White continues in normal King's Indian Attack fashion, with moves such as ♘bd2, ♘h4, f4, etc., we would reach positions of the sort that usually arise with Black having played 2...b6. In those

lines, Black usually responds to White's kingside play by countering on the queenside with ...c5, ...b5, etc. It is clear that in this position, Black could well be a tempo up on those usual lines, thanks to having played 2...b5. If he wishes to secure any advantage, therefore, White needs to adjust his usual plan to utilize the changed circumstances.

7...b4 8 a5! *(D)*

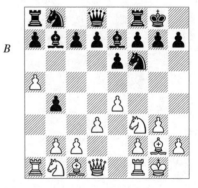

With this move, White prevents Black from supporting his advanced b-pawn with ...a5. White's further plan is to play c3 and exchange pawns on b4, after which he will bring his knight via d2 to b3. From b3, the knight will eye potentially weak squares such as c5, and White will also be able to target the b4-pawn, which is somewhat stranded in hostile territory. Instead of the queenside being Black's territory, it is White who will seek to establish the advantage on that side of the board.

Littlewood's plan is deep and well thought-out, but his task in the present game was greatly helped by his having played much the same idea some 17 years earlier, against the great Vasily Smyslov. The latter was always a connoisseur of early b4/...b5 set-ups, and had used such a line as White against Littlewood at Hastings 1962/3. However, Littlewood had found such an effective defensive plan for Black that he had soon assumed the initiative, and Smyslov was happy to draw. Here are the opening moves of the earlier game Smyslov-Littlewood, Hastings 1962/3: 1 ♘f3 ♘f6 2 g3 g6 3 b4 ♗g7 4 ♗b2 0-0 5 ♗g2 d6 6 0-0 a5 7 b5 a4! 8 d4 c6 9 c4 cxb5 10 cxb5 ♘bd7 11 ♘a3 ♘b6 12 ♖e1, and now by 12...d5!, Black could have secured an edge. As we shall see, Littlewood uses much the same plan in the present game, and soon has a substantial positional advantage.

8...c5 9 c3 d5

Exchanging pawns on c3 would avoid the weak pawn on b4, but would be in White's favour after 9...bxc3 10 bxc3. In particular, the bishop on b7 would be vulnerable along the open b-file.

10 e5 *(D)*

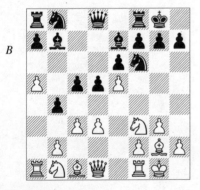

10...♘e8?!

As we shall see, Black later suffers from the weakness of the c5-square, so this knight would have done better to retreat to d7, from where it would protect that weakness. However, it is much easier to realize this when one knows what White's further plan involves. For Horner, however, this position would have been relatively unfamiliar, and it is difficult for even a strong player such as he to orientate himself in a relatively unfamiliar situation. For Littlewood, on the other hand, many of the strategic subtleties of the position would have been well-known,

thanks to his previous experience against Smyslov.

11 cxb4 cxb4 12 ♘bd2 ♗a6 13 ♘b3 ♘c6 14 ♗e3 *(D)*

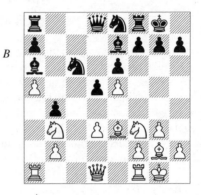

White plays consistently to seize control of the squares c5 and d4. His further plan will consist of ♕d2 and ♖fc1, bringing additional pressure to bear on the black queenside. Black, meanwhile, has great difficulty finding any active plan.

14...♖c8 15 ♕d2 ♘c7 16 ♖fc1 ♘b5 17 ♗c5! *(D)*

The exchange of dark-squared bishops is much more effective than 17 ♘c5. White wishes to retain the knight on b3, so that it can occupy c5, once Black's bishop has been eliminated.

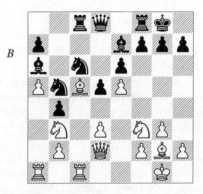

17...d4?

Horner tries to fight back on the dark squares, not wishing to allow 18 d4, but in so doing, he gives up control of the e4-square, which White soon exploits.

Passive defence with 17...♖c7 was probably better, although Black's position remains very unpleasant. It is clear that White's queenside strategy has been a complete success.

18 ♗xe7 ♕xe7 19 ♘c5 ♗b7 20 ♘xb7

Having got his knight to its long-desired outpost, White immediately exchanges it off! However, this is done in the service of a greater cause. White's next move unmasks the bishop on the freshly-opened long diagonal, and announces one of our favourite positional themes – the two weaknesses.

20...♕xb7 21 ♘g5!

The pin on the long diagonal means that White is threatening to win the b4-pawn, which has long been in its sights. However, he also has designs on Black's kingside.

21...♕d7 *(D)*

There is no way to defend the b4-pawn in any case, so Black breaks the pin and invites White to exchange twice on c6, and take the pawn.

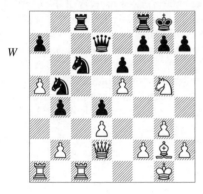

22 ♗e4!

But Littlewood refuses to be bought off so cheaply, and suddenly, Black's king comes under a lethal attack.

22...f5

This is equivalent to resignation, but the obvious 22...h6 loses to 23 ♘h7 ♖fd8 24 ♘f6+ gxf6 25 exf6, when Black has no sensible way to prevent 26 ♕xh6, followed by mate on g7.

23 exf6 gxf6

23...♖xf6 is slightly better, but the position is lost anyway.

24 ♘xh7 ♖f7 25 ♘xf6+! ♖xf6 *(D)*

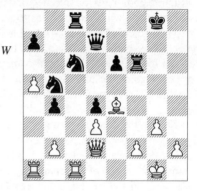

Black could have resigned with a clear conscience, but struggles on for a few more moves, probably out of shell-shock as much as anything.

26 ♕g5+ ♔f7 27 ♕xb5 e5 28 ♖c5 a6 29 ♕xa6 ♔g7 30 ♖ac1 ♘e7 31 ♕b7 ♖xc5 32 ♖xc5 ♕e6 33 ♖c7 ♖f7 34 a6 ♕f6 35 ♗f3 1-0

3 Structures

In this chapter, we shall look at some typical pawn-structures, and the plans associated with them. We covered many of the standard structures, such as IQP, hanging pawns, etc., in *50ECL*. In the present volume, we shall cover some new pawn-structures, as well as revisiting some of those covered in *50ECL*, in order to look at some additional plans and ideas associated with them.

Games 13 and 14 deal with the Modern Benoni pawn-structure. This is a typical case where the pawn-structure dominates the middlegame plans of the two sides, White seeking to exploit his central preponderance, whilst Black aims to neutralize this and capitalize on his queenside majority. Games 15 and 16 cover the Benko Gambit structure, one of the most fascinating of modern pawn-structures. Black gambits a pawn, not for the usual rapid development and tactical attacking chances, but for long-term positional compensation. He frequently seeks to exchange queens and head for an endgame, despite his material deficit.

After a brief look at the Czech Benoni, Games 18-22 deal with various aspects of the King's Indian, seeking to deepen our understanding of structures examined at a basic level in *50ECL*. One of the things which the new games show is how flexible these structures can be, with both sides frequently having the option of choosing which side of the board on which to operate. Game 19 is an especially striking example of this.

The remaining games of this chapter examine assorted pawn-structures, including various Sicilian positions, English Opening structures, Hedgehog, etc. In all cases, the examples chosen aim to bring out aspects of those formations which were not seen in the examples looked at in *50ECL*.

Game 13
Ian Watson – John Nunn
British Ch, Brighton 1980
Modern Benoni, Taimanov Attack

In this game and the next, we look at the typical Modern Benoni structure. Firstly, we see an example of Black's strategy succeeding, as he is able to exploit his queenside pawn-majority to decisive effect.

1 d4 ♘f6 2 c4 c5 3 d5 e6 4 ♘c3 exd5 5 cxd5 d6 *(D)*

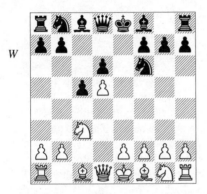

Setting up the Modern Benoni, one of Black's sharpest defences to 1 d4. A favourite of Mikhail Tal (see Game 14), it gained great popularity in the 1960s and 1970s, culminating in game 3 of the Fischer-Spassky match in 1972, when Fischer used the defence to score his first ever win against Spassky. Within a few years, however, the opening gradually lost favour, as White unearthed more effective ways of playing. Nowadays, it is a rarity at top GM level, although Topalov has occasionally ventured the black side.

The main positional themes of the Modern Benoni are derived from the unbalanced pawn-structure. Black has granted White a central pawn-majority, whilst Black has a 3 vs 2 majority on the queenside. To the classicists of Tarrasch's day, such a structure would have been regarded with virtual horror, on the assumption that White will crash through the centre with f4 and e5 long before Black can make anything of his queenside pawns. In many games, that is indeed what happens, and in the next game, we shall see an example of precisely this. However, Tal and others showed that with accurate play,

Black can usually prevent this from occurring, and that he has considerable tactical chances.

The most important thing about the Benoni is the initiative. Black usually needs to grab and hold onto the initiative, since if he loses it, White is able to prepare his central breakthrough in peace, and Black is soon in trouble.

6 e4 g6 7 f4

At the time this game was played, this line was just emerging as White's most dangerous try, and indeed, it is the line which has been chiefly responsible for the demise of the Modern Benoni at GM level. The line is so strong that most Modern Benoni die-hards, such as Psakhis and de Firmian, prefer to use the move-order 1 d4 ♘f6 2 c4 e6, waiting for White to play 3 ♘f3 before going into the Benoni by 3...c5, now that White has precluded the f4 plan. However, White also has many other good set-ups. These include 7 ♘f3 and ♗d3 (prepared by h3) or ♗e2, and 6 g3, whilst in the next game, we see White choose 7 ♗d3 and 8 ♘ge2.

7...♗g7 8 ♗b5+ *(D)*

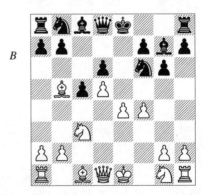

8...♘fd7

This looks a clumsy move, and indeed it is, but both of the more natural means of blocking the check are strongly met by 9 e5. In more recent years, some Benoni fans have invested great efforts in trying to keep Black's position afloat after 8...♘bd7 9 e5 dxe5 10 fxe5 ♘h5 11 e6 ♛h4+, but although no definitive refutation of Black's play has yet been found, few strong GMs seem to trust it.

9 a4!

The best move, ensuring that Black cannot expand on the queenside by means of ...a6 and ...b5.

9...0-0

9...♛h4+ has also been tried here, when Black can meet 10 g3 with either 10...♛e7 or 10...♛d8. However, here too White's powerful pawn-centre and rapid development have seen him win numerous games in short order.

10 ♘f3 ♘a6

Black takes advantage of White's 9th move, to steer his knight to an active position on the queenside. In Game 17, we see Black play a similar manoeuvre in a Czech Benoni, but the knight proves misplaced. In this position, it makes much more sense, since Black's queenside pawn-majority means that the knight has some support. For example, one plan is to play ...c4 and entrench the knight on d3.

11 0-0 ♘b4 12 ♖e1 a6 *(D)*

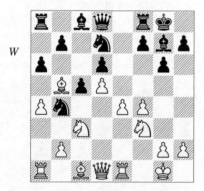

13 ♗c4?!

Up to now, White has played the opening well, but here he loses his way. The text-move is designed to meet 13...♘f6 with 14 e5, when the bishop defends d5 after 14...dxe5 15 fxe5, but Black is able to exploit the bishop's exposed position. A stronger line is 13 ♗f1 ♘f6 14 h3!, preventing Black from freeing his position by ...♗g4 and ...♗xf3. Black would then be much more badly affected by his lack of space, and White could prepare e5 at greater leisure. It was

the possibility of such a plan that put Nunn and other Benoni practitioners off this whole variation.

13...♘b6! *(D)*

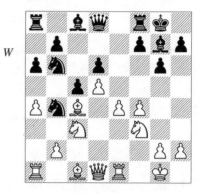

This is not usually a very good square for Black's knights in the Benoni, because the knight can be driven back by a5. However, in this position, the important thing for Black is to gain a tempo, so he can play ...♗g4.

14 ♗e2 ♗g4!

Now Black has a satisfactory position, and he soon assumes the initiative. Although he surrenders the bishop-pair, this is less important than the fact that he frees up some space in his rather cramped position. For instance, his knight can now use the d7-square, without having to compete for it with his own bishop. In addition, the exchange of White's knight on f3 means that it is much harder for White to prepare the breakthrough e5, which is his main source of play.

15 h3 ♗xf3 16 ♗xf3 ♛h4 *(D)*

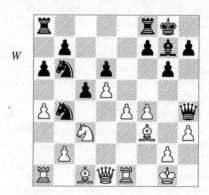

This carries the incidental tactical threat of 17...♘c2.

17 ♔h2 ♖fe8

Not 17...♘c2?? 18 g3, winning.
18 g3
This weakens the position, but it is already difficult to find a good way for White to continue. 18 ♗e3 allows 18...♘c4.
18...♕d8 19 ♖e2 ♘c4 20 ♘a2 ♕b6 21 ♘xb4 ♕xb4 22 ♖a2 *(D)*

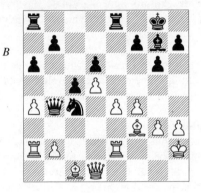

White's clumsy manoeuvres are a clear sign that he has lost the initiative, and is struggling to hold back Black's queenside pressure.
22...♘a5 23 ♗d2 ♕b3
Forcing an endgame, which normally favours Black in the Modern Benoni. With queens gone, the danger posed by White's potential central and kingside breakthrough is much reduced, whilst Black's queenside majority becomes correspondingly more powerful.
24 ♕xb3 ♘xb3 25 ♗e3 *(D)*

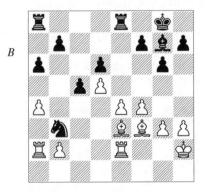

25...f5!

This is another reason why Black is usually happy to see queens come off in this opening. With queens on, Black would have to be very careful about playing this move, since although he breaks up White's centre and isolates his d-pawn, he also exposes his own king significantly. In the endgame, however, the move is much more likely to be effective.
26 exf5 gxf5
White is in a very bad way. Almost every black piece is more active than its opposite number, and Black's queenside pawns are ready to roll.
27 ♔g2 b5 28 ♗h5 ♖f8 29 ♖a3 c4 30 axb5
Opening the a-file helps Black, but otherwise, the white rook ran the risk of being buried alive after 30...b4.
30...axb5 31 ♖xa8 ♖xa8 32 ♗b6 b4 33 ♖c2 c3 34 bxc3 bxc3 *(D)*

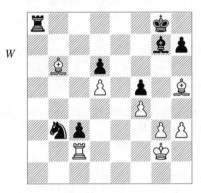

The distant passed pawn, supported by all of its pieces, will soon decide the game.
35 ♗e3 ♘a1 36 ♖c1 ♖a2+ 37 ♔f1 ♘b3 38 ♖e1 c2 39 ♗e2 ♗c3 40 ♗c4 ♘d2+ 0-1
A very typical Benoni win. White did not seem to do that much seriously wrong, yet he was beaten almost effortlessly. The possibility of such games, which arise from the unbalanced pawn-structure, is what made the Modern Benoni such an attractive opening for a long time, especially in the hands of a player facing a lower-rated opponent, and keen to play for a win.

Game 14

Jonathan Penrose – Mikhail Tal

Leipzig Olympiad 1960

Modern Benoni, ♗d3 and ♘ge2

Here, we see the other side of the Modern Benoni coin. White exploits some inaccurate play by his opponent in order to organize the central breakthrough e5, after which he soon whips up a winning attack.

1 d4 ♘f6 2 c4 e6 3 ♘c3 c5 4 d5 exd5 5 cxd5 g6 6 e4 d6 7 ♗d3 ♗g7 8 ♘ge2 *(D)*

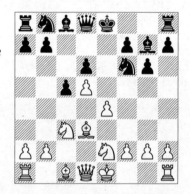

B

As explained in Game 13, White's main plan in the Modern Benoni is to use his central pawn-majority to force a breakthrough by means of f4 and e5. For this reason, he develops his kingside pieces in such a way as to leave open the path of the f-pawn. The bishop on d3 points aggressively at Black's kingside, and the knight can later move to g3, allowing White to double his major pieces on the f-file. This plan is one of White's most aggressive choices, although over the course of some years, adequate defensive methods were found for Black. Nonetheless, the line remains a reputable way of combating the Modern Benoni, and, as this game shows, it can pack a considerable punch if Black does not play accurately. One player who remained faithful to this line throughout his playing career was the East German GM, Rainer Knaak, a noted opening theoretician. Anybody interested in this variation would be well advised to study his games.

One point which probably strikes the reader is that White's knight on e2 does not control the e5-square (as it would from f3), and one may therefore wonder how White is ever going

to achieve the e5 break, on which so much of his build-up depends. Later developments in the game will supply the answer to this question.

8...0-0 9 0-0 a6

Another option for Black here is 9...♘a6, planning to bring the knight to c7, to support the ...b5 advance. The choice between c7 and d7 for his queen's knight is one of Black's most fundamental decisions in the Modern Benoni. On c7, the knight does not exert so much control over the e5-square, but on the other hand, it attacks White's d5-pawn, which in itself may make it more difficult for him to play e5. Another merit of c7 is that if White ever does achieve the breakthrough e5, Black's other knight may have the retreat-square d7, which will not be the case if the queen's knight occupies that square. On the other hand, this may be small consolation, since if White gets in e5 favourably, Black is usually in a good deal of trouble anyway.

All in all, it is often difficult to say which development of the knight is preferable, and the choice is frequently one of taste.

10 a4 ♕c7 *(D)*

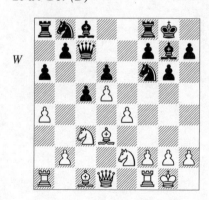

W

11 h3

This is the main thematic continuation, preparing f4 and ♘g3. White can also adopt a strategy based around playing f3 at some point. White solidifies his centre and he will later try to play on the queenside, by preparing the advance b4. White's position is strongly reminiscent of the Sämisch King's Indian. This sophisticated positional plan was played quite extensively in the 1980s by Tony Miles, who was very successful with it, and it remains a perfectly valid alternative to Penrose's more ambitious attacking strategy.

11...♘bd7 12 f4 ♖e8?! *(D)*

This is a typical move in the Modern Benoni, but in this instance, Black has cause to regret weakening the f7-square. Modern theory prefers 12...♖b8, when *NCO* quotes the game Knaak-Berend, Thessaloniki Olympiad 1988, which continued 13 ♗e3! ♖e8 14 ♘g3 c4 15 ♗c2 b5 16 axb5 axb5 17 ♖a7 ♕d8 18 ♕d2, with a small advantage to White.

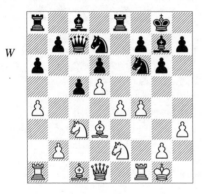

13 ♘g3 c4 14 ♗c2 ♘c5

This is one of Black's typical ideas in the Benoni, especially when his queen's knight is on d7. The move 13...c4 helps Black to prepare a later ...b5, and also clears the c5-square, so Black's knight can jump to c5, and thence to d3 or b3. The main factor Black must be aware of, when playing ...c4, is that he gives up control of d4, and so he must be careful that White cannot play his own knight into this square. From d4, a white knight could then later go to c6, once Black has played ...b5. The alert reader will note that, both in this game and in Knaak-Berend quoted above, Black only played the move ...c4 after White's king's knight had gone to g3, and can therefore only get to d4 at the cost of another tempo.

15 ♕f3 *(D)*

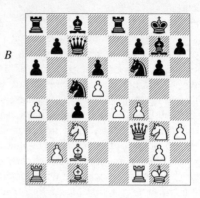

15...♘fd7

In the best Nimzowitschian style, Black over-protects the important e5-square. This decision is explained by a tactical point. The move Black would really like to play is 15...♖b8, preparing 16...b5, but this would run into an immediate 16 e5!, when Black cannot capture on e5 because after 16...dxe5 17 fxe5, both 17...♖xe5 18 ♗f4 and 17...♕xe5 18 ♗f4 ♕d4+ 19 ♖f2 ♖a8 20 ♘ge2 lose material.

16 ♗e3 b5!?

A typical Tal, and Modern Benoni, tactic. Black takes advantage of the undefended b2-pawn to force through his desired queenside break.

17 axb5 ♖b8 18 ♕f2!

A subtle move, the point of which will become clear soon. Capturing on a6 would give Black excellent counterplay after 18 bxa6 ♖xb2.

18...axb5 *(D)*

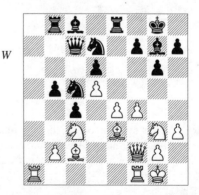

White has finished his development, whilst Black is already making progress on the queenside. It is clear that White needs to strike on the other wing, yet he has too few pieces covering the e5-square. Penrose supplies the answer to the dilemma.

19 e5! dxe5 20 f5!

This pawn sacrifice breakthrough is at the basis of White's whole set-up, and is a very common theme in such Benoni structures. For his pawn, White has powerful pressure down the f-file and against Black's king (it is already apparent that Black's rook would have been better off remaining on f8). In addition, the pawn on e5 shuts out Black's dark-squared bishop, and White plans to establish a knight on the great square e4, from where it will blockade the e5-pawn, support a possible d6 thrust, and threaten to jump to f6 or g5.

Because this e5-pawn causes Black a lot of trouble, one of the standard ways to react to the e5 and f5 breakthrough is for Black immediately to return the pawn by ...e4, so as to liberate his g7-bishop, and open the e-file for his rook. It is in this context that we can understand White's 18th move. If his queen were still on f3, ...e4 would attack the queen and force White to spend a tempo capturing on e4, or moving the queen away. Thanks to 18 ♛f2!, however, the move 20...e4? would not come with tempo, and would lose immediately to 21 fxg6.

20...♝b7 *(D)*

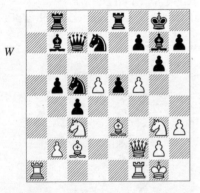

Black defends his rook on e8, thereby meeting the immediate threat of 21 fxg6, and also attacks White's d5-pawn, thereby preventing 21 ♘ce4.

21 ♖ad1!

Penrose is not distracted by the b5-pawn, and instead defends his strong passed d-pawn, thereby renewing the threat of ♘ce4.

21...♝a8 22 ♘ce4

Once again, White could have regained his pawn by 22 fxg6 fxg6 23 ♘xb5 (23...♖xb5? 24 ♛f7+), but prefers to concentrate on the kingside. Taking on b5 would open the b-file for Black's rook and give him additional counterplay.

22...♘a4 *(D)*

After this, White breaks into Black's position by a simple forcing sequence. 22...♘xe4 23 ♘xe4 ♖f8 is possibly a better try, but after 24 ♛h4, White has a ready-made attack with such moves as ♝h6, ♘g5, etc. It is hard to see how Black can possibly survive. One drastic variation runs 24...♛d8 25 f6 ♝h8 26 ♘g5 h5 27 ♛xh5!, and if 27...gxh5, then 28 ♝h7#.

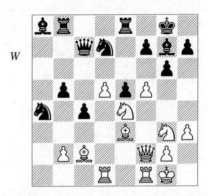

23 ♝xa4 bxa4 24 fxg6 fxg6 25 ♛f7+ ♚h8 26 ♘c5!

This wins a whole piece, since 26...♖bd8 loses to 27 ♘e6. Tal struggles on for a few moves with two pawns for his piece, but the rest is really just a mopping-up exercise for White.

26...♛a7 27 ♛xd7 ♛xd7 28 ♘xd7 ♖xb2 29 ♘b6

Immediately annexing one of the two passed pawns.

29...♖b3 30 ♘xc4 ♖d8 31 d6 ♖c3 32 ♖c1

The simplest.

32...♖xc1 33 ♖xc1 ♝d5 34 ♘b6 ♝b3 35 ♘e4 h6 36 d7 ♝f8 37 ♖c8 ♝e7 38 ♝c5 ♝h4 39 g3 1-0

Game 15
Gennadi Kuzmin – Tamaz Georgadze
Odessa 1972
Benko Gambit

In this game and the next, we encounter another typical modern pawn-structure, the Benko Gambit. Black sacrifices a pawn on the queenside to open the a- and b-files for his rooks. It is one of the most fascinating of gambits, since Black relies for his compensation on long-term positional factors, rather than seeking immediate tactical chances. In many cases, Black will happily exchange queens, something he would rarely do in most other gambits.

1 d4 ♘f6 2 c4 c5 3 d5 b5

This is the characteristic move of the Benko Gambit. Most gambits aim at rapid development and an attack on the enemy king, but the Benko is much more positionally based, and perhaps for that reason, has achieved a popularity amongst grandmasters which few other genuine gambits have managed.

4 cxb5

White has a wide variety of ways to meet the Benko, both by accepting and declining it. In this position, for example, he can refuse the pawn altogether, with either 4 ♘f3 or 4 a4.

4...a6 5 bxa6

Here too, White can play other moves, notably 5 e3, as seen in the next game, and 5 b6, seeking to keep the a-file closed. However, the old adage that the best way to refute a gambit is to accept it, still contains a fair amount of truth, and taking both pawns is certainly White's most natural and ambitious approach.

5...♗xa6 6 ♘c3 d6 *(D)*

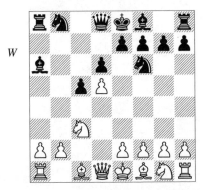

7 e4

After this move, White loses castling rights, and has to spend an extra tempo or two bringing his king into safety. The main alternative is 7 g3, aiming to develop normally on the kingside and castle. This is certainly a very respectable way for White to continue, but it is also true that in the resulting positions, his bishop on g2 is often not all that active. In addition, it becomes relatively difficult to advance e4-e5 in the centre, since with Black's bishop unopposed on the a6-f1 diagonal, White frequently has trouble defending his d3-square against invasion by a black knight after, for example, ...♘g4-e5.

For this reason, many players prefer the textmove, by which the troublesome bishop on a6 is eliminated.

7...♗xf1 8 ♔xf1 g6 *(D)*

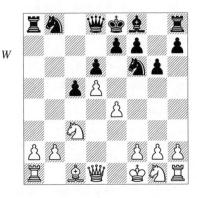

9 g3

Preparing a spot for the king on g2. Another plan is 9 h3, with a similar idea, to play ♔g1-h2. In many ways, this is preferable, since the king is safer on h2 than on g2, whilst the pawn often needs to go to h3 in such structures, to prevent Black's thematic knight manoeuvre ...♘g4-e5. However, the drawback of 9 h3 is that it takes one move longer for White to evacuate his king than is the case after 9 g3, and this extra tempo allows Black to generate his queenside counterplay more quickly. For this reason, 9 g3 has tended to be the more popular move here, although 9 h3 has also had its adherents.

9...♗g7 10 ♔g2 0-0 11 ♘f3 ♘bd7 12 ♖e1 ♕a5 *(D)*

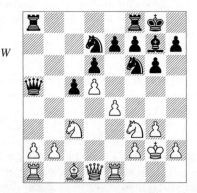

A typical Benko set-up has been reached. Black's moves are very standard in the Accepted lines of the gambit, with only the placing of his queen usually requiring any particular thought (sometimes it goes to b6 or c7, although a5 is the most active square). As a result, within reason, Black can almost "shut his eyes" and play most of these moves irrespective of what White does. Indeed, Larsen once joked that he thought this was why Pal Benko, a notorious time-trouble addict, was so fond of the opening – "12 moves, for just a pawn!". The last of Black's 'auto-pilot' moves will usually be ...♖fb8, after which the middlegame begins in earnest.

So what exactly does Black have for his pawn? After all, White has no real weaknesses, his development is almost complete, and his king is not subject to any real threats. Compared with most gambits, Black seems to have very little to show for his investment.

The subtlety of the Benko lies in the long-term positional nature of Black's compensation. In the first place he has a rock-solid pawn-structure. His single pawn-island contains only one small weakness, the e7-pawn, and this is difficult for White to attack. By contrast, White has two pawn-islands, and the a2- and b2-pawns are both under pressure down the open queenside files. Secondly, Black has an extremely harmonious and natural development.

His rooks have open files, his bishop on g7 co-operates with the rooks in bearing down on White's queenside, and his knights have a potential outpost on d3 (e.g., after the pawn move ...c4, followed by ...♘c5-d3).

One of the most unusual features of the Benko is that a queen exchange frequently favours Black. One would expect that, as with most gambits, the gambiteer would need to keep queens on the board, so as to maximize his attacking chances, but the Benko is not that sort of gambit. His compensation does not consist so much in attacking chances, as the prospect of long-term pressure on the queenside, and the endgame often favours him more than the middlegame. This is something that we shall see illustrated in the present game.

13 ♗d2

This is a very natural move, but as the further course of the game shows, Black does not really have much to fear from the opposition of the bishop on his queen, as White has no effective discoveries with the knight. As we have pointed out earlier, the manoeuvre ...♘g4-e5 is a common idea for Black in these positions, and so White's most accurate move is probably the prophylactic 13 h3, preventing this idea once and for all.

13...♖fb8 14 ♕c2 *(D)*

14 b3 would be answered in similar fashion to the game.

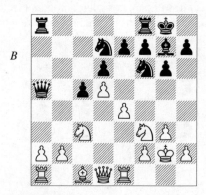

14...♘g4!

The thematic manoeuvre. The knight heads for e5, from where it will constantly threaten to jump to c4 or d3.

15 a4?!

This move is a common idea for White in Benko positions, but in this example, it does not work out well. White's idea is to block off the pressure on the b-file by playing ♘b5. If he can put his knight on b5, and keep it there, it can prove very effective in sealing off Black's queenside play, but if not, White runs the risk that the move a4 will merely create a weak backward pawn down the b-file.

Black has various ways to fight against the ♘b5 plan. If his knight is still on f6, he will in many positions challenge the knight with the standard manoeuvre ...♘e8-c7, seeking to force an exchange of knights. In other positions, he can put pressure on the a4-pawn, so as to force White to keep the knight on c3 to defend the a-pawn. If White reacts by playing b3, to support the pawn (having first removed his a1-rook from tactical threats on the long diagonal), Black will try to break up the b3-a4 pawn duo by playing ...c4.

In the present example, White never succeeds in getting his knight to b5 in the first place, because Black has too much pressure on the a4-pawn.

15...♕b4! *(D)*

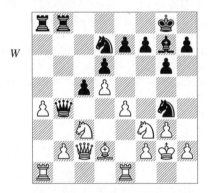

This prevents 16 ♘b5, since the b2-pawn would then be *en prise*. It looks tactically risky to place the queen on b4, where it can be hit by a subsequent ♘b5, but Georgadze has calculated accurately, and realized that everything is in order. This is another example of how tactics and strategy go together. A less tactically acute player might shy away from the move 15...♕b4. If, as a result, White managed to get his knight to b5 and gradually sit on the black position, many people would be tempted to attribute Black's loss to being outplayed strategically, whereas it was actually his failure to calculate the tactics properly after 15...♕b4

which would have sown the seeds of Black's defeat.

It is no coincidence that some of the world's greatest-ever strategists have been outstanding tacticians. I recall a Russian friend of mine telling me about his experience as a junior player, when he and some colleagues spent several hours having their games analysed by Tigran Petrosian. The latter was, and is, regarded as possibly the deepest strategist ever to be world champion, and my friend and his colleagues were expecting to be regaled with all manner of deep positional ideas. Instead, what they found was that Petrosian was simply fantastically quick at calculating tactics. It was precisely this tactical vision which allowed him to control positions and carry out his strategic plans, without allowing counterplay.

16 h3 ♘ge5 17 ♘xe5 ♗xe5!

Again, concrete tactical play. The usual move in such positions is 17...♘xe5, but here that would allow White to carry out his plan with 18 ♘b5 ♕c4 19 ♗c3, neutralizing the long diagonal and establishing his knight on the b5-square.

18 ♘d1 *(D)*

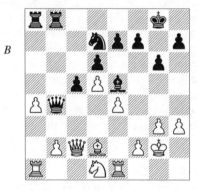

18...♕b3!

See the note to Black's 12th move. Despite his material deficit, Black is happy to exchange queens.

19 ♕xb3 ♖xb3 20 ♖e3?

This loses the extra pawn, after which there is no doubt as to Black's advantage. However, both 20 ♖a2 ♘b6 and 20 ♗c3 ♗xc3 21 bxc3 ♘b6 leave Black with good pressure for the pawn. Possibly the best line was to try to make something of the passed pawn by 20 a5!, when 20...♗xb2 21 ♘xb2 ♖xb2 22 ♗c3 ♖c2 23

罩ec1 罩xc1 24 罩xc1 f5! leads to an unclear position.

20...皀xb2 21 罩a2 罩xe3 22 ②xe3 皀d4 23 ②c4 *(D)*

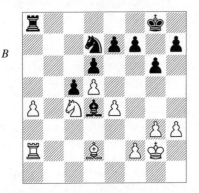

23...f5!

This move is very thematic for Benko endings, and is another reason why the exchange of queens tends to favour Black in such positions.

Black undermines the advanced d5-pawn. If White exchanges on f5, the d5-pawn is isolated and may well fall to Black's knight. On the other hand, if White shores up his pawn-structure by f3, a later exchange of pawns on e4 will leave a weakness on the e4-square. The importance of the queen exchange is that the move ...f5 is rarely good in the middlegame, because the weaknesses created on the e-file and in the vicinity of Black's king are usually more important than Black's positional gains. Once the queens are gone and the position is simplified, it is harder for White to exploit the e6-square and Black's weakened king, and the weakness of White's own pawns becomes more significant.

24 exf5 gxf5 25 皀g5?!

This leads to the bishop being out of play on the kingside, whilst the pressure against e7 proves easy to cope with. Using his passed a-pawn with 25 a5 would again have given White better chances than in the game.

25...當f7 26 f4 罩b8

Planning to get his own passed pawn rolling after 27...罩b4.

27 ②a5 h6!? *(D)*

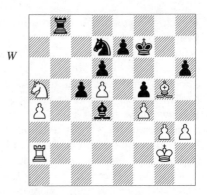

Aiming to deflect the bishop, so that after a later ②c6 by White, the pawn on e7 will not be hanging.

28 皀xh6

The tactical try 28 皀xe7 was also possible, but after 28...當xe7 29 ②c6+ 當f7 30 ②xb8 ②xb8, the two pieces would be stronger than the rook.

28...②b6

See the note to move 23. The d5-pawn can no longer be defended.

29 ②c6 罩a8 30 g4 ②xd5 31 ②xd4 cxd4 32 a5 當g6 33 皀g5 e5

White's centre has vanished into thin air, a common occurrence in Benko Gambit endings, and now Black's own passed pawns in the centre decide the game.

34 a6 ②e3+ 35 當g1 e4 36 皀e7 d3 37 皀xd6 ②c2! *(D)*

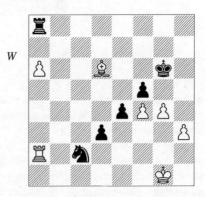

Neatly cutting both white pieces off from the d2-square.

38 gxf5+ 當f7 39 罩b2 d2 40 罩b7+ 當g8 0-1

Game 16
Walter Browne – Lev Alburt
USA Ch, Greenville 1983
Benko Gambit

Having just seen a typical win by Black in the Benko, here we see White give a fine demonstration of the merits of his position. Browne manages to neutralize Black's queenside pressure, and then breaks through in the centre with the e5 advance.

1 d4 ♘f6 2 c4 c5 3 d5 b5 4 cxb5 a6 5 e3

As we saw in the previous game, taking the pawn allows Black good play down the open a- and b-files. Once White started to realize this, attempts were made to find other ways to meet the Benko. The text-move is one of the most important, and has retained a measure of popularity to this day. Rather than develop Black's bishop by capturing on a6, White simply defends the pawn on b5, and develops his pieces.

5...g6

The normal Benko response, and probably the best move, although a more tactical solution, based around 5...axb5 6 ♗xb5 ♗b7 7 ♘c3 ♕a5, was later developed.

6 ♘c3 ♗g7 7 ♘f3 0-0 8 a4 *(D)*

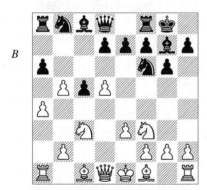

A typical part of White's plan in this variation. He intends to meet ...axb5 by recapturing with the bishop, and so prefers to keep the bishop on f1 for as long as possible, hoping to save a tempo by capturing in one move. He therefore plays a useful move on the queenside, solidifying his extra pawn, and allowing the rook to come to a3 in many variations. The latter defuses some of Black's tactical tricks, which are often based on the rook's undefended position on a1, and a consequent pin of the a4-pawn.

8...d6?!

Based largely on this game, and one or two others, Benko players soon came to the conclusion that this move is not the most accurate. Nowadays, the best move is considered to be 8...e6, when many games have continued 9 dxe6 fxe6 10 ♕d6, with unclear play.

9 ♖a3 ♘bd7

And here, 9...axb5! 10 ♗xb5 ♗a6 is a better try.

10 e4 axb5 *(D)*

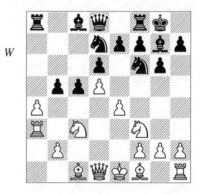

Both sides have been playing a waiting game with the pawn on b5. White has been trying to get Black to capture on b5, before White spends a tempo moving his bishop from f1, whilst Black has in turn been delaying ...axb5, hoping White would have to move the bishop first. Now Black finally admits defeat, since he has run out of useful moves.

11 ♗xb5 ♗a6 12 ♕e2 *(D)*

This was a new move at the time. Rather than capturing on a6, White defends his e-pawn with the queen, so that he can capture on b5 with the knight. The essence of White's strategy here is to use the outpost on b5 to stifle Black's queenside play. We saw in the previous game that Black's pressure down the open a- and b-files

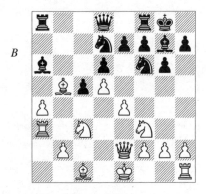

can be very difficult to meet, and so Browne is keen to avoid such a situation.

12...&xb5 13 &xb5 &e8!

A good manoeuvre, which was to become standard in such Benko positions. Black understands that, in order to create any pressure on the queenside, so as to compensate for his pawn minus, he needs to remove the powerful knight at b5.

14 0-0 &c7 15 b3!

White's play is very methodical. He intends to recapture on b5 with the queen, and also wishes to develop his queen's bishop. Since 15 &g5 &xb5 16 &xb5? &b8 would lose the b-pawn, he first moves it to a protected square.

15...&xb5 16 &xb5 &a7?!

This proves a little slow, and 16...&b8 was later suggested as a slight improvement.

17 &d2 &a8 18 &e1 *(D)*

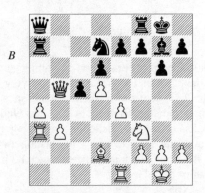

White's long-term strategy, once he has secured the queenside, is to break through the centre, in classic Benoni style, with e5.

18...&b7 19 &c4 &b6 20 &c2 &a7?!

When this game was played, the plan adopted by White was not very well-known, and many of the best counter-measures were not yet worked out. One thing which Black soon learned was that White's a4-b3 pawn-formation does a great deal to kill off Black's queenside counterplay, and therefore it cannot be allowed to stand unmolested. The correct counter is for Black to try to get in the move ...c4, undermining the a4-pawn, and hence the b5 outpost. For this reason, he should here have played 20...&c8, with better chances of counterplay.

21 a5 &d7 22 &c3! *(D)*

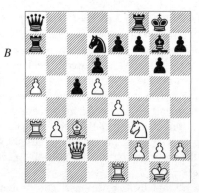

Removing Black's powerful Benko bishop, thereby both reducing Black's queenside pressure, and weakening his kingside, in preparation for White's later central breakthrough.

22...&b7 23 &xg7 &xg7 24 &d2!

An important move. Not only does the knight make way for f4 and e5, but it is on its way to the vital square c4. From there, it does almost everything White could want – prevents the black pawn-break ...c4, defends the a5-pawn, supports the e5 break, and has the option to jump into b6. In fact, one of the secrets of such Benko structures is the importance of the c4-square, which is vital to both sides.

24...f6 *(D)*

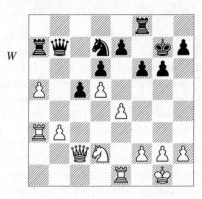

An ugly move to have to make, but Black understands that he is wholly on the defensive, and must just try to make it as difficult as possible for White to organize the e5 advance. Despite the fact that he has been outplayed, Black's position is still very difficult to break down. Indeed, one of the keys to the viability of the Benko is that Black has a superb structure, with his only pawn-weakness being on e7, which is extremely hard to get at. Even when things go wrong, as they have done here, Black's solid structure and active pieces can make it very hard for White to organize his breakthrough.

25 f4 ♘b8 26 ♘c4 ♘a6 27 ♕c3 ♘c7 28 ♖aa1 ♘b5 29 ♕d3 ♘d4 30 ♖ab1

Another move which White is always looking to achieve in these structures is b4. This is because Black's c5-pawn is the lynchpin of his queenside counterplay, and the exchange of this pawn for the white b-pawn is almost always in White's favour. It looks as though he has a chance to do so here, since 30 b4? ♕xb4 31 ♖eb1 appears to trap Black's queen. However, Black then has the tactical resource 31...♕c3!, and hence, 30 b4 is not playable.

30...♕b4 *(D)*

Walter Browne later condemned this as the decisive mistake, and recommended 30...♕b5, which pins the white knight, and so threatens 31...♖xa5. However, it is not clear what Black can play after simply 31 b4, which was clearly the move Alburt felt he had to prevent.

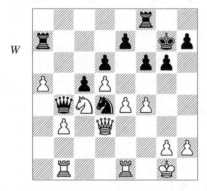

31 e5! dxe5 32 fxe5 ♖d7

32...fxe5 33 ♖xe5, followed by ♖be1, is no better.

33 exf6+ ♖xf6

33...exf6 34 d6 is also hopeless for Black.

34 ♕e4 ♖f5

If 34...♘xb3, then 35 ♘b6!, and Black cannot defend both d7 and b3.

35 d6! *(D)*

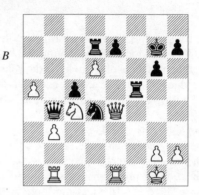

35...e6

35...exd6 36 ♘xd6 ♖xd6 37 ♕e7+ ♔g8 38 ♕xd6 wins for White.

36 ♖f1 ♕c3 37 ♖fc1

Browne was in time-trouble at this point, hence the repetition to gain time on the clock.

37...♕b4 38 ♖f1 ♕c3 39 ♖xf5 gxf5 40 ♕e5+ ♔f7 41 ♕xc5 ♘e2+ *(D)*

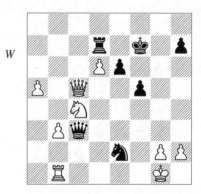

Black's position is clearly hopeless, and he should resign. The remaining moves just represent a rather desperate attempt to swindle his opponent.

42 ♔f1 ♘g3+ 43 hxg3 ♕d3+ 44 ♔f2 ♕c2+

44...♕xb1 45 ♘e5+ ♔e8 46 ♕c8+ is winning for White.

45 ♔e3 ♕e4+ 46 ♔d2 ♕xg2+ 47 ♔c3 ♖b7 48 ♕e3 ♕a2 49 ♖b2 ♕a1 50 ♕d2 ♔e8 51 ♕e3 ♔d7 52 b4 1-0

Game 17
Rory O'Kelly – Jonathan Penrose
English Counties Ch 1978
Czech Benoni

Here, we see a relatively rare formation, the Czech Benoni. This is a much less dynamic system than either the Modern Benoni or the Benko, and has never been all that popular in itself. However, such structures quite often arise via the King's Indian Defence, and hence it is useful to have some knowledge of them. The present game illustrates, in particularly gruesome style, a typical strategic error by Black in King's Indian positions – conceding White a piece outpost on e4.

1 d4 ♘f6 2 c4 c5 3 d5 e5

The move which characterizes the so-called Czech Benoni structure. By contrast with 3...e6, which leads to an unbalanced pawn-structure and very sharp play, the text-move produces a blocked position, where positional manoeuvring is generally the order of the day. It had a strong burst of popularity in the late 1960s, mainly in the hands of the Czech GMs Hort, Jansa and Kavalek, hence its nomenclature. In England, Bill Hartston was also a firm fan, and won a number of impressive games with it. After the mid-1970s, however, the popularity of the line fell sharply, and it has never really recovered, although in more recent times it has been successfully employed by the Romanian grandmaster Liviu-Dieter Nisipeanu.

4 ♘c3 d6 5 e4 ♗e7 *(D)*

The alternative is 5...g6, but the text-move is the most popular choice.

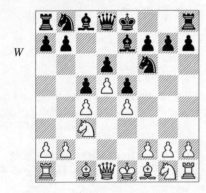

W

Although the bishop looks passively placed on e7, one of Black's main strategic plans is to exchange off this bad bishop by ...0-0, ...♘e8 and ...♗g5. Black also has the idea to play ...♘e8, ...g6, ...♘g7 and gradually prepare ...f5,

whilst a blow on the other flank, with ...b5, is sometimes also possible. To some extent, it will depend on how White develops, as he has a wide choice of possible set-ups. Black's play looks rather slow, but is justified by the blocked nature of the position.

6 ♕d3!?

An interesting and little-explored idea. The main point is that against the immediate 6 g3 0-0 7 h4, Black has the Benko-style gambit 7...b5 8 cxb5 a6, when practice suggests that Black has reasonable compensation. O'Kelly's move stops this by protecting the e4-pawn, and thus allowing ...b5 to be met by ♘xb5.

6...0-0 7 g3 ♘a6 8 h4!?

Another interesting idea. Rather than merely fianchettoing his bishop on g2, White plans to play the bishop to h3, angling to exchange light-squared bishops. With the respective central pawn-structures, the light-squared bishop is White's bad bishop, and Black's good one, so the exchange of the bishops favours White. In addition, the pawn on h4 prevents Black from exchanging off his own bad bishop by ...♗g5. Of course, White's play with ♕d3, g3 and h4 is also rather slow, but once again, the blocked nature of the position means that such long-term strategic manoeuvring, at the expense of development, is much easier to justify than would be the case in a more open position.

8...♘c7 9 a4 *(D)*

9...♘a6?!

Playing the knight into b4 at move 8 would have made no sense at all, since it would soon be driven back by a3, but now that White has irrevocably weakened the b4-square with his last move, Black decides to return the knight to the b4 outpost. Nonetheless, although this square is

superficially attractive, the knight is not terribly effective, since it is cut off and has no support from the rest of his forces. As the Russians like to say in such situations, "one soldier in a field is not a warrior"! 9...♞fe8 is more logical.

10 ♗h3 ♞b4 11 ♕e2 ♗xh3 12 ♞xh3 ♕d7 13 ♔f1

White has carried out the strategically favourable exchange of light-squared bishops. Now he takes his king to g2. The fact that he has to do so by hand, rather than by castling, is of little importance, because once again, time is not of so much importance in a closed position.

13...♞e8 14 ♔g2 *(D)*

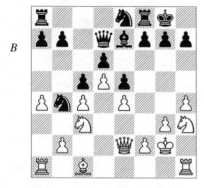

14...f5?

A most tangy positional lemon. As Botvinnik allegedly once claimed, every Russian schoolboy knows that in such Benoni and King's Indian positions, Black must usually be able to recapture with a pawn on f5, so as to keep control over the e4-square. After the text-move, White is able to use e4 as a base for his knights, and Black will be killed on the light squares. It was essential to prepare the ...f5 advance with 14...g6.

15 exf5 ♕xf5 16 ♞e4 ♞f6 17 ♞hg5

Black is able to exchange off one knight, but not both. This is where we see how badly-placed the other black knight is on b4, where it is effectively doing nothing. Put this knight on d7, in easy reach of f6, and Black would be able to get rid of both white knights on e4, in which case he would not stand too badly. As it is, though, White can maintain his remaining horse on the magnificent e4 outpost, and use it as the basis of a crushing attack on the kingside.

17...h6 18 ♞xf6+ ♖xf6 19 ♞e4

The knight is even better here than on e6.

19...♖f7 20 ♖a3! *(D)*

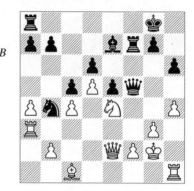

An excellent move. White plans to swing the rook along the third rank, to join the attack on Black's king.

20...♖af8 21 g4 ♕d7 22 g5

Black has no counterplay. The e4-knight dominates the position, attacking d6, defending f2 and supporting g5.

22...♔h7 23 ♖g3 ♖f5 24 gxh6 g6

24...gxh6 25 ♕g4 is curtains.

25 h5 g5

Desperation. 25...gxh5 26 ♖xh5 is no better.

26 ♗xg5 ♗xg5 27 ♞xg5+ ♔xh6 28 ♞e4

Returning to the beloved outpost, just to rub it in. Actually, of course, this is objectively better than 28 ♞e6, when Black could at least defend his g6-square by 28...♖8f6 or muddy the waters by 28...♖xf2+. Now he cannot even do that.

28...♖f4 29 ♖g6+ ♔h7 30 ♞g5+ ♔h8 31 ♖h6+ 1-0

The knight will finally come to e6 next move. Black had seen enough. A drastic example of the dangers of ceding the e4-square in such structures.

Game 18
Aaron Summerscale – Ian Snape
Coulsdon 2002
King's Indian Defence, Classical Variation

The Classical Variation of the King's Indian is just about the sharpest line of the opening. White advances his queenside pawns, and tries to break through on that wing, whilst Black advances ...f5-f4 and ...g5-g4, and tries to crush the white king under a pawn-avalanche. In the present game, we see some crucial aspects of White's strategy in such structures.

1 d4 ♘f6 2 c4 g6 3 ♘c3 ♗g7 4 e4 d6 5 ♘f3 0-0 6 ♗e2 e5 7 0-0 ♘c6 8 d5 ♘e7 9 ♘e1 *(D)*

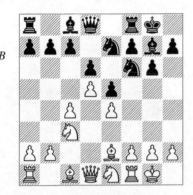

B

We saw this standard position from the King's Indian in *50ECL*, Game 36 (Shamkovich-Nezhmetdinov). White plans to attack on the queenside, primarily by the break c5, whilst Black will counter on the kingside, with ...f5-f4 and a pawn-storm. As Shamkovich-Nezhmetdinov showed, in spectacular style, the black attack can be lethal in such positions, and extremely accurate play is required from White if he is to make progress on the queenside, as well as holding up Black's counterplay. Shamkovich failed to do so, but the present game gives an excellent example of how White should go about handling the position.

9...♘d7 10 ♗e3

This is a double-edged choice, but the most critical move in the position. From the e3-square, the bishop supports White's queenside attack, whilst at the same time having the chance to help defend the white king. However, the move also involves investing a couple of tempi, since a subsequent ...f4 by Black will hit the bishop. In such positions, with attacks on opposite flanks, time is frequently of the essence, so

it is a moot point whether it is worth expending two tempi to have the bishop on f2. A great deal of analysis and practical experience over the years has still not come to a definitive answer. White has an alternative plan of 10 ♘d3, followed by a later ♗d2, but this too has been tested extensively, without any definite conclusions being reached.

10...f5 11 f3 f4 12 ♗f2 g5 *(D)*

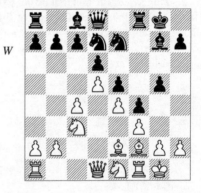

W

13 a4!?

This move may look a little strange. Given that White's main plan is to break with c5, one would rather expect the move 13 b4 to support this break (indeed, this is how Shamkovich played in a similar position in the earlier game). However, this is generally regarded as a little slow nowadays, and White usually employs more subtle means of conducting his queenside play.

In the context of Shamkovich-Nezhmetdinov we made the point that in such structures, Black's light-squared bishop is frequently his most important minor piece. Given the kingside pawn-structure, the bishop plays a vital role in supporting the breakthrough ...g4, and in threatening a sacrifice on h3, if White should play h3 to hold up Black's pawn-storm. In view of this, queenside play by White is frequently linked not so much with an immediate desire to win material, as to eliminate the enemy light-squared bishop. There are several ways of doing this. The main plan is to play c5 and cxd6, and then follow up with ♘b5. White may then be able to play ♘xa7, followed by ♘xc8. Alternatively, he may play ♘c7-e6, forcing Black to give the bishop for the knight.

In the present position, White could initiate this plan with the immediate 13 ♘b5, and indeed, this was a popular line for a period in the late 1980s. Black should avoid 13...a6? 14 ♘a7 ♖xa7 (otherwise White captures the important light-squared bishop) 15 ♗xa7 b6. This might look at first attractive for Black since it is not clear how White's bishop will escape, and meanwhile, it seems that Black can proceed with his kingside attack. However, the specific tactics work strongly against Black, as White makes much more rapid progress on the queenside than Black can with any of his plans. Black does better to meet 13 ♘b5 with 13...b6 14 b4 a6 15 ♘c3, when practice has shown that it is not easy for White to exploit the weakness of Black's queenside pawns, whereas Black has his normal vigorous kingside counterplay.

In view of all these considerations, White (represented notably by Viktor Korchnoi, a specialist in the white side of this variation) came up with the move 13 a4. The idea is that now 14 ♘b5 will be more effective, since 14...b6 can be met by 15 a5. A further, more subtle, point is that White may be able to achieve a successful c5 advance (sometimes as a sacrifice) without needing to support it with b4, and thus saving a tempo.

This long explanation is typical of the depth of strategy to be found in many modern opening variations. Of course, it has taken many years of research and practice to develop these ideas, and to find the best plans for both sides. In the game Shamkovich-Nezhmetdinov, played almost 50 years ago, we saw much more naïve play by White, for which he was drastically punished.

13...a6?!

This move, preventing ♘b5, may look insignificant, but in fact, it is a crucial and rather questionable decision by Black. The problem is that he weakens the b6-square. Currently this square is covered by the c7-pawn, but White will later be able to eliminate that pawn by means of c5 and cxd6. The importance of the b6-square is again linked with the fate of Black's light-squared bishop on c8. White now has the plan of c5 and cxd6, followed by ♘a4-b6, again going after the vital bishop. If he can eliminate the bishop, he usually finds it much easier to withstand Black's kingside attack, and if given enough time, he can then finish off the demolition of Black's queenside, which is generally indefensible in the long run.

The modern preference for Black is the more radical 13...a5 14 ♘d3 b6, with an unclear position.

14 a5! *(D)*

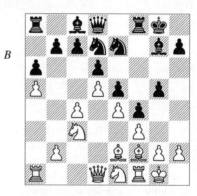

B

Seizing control of the vital b6-square.

14...♖f6 15 ♘a4 ♖h6

Each side pursues its plans. Black will transfer his queen to h5, to join in the attack on White's king.

16 c5 ♕e8 17 ♔h1!

An important piece of prophylaxis. Black threatens 17...♕h5, attacking h2. White cannot afford at this stage to meet that with 17 h3, since Black will play 17...♘f6 and then sacrifice the bishop on h3 next move, with a devastating attack. White therefore makes room for his bishop to defend from g1.

17...♕h5 18 ♗g1 ♘f6 *(D)*

This is also a key moment. Black would prefer to do without this move, since from d7, the knight controls the b6-square, and so prevents the white knight from entering and removing the c8-bishop. However, Black has no real way to make further progress on the kingside without bringing the knight over. He cannot play

18...g4, since White simply captures by 19 fxg4. He is therefore forced to support the ...g4 break with the knight.

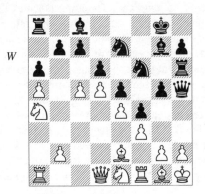

19 cxd6 cxd6 20 ♘b6!

Vital. White eliminates the bishop in the nick of time, before Black can play 20...g4.

20...♕h4

Planning ...♘h5, with a threat of mate on g3. Black loses material after 20...g4 21 fxg4; e.g. 21...♗xg4 22 ♗xg4 ♘xg4 23 ♘xa8, 21...♘xg4 22 ♘xc8 or 21...♕g6 22 ♘xa8.

21 ♘xc8 ♖xc8 22 h3!

Having carried out his plan to remove the enemy light-squared bishop, White can now place his kingside pawns on light squares and aim to hold the attack. Black cannot get enough pieces attacking the g4-square to support the ...g4 break, since the direct way 22...♖g6 23 ♘d3 h5?? drops the queen after 24 ♗f2. Black should probably seize his chance and play 22...g4 immediately, based on the fact that White's e4-pawn is unprotected after 23 fxg4 ♘xe4. In fact, the game Summerscale-Hebden, British Rapid Ch, Bradford 2002 saw Black try this move. After 23 ♗f2 ♕g5 (23...g3? would just block the kingside to White's advantage) 24 fxg4 ♘xe4 25 ♖a4 ♘f6 26 ♗f3, White had established a blockade on the light squares, and went on to win. Even so, this would have offered Black better practical chances than the game.

22...♘h5 23 ♗f2 ♘g3+ 24 ♔g1 ♖f6 25 ♘d3 ♖ff8 *(D)*

Black's problem is that his queenside is likely to prove untenable in the long run. Once White has consolidated the other flank, he will bring a rook to the c-file and/or attack the weak pawns on b7 and d6. Black must therefore continue to seek counterplay on the kingside.

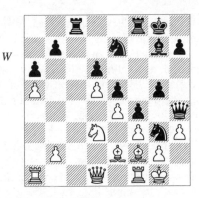

26 ♖e1 ♕h6 27 ♕a4 ♘xe2+?

Here Black missed his last chance to create play by means of 27...g4!. Then both 28 fxg4 ♘xe2+ 29 ♖xe2 f3, and 28 ♗xg3 fxg3 29 fxg4 ♕e3+ 30 ♔h1 ♖f7 give him better chances of distracting White from his queenside plans.

28 ♖xe2 ♕f6 29 ♖c1 ♖xc1+ 30 ♘xc1 ♘g6

After 30...♖c8 31 ♘d3, Black cannot make use of the c-file, and meanwhile, White threatens to penetrate by 32 ♕d7 (31...♖c7 32 ♗b6 does not help).

31 ♖c2 ♖f7 32 ♗b6 ♗f8 33 ♘d3 h5 34 ♘f2! *(D)*

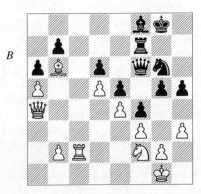

White continues to hold up the ...g4 break, which is Black's only source of counterplay. The white knight is not needed on the queenside.

34...♘h4 35 ♕e8 ♔g7 36 ♕c8

Now 37 ♗c7 will annex the b-pawn.

36...♘g6 37 ♗c7 ♗e7 38 ♕xb7 ♗d8 39 ♕c8 ♗xc7 40 ♖xc7 ♖xc7 41 ♕xc7+ ♔h6 42 b4 g4 43 hxg4 ♕h4 44 gxh5 1-0

A perfect illustration of White's strategy in such positions – eliminate the enemy light-squared bishop, and then hold firm against the kingside attack and win on the other flank.

Game 19
Ivan Cheparinov – Daniel Stellwagen
Amsterdam 2005
King's Indian Defence, Classical Variation

This game again features the Classical Variation of the King's Indian, but this time White adopts an altogether different strategy. Rather than defending on the kingside and pursuing a pawn-break on the other flank, White chooses to play the move g4, in front of his own castled king! This highly unusual strategy is based on a deep positional idea, which achieves total success in the present game.

1 d4 ♘f6 2 c4 g6 3 ♘c3 ♗g7 4 e4 d6 5 ♘f3 0-0 6 ♗e2 e5 7 0-0 ♘c6 8 d5 ♘e7 9 ♘e1

We also saw this standard King's Indian position in the previous game. It very often involves a race between the opposing attacks, with White coming down the queenside and Black the kingside. In the present game, though, White shows another idea.

9...♘d7 10 f3 f5 *(D)*

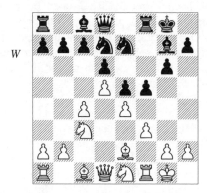

11 g4!?

To anyone brought up on classical principles, this move looks completely crazy at first sight, and I am sure that Steinitz would be revolving in his grave at such a move. White advances his pawns, in front of his own castled king, on the side of the board where Black stands better! However, far from having taken leave of his senses, White is actually employing a very sophisticated positional idea, which was developed by the Hungarian-born grandmaster, Pal Benko.

The essence of White's idea is that he wishes to make it difficult for Black to open lines on the kingside. As Shamkovich-Nezhmetdinov (Game 36 in *50ECL*) demonstrated, if Black can play ...f4, and then ...g5-g4, he has an extremely strong attack, and even the slightest inaccuracy by White can be fatal. Once Black gets his pawn to f4, he will always have the f3-pawn to 'bite on', and White can hardly hope to keep the kingside closed. The point of 11 g4 is to try to avoid this. Now if Black plays 11...f4, White intends 12 h4!, after which it becomes very difficult for Black to open lines on the kingside. If he ever plays ...g5, White will reply h5, and if instead Black plays ...h5, White answers with g5, in either case keeping the kingside files closed. Black would be reduced to a piece sacrifice in order to open lines, and if White is careful, he should be in a position to deal with any such sacrifice.

A typical example was the game Benko-Eliskases, Buenos Aires 1960, which continued 11...f4? 12 h4 a5 13 ♘g2 ♘c5 14 ♗d2 ♔h8 15 ♗e1 ♗d7 16 ♗f2 b6 17 ♘e1 ♘g8 18 ♔g2 ♘f6 19 ♘d3 ♕e7 20 ♖b1 ♖fb8 21 b3 ♗e8 22 ♘c1 h6 23 a3 ♘fd7 24 b4 *(D)*.

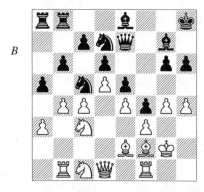

Black never succeeded in creating the ghost of a threat on the kingside, and was eventually ground down on the other flank.

Another strategy for Black is to exchange pawns on g4, but although this opens up one file, it again does nothing for Black's attacking chances. White can easily cover the entry-squares down the f-file, and once again, Black will be unable to create threats on the kingside. Portisch-Attard, Madrid 1960 was typical: 11...fxg4 12 fxg4 ℤxf1+ 13 ♔xf1 ♘f6 14 ♘d3 c5 15 ♗e3 ♗d7 16 ♔g1 ♔h8 17 ♔h1 ♕c7 18 g5 ♘fg8 19 ♘b5 ♕b8 20 b4! *(D)*.

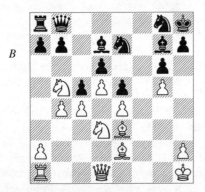

White's king was as safe as the Bank of England, and he won easily on the queenside.

In view of these problems, the best strategy for Black is reckoned to be to retain flexibility on the kingside, and avoid committing the pawn-structure too soon. This makes it more difficult for White to make progress on the other flank, since he must constantly keep one eye on possible developments on the kingside.

11...♔h8

Generally considered to be the best move. The king frees the g8-square for the knight, which currently stands rather awkwardly on e7. Once it reaches g8, Black will have the possibility of ....♗h6, trying to exchange off his bad bishop.

12 h4!

A relatively rare move, but I think it is a very good one. White anticipates Black's plan of ...♘g8 and ....♗h6 by establishing his pawns on h4 and g5. In most previous games, White has prepared this move with 12 ♘g2, planning to meet 12...♘g8 with 13 h4, but Cheparinov's move-order introduces a different set-up. The e1-knight will go to its best square at d3, from where it supports the standard c5 break, whilst g2 is left free for the white king.

12...♘g8 13 g5 f4 *(D)*

Clearly the critical choice. Black's only real plan of kingside counterplay is to break up

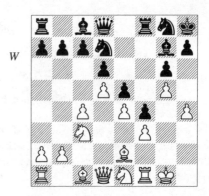

White's advanced pawns by ...h6, so first he cuts off the g5-pawn from its supporting bishop on c1.

14 ♔g2!

Just in time. Now the rook will come to the h-file, when the position of Black's king on h8 will make it difficult for him to capture on g5.

14...h6 15 ℤh1 ℤf7 16 ♘d3 ♗f8 17 ♕g1

White is keen to avoid having to capture on h6, which would free Black's position. He therefore maintains the g5-pawn for as long as possible, whilst also transferring his major pieces to the kingside. As will become evident, he intends to sacrifice the g5-pawn and exploit the open lines on the kingside himself.

17...♔g7

Remarkably, this is the first new move of the game. In three previous encounters, Black tried 17...ℤh7 in this position, but this move also fails to solve Black's problems. One example, which is very similar to the present game, was Gipslis-Muchnik, Moscow 1970, which went 18 ♔f1 hxg5 19 hxg5 ℤxh1 20 ♕xh1+ ♔g7 21 ♕h4 ♗e7 *(D)*.

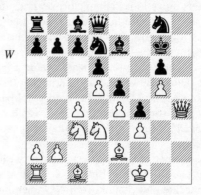

Now Black has again won the g5-pawn, but as later in the present game, a piece sacrifice breaks

open his king's position fatally: 22 ♘xf4! exf4 23 ♗xf4 ♘e5 24 ♔f2 ♘f7 25 ♖g1 c5 26 ♗d2 a6 27 a4 ♗d7 28 f4 ♗xg5 29 fxg5 ♔f8 30 ♔e1 1-0.

This predecessor game is another example of the value of studying not just sequences of opening moves, but the underlying middlegame plans. From the above game, Cheparinov was able to develop a whole strategy for the position, including elements such as the sacrifice of the g5-pawn, and the use of a timely piece sacrifice, to open the position and exploit Black's exposed king and lack of queenside development. At the board, he had to find the precise form in which to execute these ideas, and he had to calculate the variations, but virtually his entire underlying strategy was taken from the previous game.

18 ♔f1 ♗e7

Black has finally forced an issue with the pawn on g5, which cannot be defended any further.

19 ♗d2! *(D)*

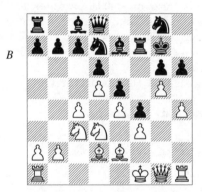

White sacrifices the g5-pawn, proceeding with his development in the meantime. Black's own development is seriously lagging, with the queen's rook and queen's bishop still at home, and White's initiative grows very quickly.

19...hxg5 20 hxg5 ♗xg5 21 ♘b5!

Now 22 ♘xc7 is threatened, so Black must lose another tempo to remove his g5-bishop from the vulnerable square.

21...♗h6 22 c5!

White's queenside attack hits home, whilst Black has only weaknesses on the kingside and undeveloped pieces on the other wing.

22...a6 23 ♘a3

This is better than 23 ♘c3, as the knight is heading to c4, from where it will exert pressure on d6, and also eye the b6-square, after an exchange of pawns on d6.

23...♘df6 24 ♘c4 ♘e8 *(D)*

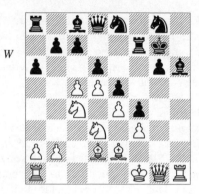

25 ♘cxe5!

Just as in Gipslis-Muchnik in the note to Black's 17th move above, a piece sacrifice breaks open the position decisively.

25...dxe5 26 ♘xe5 ♖f6 27 ♗c3 ♔h7 28 ♕g5!

This very nice move ties Black hand and foot, pinning the rook on f6, tying the knight on g8 to the defence of the h6-bishop, and freeing g1 for the other rook to join the attack.

28...♕e7

Note that the tactical defence 28...♖d6 loses to 29 ♘f7.

29 ♗d4

Another calm move. White simply defends his c5-pawn before proceeding with ♔f2 and ♖ag1. Black is too tied up to be able to do anything about this apparently slow build-up.

29...♕f8 30 ♔f2 ♘g7 31 ♖ag1 ♘h5 32 ♖xh5

A further sacrifice to finish the game off, but the simple 32 ♘xg6 was also winning.

32...gxh5 33 ♕xh5 ♘e7 34 ♗d3 ♗f5

Complete desperation in the face of the threat of moving the knight from e5, and then playing e5. The fact that this is the first move by either Black's queen's bishop or queen's rook sums up his plight.

35 exf5 ♖d8 36 ♘g4 1-0

Game 20
Jan Timman – Mikhail Tal
Tallinn 1973
King's Indian/Benoni

Another standard way for White to answer Black's ...f5 advance in the King's Indian is to exchange pawns on f5 and then play f4. In *50ECL*, we looked at the game Flohr-Suetin (Game 37), where White won a fine strategic game with this approach. Here, we see White employ the same strategy, but Black is able to exploit a slight difference in the pawn-structure to demonstrate that that this particular version favours him.

1 d4 ♘f6 2 c4 c5 3 d5 g6

A slightly unusual move-order. Instead of the Modern Benoni with 3...e6, or the Benko with 3...b5, Black chooses to fianchetto on the kingside, retaining options as to his central formation. This is a valid enough idea in itself, although White too is granted additional possibilities.

4 ♘c3 ♗g7 5 e4 d6 6 ♘f3 0-0 7 ♗e2

In addition to this move, White also has the attractive alternative 7 h3, planning to put his king's bishop on d3. Then, if Black tries to transpose into a Modern Benoni by 7...e6, after 8 ♗d3 exd5, White can either play 9 cxd5, with a Modern Benoni line which is nowadays regarded as rather promising for White, or play the quieter 9 exd5. Although this produces a symmetrical pawn-structure, practice has shown that White has good chances of a small advantage, chiefly because of his extra space. Note that the pawn on h3 is very useful in such a position, preventing Black from freeing up some space in his position by ...♗g4 and ...♗xf3. In many Benoni positions, this exchange is an important theme. The nature of the pawn-structure rather suits knights, so Black is frequently happy to surrender the bishop-pair, whereas if he cannot do so, it is often hard to find an effective post for the bishop.

7...e5?!

An unusual choice at this juncture, reaching a kind of King's Indian/Czech Benoni. There are many positions where the combination of ...e5 and ...c5 is satisfactory for Black, but he has to be careful about when to choose this formation. In particular, it is often dubious when White has not yet castled kingside, as here.

8 0-0?!

White, in his turn, does not try to exploit Black's move-order directly. He could have done so by 8 ♗g5, when it is dangerous for Black to chase the bishop away by 8...h6 and 9...g5. With his king still uncastled, White would be able to attack Black's weakened kingside by h4, with the option of taking his own king to the queenside. On the other hand, if Black allows the bishop to remain on g5, it is extremely difficult to organize his standard pawn-break ...f5. White would therefore have a definite edge after 8 ♗g5. After the text-move, we transpose back into a more normal King's Indian line.

8...♘e8

Black prepares his normal kingside counterplay by ...f5.

9 ♘e1 ♘d7 10 ♘d3 f5 *(D)*

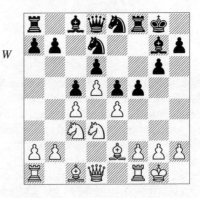

11 f4

In both this book and *50ECL*, we have examined games in which White played the move 11 f3 in similar positions, and Black pressed on with his kingside attack by ...f4, ...g5, etc. As those games showed, such positions are extremely double-edged, and basically come down to a race between White's queenside attack and

Black's counterplay on the kingside. In the present position, things are changed slightly by the fact that Black's pawn is on c5 rather than c7. With the pawn on c7, White's standard plan is to play the pawn-break c5, trying to break through on the c-file, and get a knight into c7, via b5. Here, this plan is much more difficult to achieve, and the white queenside play is slower, thanks to Black's pawn on c5. As a result, entering the 'race' by playing 11 f3 would be rather risky for White, whose queenside play is likely to take too long to get going.

Timman's move aims to exploit the changed situation by opening the position up on the kingside and in the centre. Partly thanks to the tempo spent on the move ...c5, Black is rather behind in development, so opening the position should, in principle, favour White.

11...♕e7

Exchanging pawns in the centre would favour White, whose knights would be brought into contact with Black's weaknesses on d6 and e6. Tal therefore retains the tension, and invites White to find the best means of clarifying matters.

12 exf5?!

This and the next move do not work out well for White, and he would probably have done better to maintain the tension by 12 ♗f3.

12...gxf5 13 ♔h1 *(D)*

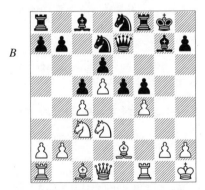

Now we reach another standard King's Indian formation that was discussed at some length in *50ECL*, in the context of Game 37, Flohr-Suetin. There, we saw Black play ...e4 in a similar position, and be soundly crushed, as White arranged his pieces on the central squares d4 and e3. I pointed out in the notes to that game that the move ...e4 is usually only

good in these structures if Black's c-pawn is on c5 rather than c7, since then his enhanced central control (notably of the d4-square) makes it more difficult for White to manoeuvre successfully. Here, the black pawn is already on c5, and Tal therefore chooses the ...e4 formation.

13...e4! 14 ♘f2 ♗xc3!

Another really excellent positional decision. Black would not usually exchange off his King's Indian bishop in this way, the piece traditionally being the pride of his position. However, here, with Black's pawn on c5, and White's pawns fixed on c3 and f4, it is extremely difficult to activate White's dark-squared bishop in the resulting pawn-structure. White's main plan in such positions, after the move ...e4, is to undermine the e4-pawn by some such regrouping as ♕c2, ♘d1-e3, and eventually the move g4. After the exchange of bishop for knight on c3, this plan becomes impossible to achieve, as White misses the effect of his queen's knight. Black, meanwhile, is able to put his major pieces on the g-file and attack on the kingside himself, whilst White has little or no counterplay on the other wing.

Tal's decision to exchange on c3 is an excellent one, and a player of his class is naturally capable of finding such ideas over the board. However, it is worth noting that he almost certainly did not need to do so, since he would have been familiar with the following classic example:

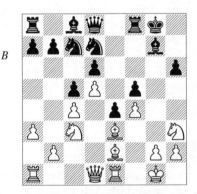

Bronstein – Petrosian
Candidates, Amsterdam 1956

Here, Petrosian played 17...♗xc3! 18 bxc3 ♘f6, obtaining an edge. Unfortunately, the players agreed a draw a few moves later, so the full value of Petrosian's positional idea was not demonstrated, but it did not escape Tal's attention, and was doubtless there in his memory banks some 17 years later, during his game with Timman – a striking example of the value of erudition!

15 bxc3 ♘df6 *(D)*

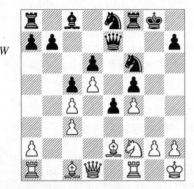

16 ♗e3

After this move, White never does achieve g4, and falls into a passive position. He could have tried 16 g4 immediately, but Black has a couple of attractive replies. Firstly, there is the simple 16...fxg4 17 ♘xg4 ♘xg4 18 ♗xg4 ♘g7, intending to maintain the blockade on f5, when Black stands better. Alternatively, Black can fish in troubled waters with the materialistic 16...e3, when after the forcing sequence 17 g5 exf2 18 gxf6 ♕e4+ 19 ♗f3 ♕xc4 20 ♖xf2 ♘xf6, White does not have enough for his pawn. In both lines, one is struck by the impotence of White's queen's bishop, obstructed by its own pawns on c3 and f4. White would very much like to be able to remove the c3-pawn from the board, and get his bishop on the long a1-h8 diagonal, when he would suddenly have a splendid game.

16...♔h8

Preparing to bring a rook to g8.

17 h3?!

Given that it proves impossible to achieve the advance g4 anyway, this weakening of the kingside could have been avoided, and the immediate 17 ♕d2 preferred.

17...♖g8 18 ♕d2

Note that 18 g4? is impossible because of 18...fxg4 19 hxg4 ♘xg4 20 ♘xg4 ♗xg4 21 ♗xg4? ♕h4+, winning.

18...♘g7

See the note to White's 17th move. This knight is on its way to h5, eyeing the weakened g3-square.

19 ♘d1 ♘gh5 20 ♗xh5

Not a move that White will have played lightly, but 20 ♗f2 ♕g7 is also fairly grim. White simply has no counterplay, and can only watch as Black builds up on the g-file.

20...♘xh5 21 ♗f2 ♗d7 22 ♗e1

White's contortions present a rather pathetic spectacle. This move is played in order to defend the f4-pawn, so that White can play ♘e3.

22...♖af8 23 ♘e3 ♕f6

The queen is coming to h6, attacking the f4-pawn.

24 ♔h2 ♕h6 25 g3 ♖f6 26 ♖g1 ♖fg6 27 ♖g2?! *(D)*

Black's pressure has reached its zenith, and it is no surprise that a winning sacrificial breakthrough is available.

27...♘xf4! 28 gxf4 ♕xf4+ 29 ♔g1 ♕f3 30 ♕f2

30 ♖xg6 ♖xg6+ 31 ♘g2 e3 32 ♕c2 e2 wins.

30...♕xh3 31 ♖b1 f4 32 ♖b2 f3 0-1

It is worth comparing this game with Flohr-Suetin. The difference in the activity of White's position between the two games is very striking, and all arises basically because of the position of Black's c-pawn, which is on c7 in one case, and c5 in the other. Such a seemingly small difference, yet so significant!

Game 21
Jaan Ehlvest – Maxim Novik
St Petersburg 1994
King's Indian Defence, Gligorić Variation

In our final King's Indian example in this chapter, we see a typical slow manoeuvring struggle. White gradually outplays his opponent, demonstrating along the way a number of instructive positional points. As so often, the principle of two weaknesses comes into the picture in an important way during the final stages of the game.

1 d4 ♘f6 2 ♘f3 g6 3 c4 ♗g7 4 ♘c3 0-0 5 e4 d6 6 ♗e2 e5

White has an important decision to make at this point. Essentially, he has three ways to respond to Black's last move. He could exchange pawns on e5, close the centre by 7 d5, or retain the tension.

7 ♗e3

Ehlvest follows the third strategy, but rather than do so by 7 0-0, which is the most common method, he chooses to support his centre with the bishop. This is a line popularized by the Yugoslav grandmaster Gligorić, and is named after him.

7...c6

Black has a number of ways to react to White's last move. Chasing the bishop by 7...♘g4 is popular, whilst preparing the chase by 7...h6, which cuts out the reply ♗g5, is also an option. Note that the move 7...♘c6, however, is probably less good here than after 7 0-0. This is because after 7 ♗e3 ♘c6 8 d5 ♘e7 9 ♘d2!, White's minor pieces are more conveniently placed, and the fact that he has not castled kingside offers him additional options against Black's programmed ...f5 advance.

8 d5 ♘g4 9 ♗g5 f6 10 ♗h4 ♘a6 11 ♘d2 *(D)*

Forcing Black to make a decision with the knight on g4.

11...♘h6

The alternative is 11...h5, which has a couple of points. The minor one is that a later ...g5 and ...h4 may threaten to trap the white bishop. More significantly, maintaining the knight on g4 makes it difficult for White to play the move f3, because of the reply ...♘e3. Of course, White could always meet 11...h5 with 12 h3, forcing the knight back, but this move does not really fit

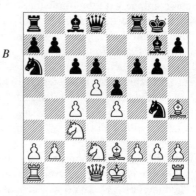

in with his plans in such positions. White's typical plan is to play f3 and ♗f2, in which case the move h3 would just weaken his kingside unnecessarily.

12 0-0 ♘f7 13 ♗d3!? *(D)*

A slightly unusual move in such positions. The most normal plan would be 13 ♖b1, preparing a queenside pawn advance. After the likely reply 13...h5 (threatening 14...g5 15 ♗g3 h4, winning a piece), White would continue 14 f3, preparing to drop the bishop back to f2. From there, the bishop helps to defend the king, as well as exerting pressure against Black's queenside.

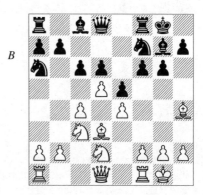

Ehlvest's choice supports the e4-pawn with the bishop, as well as envisaging the activation of the bishop on the queenside by a subsequent ♗c2-a4. As we shall see, this later proves a valuable idea for White, although against more energetic play by Black, the bishop move may have proved to be a loss of time.

13...♗h6

One point of White's last move was to tempt Black into the reflex action 13...♘c5?!. This would not be good here, since after 14 ♗c2 a5, White can continue with the immediate 15 a3, preparing to kick the knight away by b4. This is where the bishop on c2 proves well placed, since it prevents Black from meeting 15 a3 with 15...a4. Usually in such positions, this possibility means that White must lose a tempo to play first b3, and only then a3 and b4, whereas here he is able to dispense with that necessity.

Nonetheless, although Black avoids the positional error 13...♘c5?!, his last move may still not be best. 13...h5 is more thematic, forcing White to provide a retreat for his bishop by 14 f3. Then the move 14...♗h6 would activate Black's dark-squared bishop on the weakened squares around e3. Novik instead forms a different plan, involving forcing White to exchange bishops on g5.

14 ♖b1 ♗g5 15 ♗xg5 fxg5

This is Black's idea. He hopes that the open f-file will provide an avenue of attack against White's king.

16 f3 c5 17 a3 ♗d7 18 ♕e2 h5 19 ♕e3 b6 *(D)*

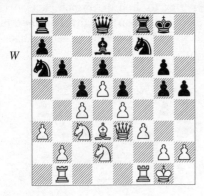

20 ♗c2!

Often a very important move in such positions. With White's pawns fixed largely on light squares, and Black's on dark squares, the bishop

on d3 is not usually an effective piece for White, and its exchange for its opposite number is generally favourable for White. In such blocked positions, strategic manoeuvring is usually the key, and it is such apparently insignificant exchanging operations which frequently play a key role in deciding the outcome.

20...♕e7 21 ♗a4 ♗xa4 22 ♘xa4 ♘d8!? 23 b4 ♘b7 24 ♘c3

The exchange of light-squared bishops has weakened many key squares in Black's camp, and one can easily see how strong a white knight would be, were it ever to penetrate to c6 or e6. This may seem a long way off at present, but it is not so far-fetched an idea as one may think. For example, if Black plays ...g4 and ...gxf3, and a white knight recaptures on f3, it would only be one step away from g5 and thence, e6. Even though this never happens, it is something Black must always worry about.

24...♖fc8?! *(D)*

With his last few moves, Black goes wholly over to defence on the queenside, and abandons any hope of counterplay on the other wing. 24...♖ac8 was a more active choice. Although White is in no danger, and can manoeuvre quietly, he has only a small advantage.

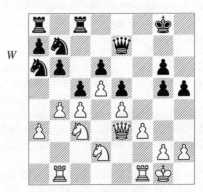

25 ♘d1!

Another regrouping move, typical of such structures. The knight is heading to d3, exerting additional pressure on c5. White wishes to have the possibility of exchanging on c5, opening the b-file, without allowing a black knight to settle on c5.

25...♘d8

The knight has only just gone to b7, and now heads back again, but White also had the threat of ♘f2-h3, attacking the weak g5-pawn. Black anticipates this by preparing to defend the pawn by ...♘f7, if necessary.

26 ♘f2 ♚g7 27 ♘d3 ♘b7?! *(D)*

Black continues to waste time with this knight, whilst the other sits relatively idle on a6. Krasenkov suggested 27...♘b8, aiming to recycle the knight to d7.

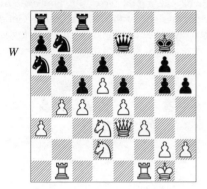

28 g3!

A very typical move, and another example of the principle of two weaknesses. Up to now, White has been manoeuvring with a view to breaking through on the queenside, but even a glance at the diagram is sufficient to show that Black is very well-prepared to meet this. However, what also stands out in the diagram is that Black's kingside bears a marked resemblance to the *Marie Celeste*, having been abandoned by almost all of his pieces. White therefore switches his attack to that side of the board, exploiting his extra space, which allows him to transfer his forces to the other flank more quickly and easily than the more cramped defender is able to do.

28...♘b8 29 f4 g4

Note that after 29...gxf4 30 gxf4 exf4 31 ♘xf4, White's knight is suddenly hopping into e6, something which seemed highly unlikely just 7 or 8 moves ago. Novik instead tries to keep lines closed on the kingside.

30 f5 ♘d7 31 fxg6 ♚xg6 32 ♖f5

White has made the breach on the kingside, and now only needs to bring one or two more pieces to bear.

32...♖h8 33 ♖bf1 ♖af8 34 ♘e1!

Another fine knight manoeuvre. The knight now heads to h4, with decisive effect.

34...♘d8 35 ♘g2 ♘f7 36 ♘h4+ ♚g7 *(D)*

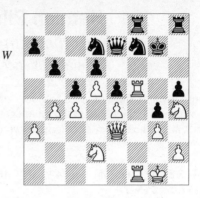

37 h3!

The final blow to Black's crumbling fortifications on the kingside. Now 37...gxh3 38 ♘df3 sees the last white piece join the attack.

37...♕d8 38 hxg4 hxg4 39 ♖1f2!

Another nice little move, simply clearing a path for the knight to come, via f1 and h2, to attack the g4-pawn. White's handling of his cavalry in this game is exemplary.

39...cxb4 40 axb4 a5

Black starts a thoroughly belated bid to stir up trouble, but his position is hopeless anyway. A move such as 40...♘h6, for example, loses to 41 ♖g5+ ♚h7 42 ♖g6 ♘g8 43 ♖h2.

41 ♘f1 axb4 42 ♘h2 *(D)*

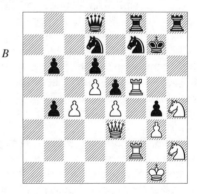

42...♕a8

Here too, 42...♘h6 43 ♖g5+ ♚h7 44 ♖g6 ♘g8 45 ♘xg4 is hopeless for Black.

43 ♖g5+! ♚h7 44 ♖g6 1-0

There is no defence to 45 ♖xf7+ and 46 ♕h6#. A beautiful example of patient and elegant positional manoeuvring by Ehlvest.

Game 22
Herman Pilnik – Efim Geller
Gothenburg Interzonal 1955
Sicilian Defence, Boleslavsky Variation

The present game starts out as a Sicilian Defence, with Black playing an early ...e5. However, the pawn-structure arising later in the middlegame is more characteristic of the King's Indian. Geller demonstrates a thematic pawn sacrifice, typical for such structures, and which is well worth knowing.

1 e4 c5 2 ♘f3 ♘c6 3 d4 cxd4 4 ♘xd4 ♘f6 5 ♘c3 d6 6 ♗e2 e5 (D)

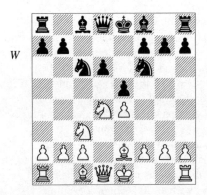

In *50ECL*, we looked at the game Matulović-Fischer (Game 30), as an example of a Sicilian structure, with Black playing ...e5. That game arose from a Najdorf, but the present game sees the Boleslavsky Variation, which was really the first of the ...e5 Sicilian structures to become respectable. Indeed, so successful was Black in this line, that the move 6 ♗e2 was driven right out of fashion, and replaced by more aggressive tries, such as 6 ♗c4 and 6 ♗g5.

As explained in *50ECL*, Black's strategic idea in these ...e5 structures is to use his central pawn-majority to stake out territory in the centre, hoping that his dynamic chances will counter-balance the weakness of the d5-square and the backward d6-pawn.

7 ♘b3 ♗e7 8 0-0 0-0 9 ♗e3 ♗e6 10 ♗f3

This is a rather clumsy-looking move, but White wishes to play ♘d5. In order to do so, he needs to defend his e4-pawn, and since 10 f3 is well met by 10...d5, he has to do so with the text-move.

10...a5 (D)

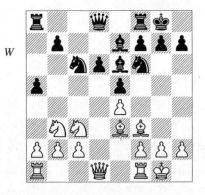

This is another move which looks strange at first sight. Usually, in the Sicilian Defence, Black plays ...a6 and ...b5, hoping to put pressure on the enemy knight on c3, combined with play down the half-open c-file. The text-move looks rather ugly, since it leaves another hole in Black's position, namely on b5, and virtually gives up the idea of a later ...b5. However, it is quite a common idea in positions where Black has played ...e5. The white knight on b3 is a target, and Black threatens to play ...a4, when the knight would lack a good square (this is why ...a5 is usually only good when Black has a pawn on e5; if the pawn were on e6, the white knight could go to d4). In addition, the pawn can go on all the way to a3, breaching White's queenside pawn-structure.

The obvious response to 10...a5 is 11 a4, stopping the pawn in its tracks, and fixing the hole on b5. However, Black will usually continue with 11...♘b4, when the knight is actively placed, attacking the c2-pawn and covering the hole on d5. In theory, White could move his knight from c3 and play c3, to expel the enemy knight, but in practice this is often difficult to achieve. White usually needs the knight on c3, defending his e4-pawn and stopping Black from breaking with ...d5. Effectively, this is another case of statics vs dynamics. Black's initiative stops White from carrying out his plans and driving the black pieces into passivity.

11 ♘d5 ♗xd5 12 exd5

The exchange on d5 has changed the character of the position somewhat. Black no longer has a hole on d5, and his d6-pawn is no longer exposed on an open file. On the other hand, White has a queenside pawn-majority, which he hopes to exploit by means of a later advance, with c4, b4 and eventually c5. Black, on the other hand, has a majority on the kingside, and will seek to create counterplay on that wing, starting with ...f5.

12...♘b8 (D)

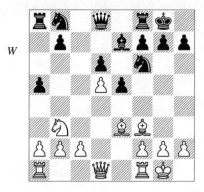

13 c4?

This looks like a logical continuation of White's plan, but in fact, it proves to be a serious positional error as Black is able to blockade the queenside and thereby stop White's play. Geller recommended that White first transfer his bishop to b5, utilizing the fact that Black has weaknesses on the light squares. This is a good illustration of one of the strategic principles involved in positions where one player has two bishops against bishop and knight. A good rule of thumb in such cases is to look for a way of making maximum use of the unopposed bishop. In this case, it is the light-squared bishop which has no opponent, and so it is logical that White should seek to use this piece to the maximum effect. From the b5-square, the bishop would exert unpleasant pressure on Black's position, making it more difficult for him to develop his counterplay on the other wing.

13...♘a6 14 ♗d2 b6 (D)

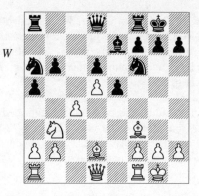

Now it is extremely difficult for White to create any activity on the queenside, and the black knight will be well placed on c5.

15 ♗c3 ♘c5 16 ♘xc5

The white knight on b3 does not have a good post, and is clearly less effective than the enemy steed on c5 – hence this exchange. But now White has no chance of any active play on the queenside, and his position becomes very passive.

16...bxc5 17 ♕e1 (D)

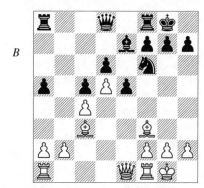

Making room for the bishop to come from f3. White has belatedly got the idea of activating this bishop on the queenside but Black nips this in the bud.

17...♘d7 18 ♗d1 a4!

Preventing the bishop from going to a4.

19 ♗c2 f5 20 ♖d1

White sticks to passive tactics. The pawn-structure on the kingside is similar to that which often arises from the King's Indian, such as we saw in Game 20. As Geller points out, White's last chance of activity was with the typical King's Indian idea 20 f4 e4 21 g4!. In this way, White undermines the support of Black's pawn on e4, since Black has no time for 21...g6

in view of 22 gxf5 gxf5 23 ♕g3+. Instead, after
21...♗f6 22 gxf5 ♖e8!, Geller considers that
the position still favours Black, but at least
White has some counter-chances. In the game,
he never gets any.

20...g6!

This precludes the possibility mentioned in
the previous note, since now 21 f4 e4 22 g4
would be met simply by 22...♗f6, when the
e4-pawn is securely defended.

21 ♕e2 ♗f6 22 f3 *(D)*

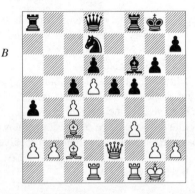

White's formation is aimed at preventing
Black from playing ...e4 followed by ...♘e5.
However, Geller proceeds to play just that, with
a thematic positional pawn sacrifice.

22...e4! 23 ♗xf6 ♕xf6 24 fxe4 f4!

This is the point of Black's play. In return for
his pawn, he has secured a marvellous outpost
on e5 for his knight, and has fixed White's
pawns on light squares, behind which his bishop
is crippled. White has absolutely no counterplay against Black's plan of ...♘e5, followed by
a pawn-storm on the kingside with ...g5-g4, etc.

25 ♖f2 ♘e5

But not 25...♕xb2? 26 ♕g4, when White has
serious counterplay. It is much more important
to keep White bottled up than to snatch back the
sacrificed pawn.

**26 ♖df1 ♕h4 27 ♗d1 ♖f7 28 ♕c2 g5 29
♕c3 ♖af8 30 h3**

30 ♗xa4? is impossible due to 30...♘g4.
30...h5 *(D)*

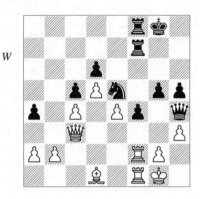

31 ♗e2

White could have snatched another pawn by
31 ♗xa4, when following 31...g4 32 ♗d1, there
is no immediate win after 32...f3 33 gxf3. However, the preparatory move 32...♔h7!, freeing
the g8-square for the rook, leaves White defenceless against the threat of 33...f3.

31...g4 32 ♖xf4

This loses quickly, but otherwise, 32...f3 will
decide.

32...♖xf4 33 ♖xf4 ♖xf4 34 g3 *(D)*

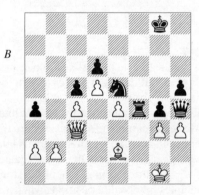

34...♘f3+

34...♕xh3 35 gxf4 g3 was even simpler.

**35 ♔f2 ♕xh3 36 gxf4 g3+ 37 ♔xf3 g2+ 38
♔f2 ♕h2 0-1**

Game 23
Alexei Sokolsky – N.P. Andreev
USSR correspondence Ch 1960-3
Sokolsky Opening

The opening of this game is an unusual one, but the pawn-structure reached in the early middle-game is similar to many Sicilian Defence positions, with colours reversed. White applies a typical Sicilian plan, using his extra central pawn to control space. This is a good example of how an understanding of one standard type of position can often be useful in positions which have arisen from an entirely different opening. Many players make the mistake of only studying games from openings they themselves play, whereas having a wider degree of erudition can often benefit a player.

1 b4!?

Variously known as the Polish, the Orang-Utan and the Sokolsky, this is a very unusual move at master level. However, it is not as bad as its reputation. White stakes out space on the queenside, and prepares to bring his bishop to the long diagonal, from where it attacks the e5-square. Tony Miles famously beat Karpov with 1 e4 a6 2 d4 b5 as Black, and later said of the opening that "it's only 1...b6, with a bit more space". White can say the same after 1 b4, which has ideas in common with Larsen's Opening, 1 b3. Having said that, the opening does not really pose any theoretical problems to Black, but it does lead to interesting, non-standard positions. Sokolsky himself played it with great success, over many years, including numerous games against Soviet grandmasters.

1...e6 *(D)*

Black selects a type of Queen's Gambit Declined set-up, one of his most solid options. 1...e5 is the main alternative, whilst 1...♘f6 2 ♗b2 g6 leads to a type of Réti/King's Indian set-up.

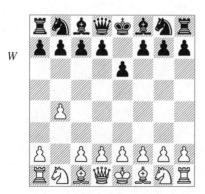

2 ♗b2 ♘f6 3 b5

3 a3 is another interpretation, but Sokolsky generally preferred to take additional space in such positions. White's basic idea is to develop by e3, ♘f3, ♗e2, etc., and then pursue an initiative on the queenside.

3...d5 4 e3 ♗d6 5 ♘f3 0-0 6 c4 c5 7 ♗e2 ♘bd7 8 0-0 *(D)*

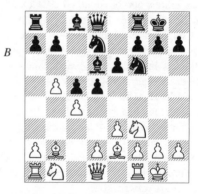

8...b6 9 a4 ♗b7 10 a5 dxc4?!

Sokolsky was critical of this move, which gives White a nice outpost on c4. The move also cedes White a central pawn-majority, which he subsequently utilizes in instructive fashion. Sokolsky preferred 10...bxa5, after which White will continue 11 cxd5 exd5 12 ♕a4, with approximately equal chances.

11 ♘a3!

The knight will be excellently placed on c4, attacking b6 and controlling d6 and e5.

11...♖c8 12 ♘xc4 ♗b8 13 d3 ♕e7 14 e4! *(D)*

A very interesting positional decision. At first sight, it looks strange to create a backward pawn on d3 and a hole on d4. However, readers

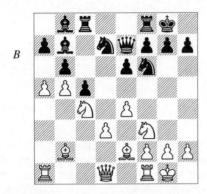

familiar with the game Matulović-Fischer, examined in detail in *50ECL*, may recognize the pattern. Despite the unusual opening, we have actually reached something close to a type of Sicilian pawn-structure, with colours reversed. As the Fischer game showed, the central pawn-majority can often be used most effectively by placing the pawns on e5 and d6 (as Black), maximizing the central control. In the present case, the pawns on d3 and e4 control a lot of central squares, notably depriving Black of the use of the d5-square. The formal weakness of d3 and d4 is of little importance, since these squares are well covered by White's pieces, and Black's knights are some distance away from ever threatening to occupy d4.

14...♖fd8 15 ♕b3 ♘e8 16 ♘fd2

White already has the initiative on the queen-side, and now prepares f4, taking the whip hand on the other flank too. As will become clear, his knights are already eyeing the d6-square as a potential outpost. Black's biggest problem is that his position is very passive.

16...♗c7 17 f4 ♔h8 18 axb6 axb6 19 ♖a7 ♖b8 *(D)*

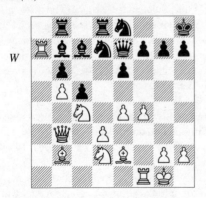

20 e5!

A very interesting and well-judged move, which shows the importance of being able to assess the relative importance of different positional factors. The move is certainly not without its drawbacks – it blocks the long diagonal of White's bishop on b2, cedes control of d5, and opens the long diagonal for Black's bishop on b7. However, the b7-bishop will immediately be exchanged by ♗f3, whilst the two black knights need time to reach the d5-square. In the meantime, White can bring his knight to e4, threatening to jump into a huge outpost on d6, whilst a later f5 will create dangerous threats on the kingside. Sokolsky correctly judged that the move's benefits outweigh its drawbacks.

20...♘f8 21 ♗f3 ♗xf3 22 ♖xf3 ♖d7 *(D)*

Removing the active rook by 22...♖a8 may be a little better.

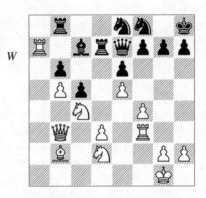

23 ♘e4 ♘g6

The knight sets off on its trek to d5.

24 g3 ♕d8 25 ♖a1 ♘e7 26 g4

Black's knight is almost at journey's end, but now White commences the final assault on Black's king.

26...♘d5 27 ♖af1 ♕h4 28 ♖g3 ♖bd8 *(D)*

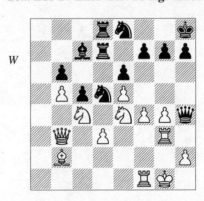

With his rooks doubled on the d-file, Black finally has a breath of counterplay in the form of a possible ...♘b4. Sokolsky points out that even this is often not a particular threat, since in many cases, it can be met by d4, but as it is, White is ready to launch his decisive breakthrough. Up to now, the game has been dominated by positional manoeuvring, but now it becomes much more concrete and tactical. This is where a player's all-round ability becomes important. No matter how good one's positional and strategic understanding, the moment always comes in a game when it is necessary to calculate concrete variations in order to convert one's advantage into victory (of course, in the present game, Sokolsky was playing by correspondence, and so was able to analyse the tactics at his leisure).

29 f5 exf5 30 ♖xf5 ♔g8 *(D)*

After 30...♘b4, Sokolsky gives a spectacular variation: 31 e6 ♗xg3 32 hxg3 ♕xg4 33 exd7 ♕xf5 34 dxe8♕+ ♖xe8 35 ♘cd6 ♕e6 36 ♘xe8!?, and if 36...♕xb3, then 37 ♗xg7+ ♔g8 38 ♘4f6#. However, attractive though this is, the computer points out that it is unnecessary, since both 31 ♘cd6 and the prosaic 31 ♘e3 also give White a winning advantage.

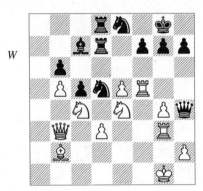

31 ♗c1

The bishop switches effectively to the c1-h6 diagonal, threatening to win material by 32 ♗g5.

31...♕e7

The alternative is 31...h6. Sokolsky then recommends 32 ♖h5 ♕e7 33 ♗g5, with the point that 33...hxg5 34 ♖gh3 f6 35 ♘cd6! wins for White, but instead, Black can hang on with

33...f6. For this reason, the simple 32 g5 should be preferred, when White will break through in short order.

32 ♗g5 f6 *(D)*

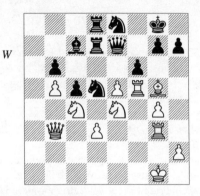

33 ♖gf3! fxg5

33...♕e6 is slightly more stubborn, although after 34 exf6 ♘exf6 35 ♗xf6 gxf6 (35...♘xf6 loses to 36 ♖e3!) 36 ♘e3, White should win.

34 e6! ♘ef6

Obviously, the pawn cannot be taken because of mate on f8.

35 exd7 ♔h8

35...♘xe4 is refuted nicely by Sokolsky's 36 ♘e3!; e.g., 36...♘d2 37 ♕xd5+ ♔h8 38 ♖h3 ♗f4 39 ♖f7! ♗xe3+ 40 ♔h1 and wins.

36 ♘xg5 ♖xd7 37 ♘e4 *(D)*

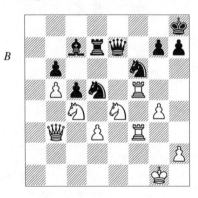

White has an extra exchange, as well as an ongoing attack.

37...h6 38 g5 ♘xe4

Or 38...hxg5 39 ♖h3+ ♔g8 40 ♘e3!.

39 dxe4 ♕xe4 40 ♕d3 ♕d4+ 41 ♔h1 ♘e7 42 ♖f8+ ♘g8 43 ♕xd4 ♖xd4 44 ♖3f7 ♗d6 45 ♘xd6 ♖d1+ 46 ♖f1 ♖xd6 47 ♖e1 1-0

Game 24
Nikolaus Stanec – Alexander Beliavsky
Graz open 1996
Nimzo-Indian Defence, Rubinstein System

In *50ECL*, we examined several examples of the IQP structure. Here we see another, in which Black demonstrates a defensive idea that we have not seen before. He allows his own queenside pawns to be split, and succeeds in proving that Black's apparent weakness on c6 is less important than the white weaknesses.

1 c4 e6 2 d4 ♞f6 3 ♞c3 ♝b4 4 e3 c5 5 ♝d3 ♞c6 6 ♞e2

This move is nowadays more popular, and probably also stronger, at move 5. The main point of playing the move at this moment is to avoid the Hübner Variation, which arises after 6 ♞f3 ♝xc3+ 7 bxc3 d6. We saw a similar line in Game 25, Speelman-Agdestein, in *50ECL*. It is very difficult for White to activate his bishop-pair in such Hübner structures, and most grand-masters prefer to avoid the line with White.

6...cxd4 7 exd4 d5 8 0-0 dxc4 9 ♝xc4 0-0 *(D)*

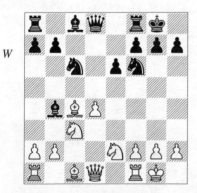

We have reached a typical IQP structure, of the type we examined in several games in *50ECL*, but with the difference that here White's knight is on e2, rather than f3. As we discussed at some length in *50ECL*, White's main plan in such IQP structures is to use his extra central space and freer development to prepare a king-side attack. One of the main features in such at-tacks is the possibility of the king's knight posting itself on e5, from where it threatens a variety of sacrifices around the squares f7 and g6. In the present position, however, the knight is not in contact with the e5 outpost, and this

makes it slightly more difficult for White to or-ganize his kingside play. In general, this version of the typical IQP structure should be fairly comfortable for Black, although one should not overstate the case.

10 ♝g5 ♝e7 11 a3

It looks a little strange that White plays a3 only after the bishop has already retreated, but the move is quite logical, and is a common idea in IQP structures. There are two main points to the move. Firstly, White prevents Black from transferring his queen's knight to the standard blockading post by means of ...♞b4-d5, and secondly, he prepares ♛d3 and ♝b3-c2.

11...♞d5 *(D)*

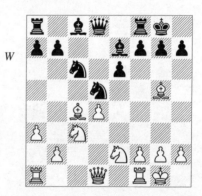

As usual in IQP positions, Black is happy to trade minor pieces, since his position is a little more cramped, and exchanges reduce White's dynamic potential.

12 ♝xe7 ♞cxe7 13 ♞xd5?!

This further unnecessary exchange does not meet the logic of the position. White should be looking to retain minor pieces, not exchange them off. 13 ♞e4 looks better.

13...♞xd5 14 ♛b3 ♞b6 15 ♜fd1 ♝d7 16 ♞c3 ♜c8 17 ♝b5 ♜c7 18 a4?! *(D)*

White's play has not been calculated to retain the initiative, and he already has to be careful not to end up standing worse. Instead of this gratuitous weakening of the queenside, he should play 18 d5, looking to exchange off what is by now just a potential weakness.

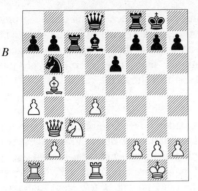

18...♗c6 19 ♗xc6 bxc6!

An excellent positional idea, worthy of note. At first sight, it looks wrong to accept an isolated pawn on the open c-file, but Beliavsky is already playing to unbalance the position. Such a structure arises quite often in IQP positions, and very often, the apparent weakness of the c6-pawn proves much less significant than the weakness of d4. The former can be defended comfortably by a knight on e7, whilst the pawn duo c6 and e6 give Black eternal control over d5. In this position, the presence of White's pawn on a4 is an additional factor, since it means that he has another weakness on b2. White is not yet clearly worse, but he must be very careful.

20 ♘e4 ♖d7 21 a5?!

This weakens the a-pawn further, and drives the knight where it wants to go anyway. 21 ♕c3 was probably better.

21...♘c8 22 ♕a4 ♘e7

The knight is ideally placed on e7. It defends c6, and prepares at some later moment to jump out to f5, attacking the d4-pawn, or to the traditional blockading square, d5. Meanwhile, White has no positive plan, and can only mark time.

23 ♘g5 ♖d5 24 ♘f3 ♕d6 25 h3 ♖b8

Reminding White of his weakness on b2.

26 ♖d2 ♕b4 27 ♕xb4 ♖xb4 *(D)*

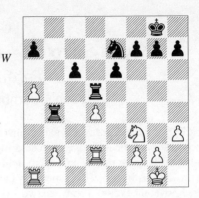

This ending is very unpleasant for White, who has to worry about three weak pawns on a5, b2 and d4, and has no active counterplay. The next step for Black is to bring his king to d7, where it defends the c6-pawn, and thus frees Black's knight for further action.

28 ♖c2 f6 29 a6 ♔f7 30 ♖e1 h5

Black could already go after the a6-pawn by means of 30...♖a4, but there is no hurry.

31 h4 ♖d6 32 g3 ♘f5 33 ♔g2 ♔e7 *(D)*

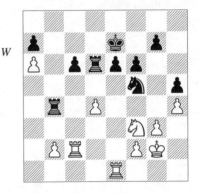

Once the king reaches d7, Black can safely help himself to a pawn or two. It is remarkable how quickly White's position became hopeless after the exchanges on c6.

34 ♖ec1 ♔d7 35 ♖a1 ♘xd4 36 ♘xd4 ♖dxd4 37 ♖a5 ♖d5 38 ♖a3 e5 39 ♖f3 ♖b6 40 ♖a3 ♔c7 41 ♔f3 ♖db5 42 ♖a2 ♖b3+ 43 ♔e2 ♖6b4 0-1

White's resignation is a trifle premature, but he was no doubt demoralized by his lack of active counterplay. Black will put his king on b6, and then think about how to strengthen his position. One of many plans is to advance ...f5-f4, forcing new weaknesses in White's kingside.

Game 25

Ivan Sokolov – Alexander Khalifman

Pardubice 1994

Queen's Gambit, Semi-Slav Defence

In *50ECL*, we looked at several games involving 'hanging pawns'. Such pawns can be strong if their possessor has the initiative, but can prove a static weakness. The games in *50ECL* showed the two sides of hanging pawns, and were deliberately chosen because they were one-sided games, where the various factors were especially clearly demonstrated. This game, by contrast, is a much more heavyweight example between two world-class GMs, which shows the various aspects of the hanging pawns structure.

1 d4 d5 2 c4 c6 3 ♘c3 ♘f6 4 e3 e6 5 ♘f3 ♘bd7

The Semi-Slav is one of Black's most popular and reputable defences. His basic strategy is to exchange pawns on c4, then play ...b5, ...♗b7 and/or ...a6 and finally ...c5. If he can achieve these moves without hindrance, he can usually expect an excellent game, so White needs to fight against Black's idea.

6 ♕c2

Immediately side-stepping the Meran, which runs 6 ♗d3 dxc4 7 ♗xc4 b5. The text-move has long been a favourite of Karpov's.

6...♗e7 *(D)*

Slightly unusual. The more active 6...♗d6 is generally preferred, but Khalifman did not wish to face the sharp reply 7 g4!?.

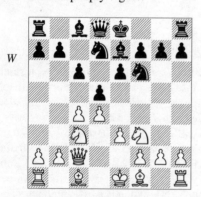

7 b3

This finally puts paid to the plan outlined in the note to Black's 5th move, because now White will meet ...dxc4 by recapturing with the pawn.

7...b6 8 ♗d3 ♗b7 9 0-0 0-0 10 ♗b2 ♖c8 11 ♖ad1 c5

Both sides have developed their pieces in logical fashion, and Black now strikes in the centre. White must decide how to deal with the central pawn-formation, i.e. whether to give Black hanging pawns, or to accept such pawns himself. If his queen were on e2, he might well be tempted to do the latter, but with his queen on c2, the opening of the c-file after ...cxd4 would leave the queen feeling slightly uncomfortable, so he decides to exchange pawns himself.

12 cxd5 exd5 13 dxc5 bxc5 *(D)*

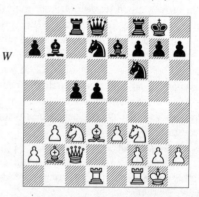

Thus we have the characteristic 'hanging pawns' formation on c5 and d5. As emphasized in *50ECL*, the pawns control a lot of central squares, and can give their possessor many dynamic possibilities, but they can also be subject to pressure, and may prove a weakness. It is essential for White to exert pressure against the pawns, which Sokolov proceeds to do.

14 ♗f5

A typical manoeuvre in such positions. The bishop unmasks an attack on d5 from the rook on d1, and also pins the knight on d7, which in turn defends the c5-pawn. Thus, in one move, the pressure is augmented on both c5 and d5.

14...g6?!

This weakens the long diagonal, without actually driving White's bishop off the h3-c8 diagonal, and so Black may have been better off dispensing with this move and playing 14...a6 immediately.

15 ♗h3 a6

Black wishes to unpin his knight by means of ...♖c7, so this preliminary pawn move is necessary, to prevent the rook from being hit by ♘b5.

16 ♘e2! *(D)*

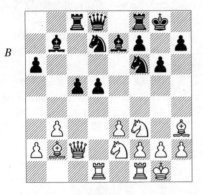

Another excellent and thematic move in such hanging pawns structures. The knight unmasks the b2-bishop, which puts pressure on Black's hanging pawn duo by constantly threatening ♗xf6. Then both recaptures ...♘xf6 and ...♗xf6 would involve removing one of the guards of the c5-pawn. Meanwhile, the knight is on its way to f4, attacking the d5-pawn. The manoeuvre is especially effective in this position, since the long a1-h8 diagonal has been weakened by Black's 14th move.

16...♖c7 17 ♕c3!

Another link in the chain, stepping up the pressure on the long diagonal. Now, if Black does nothing, the follow-up ♘f4 will already threaten to win the d5-pawn by ♘xd5, in view of the mate threat on g7.

17...♘b6 18 ♕a5

This manoeuvre ♕c3-a5 is an instructive and typical idea in hanging pawns positions, and is worth remembering. As Sokolov himself acknowledged, it was seen in some of Rubinstein's games. Curiously, in *Informator 61*, Sokolov claims that 18 ♘f4 would be answered by 18...♗d6, but this just leaves a piece hanging

on f6! More to the point, though, 18 ♘f4 would no longer threaten anything, since Black has overprotected d5. Sokolov's move attacks the knight on b6, which cannot be defended conveniently, and so has to retreat.

18...♘bd7 19 ♘f4 *(D)*

The pressure on the hanging pawns is mounting inexorably, and White now has the unpleasant threat of 20 ♘e5. Khalifman understands that things have already gone wrong for Black, and that continued passive play will lead to disaster, so he adopts dynamic measures, sacrificing a pawn to expose White's king.

19...d4! 20 exd4

Sokolov points out that the apparently powerful move 20 ♘g5, avoiding the doubling of his kingside pawns and threatening 21 ♘ge6, is well met by 20...♗d6! 21 ♘ge6 fxe6 22 ♘xe6 ♕b8 23 exd4 c4!, with counterplay. This position would be quite unclear, with approximate material equality (after taking back the exchange, White will have rook and two pawns for two minor pieces), so Sokolov instead decides to accept the pawn sacrifice.

20...♗xf3 21 gxf3 c4 22 bxc4 ♖xc4 23 ♕xa6 ♖c2

As a result of the forced sequence beginning 19...d4!, White has won a couple of pawns, and although it is difficult to hold the a-pawn, he objectively still stands clearly better. However, Black has some compensation, in the form of White's slightly exposed king and the active black rook. Although it is not really enough, Khalifman would rather take his chances in this position than continue to play passively. This is typical of modern grandmaster play, where activity and counterplay are almost always preferred to passive defence.

24 ♗c1 ♛a8 *(D)*

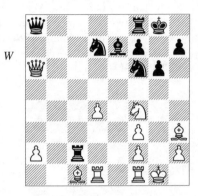

Black would prefer to retain queens, in the hope of exploiting the exposed white king, but this is not really feasible, so he settles for regaining the a-pawn.

25 ♕xa8 ♖xa8 26 ♗e3 ♖axa2 27 ♖b1

Threatening 28 ♖b7, and also preventing Black from establishing a blockading knight after ...♘b6-d5. In order to stop ♖b7, Black is forced to exchange off one of his active rooks.

27...♖ab2 28 ♘d3 ♖xb1 29 ♖xb1 ♖c7 *(D)*

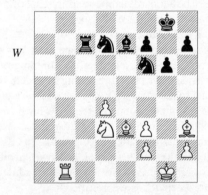

The first wave of Black's initiative has been repulsed, and now White must find a way to advance his passed d-pawn decisively.

30 ♖b5!

Again preventing Black from establishing a blockade with 30...♘d5 followed by 31...♘7f6.

30...♚g7 31 ♚g2 ♘e8 *(D)*

32 ♘c5?

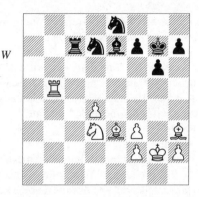

An inaccuracy in time-trouble, which could have imperilled the win. Correct was 32 ♗f4.

32...♘df6?

Black misses his chance. After 32...♘xc5! 33 dxc5 f5!, it is very difficult for White to make progress.

33 ♖b8 ♗d6 34 ♖a8 ♖e7 35 ♗g5

Now White's two bishops and active rook slowly break the coordination of Black's pieces.

35...♖e1 36 ♘e4 ♗b4 37 ♖b8 ♗a3 38 ♗f4!

Threatening 39 ♗e5.

38...♘d5 *(D)*

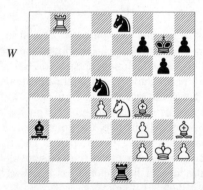

39 ♗e5+?

39 ♗d2 would have won immediately, but the text-move does not spoil anything.

39...f6 40 ♗g3 ♚f7 41 ♗d7 ♘ec7

41...♘g7 is met by 42 ♗a4 and 43 ♗b3.

42 ♖b7 ♖c1 43 ♗a4 g5 44 ♗xc7! 1-0

A piece is lost after both 44...♖xc7 45 ♗b3 and 44...♘xc7 45 ♘c5.

Game 26
Alexander Chernin – Paul van der Sterren
Amsterdam 1980
English Opening, Reversed Sicilian

In *50ECL*, we looked at the game Dragomaretsky-Maximov (Game 40), a classic demonstration of White's plan in the typical English Opening structure. In that game, Black played very passively and allowed White to carry out his plan unhindered. Here we look at a rather higher-class game, where Black makes greater efforts to drum up counterplay on the kingside. As a result, White is forced to play more imaginatively in order to pursue his own ideas, and the result is another highly instructive and impressive game, which illustrates many of the typical themes and ideas in such positions.

1 c4 g6 2 ♘c3 ♗g7 3 g3 e5 4 ♗g2 d6 5 d3

With this move, White shows that he is not interested in reaching a King's Indian-type position, but prefers an English formation. His plan is to exert pressure on the central light squares, and to advance on the queenside, using his bishop on g2 to complement the assault.

5...♘c6 6 ♖b1 *(D)*

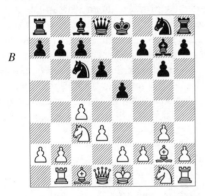

Effectively, this is a Closed Sicilian with colours reversed. In standard fashion, Chernin's last move sets in motion the usual queenside pawn advance.

6...♗e6

In such positions, the question always arises as to whether Black should play the move 6...a5. This does not really prevent the white queenside advance, because White can simply play a3, and then b4. What it does mean, is that when White's pawn gets to b4, Black can open the a-file by ...axb4. This has several features, some good, some bad.

On the plus side, the a-file is opened for Black's rook, which may prove useful. One

specific point is that White may then have more trouble playing ♗a3 to support a later c5 thrust, since on a3, the bishop would need protecting from the black rook. Another point of exchanging on b4 is that Black rids himself of his a-pawn, which in many situations may be a weakness on a7, if White breaks in through the queenside files.

So far, so good, but playing ...a5 and ...axb4 also has its downside. In particular, although Black's rook initially stands on the open a-file, he will frequently lose control of the file when White plays ♖a1. In such positions, the queenside is not really Black's territory. His play generally comes on the kingside, and there is a real danger that opening the a-file will play into White's hands, by helping to accelerate his queenside attack. Steinitz always insisted that the defender should not weaken himself in the area of the board where he stands worse, and this is a rule which is well worth remembering.

Overall, there are few hard-and-fast rules about whether ...a5 is good or bad in such positions, and it is often a mater of taste. One curious practical phenomenon, which I am at a loss to explain, is that whereas in such English structures Black quite often plays ...a5, one almost never sees White play the equivalent move a4 in the Closed Sicilian!

7 ♘f3

In Dragomaretsky-Maximov, White developed his knight by means of e3 and ♘ge2, which is very common in such structures. However, the development of the knight to f3 also has its points. Here, it is slightly more attractive than usual, because Black's bishop is already committed to e6, and hence, after 7 ♘f3, he will have to spend a tempo on 7...h6, to prevent ♘g5. This is not a huge point, but is enough to persuade Chernin to prefer f3 for his knight. Of course, playing e3 and ♘ge2 slightly weakens White's light squares, notably f3, but on the other hand, he is ready to meet Black's later ...f5-f4 plan by playing f4 himself, stopping the enemy pawn in its tracks. Once again, the choice between f3 or e2 for the knight is largely a matter of taste.

7...h6 8 0-0 ♘ge7 9 b4 ♕d7 10 b5 ♘d8 11 ♖e1 *(D)*

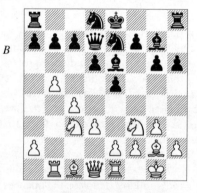

A common idea in such positions. Rather than go pell-mell on the queenside, White also pays some attention to his opponent's plans on the kingside, and employs prophylactic measures where he thinks fit. In this instance, Black is clearly preparing to exchange light-squared bishops by ...♗h3, which would both weaken the defences around White's king, and also deprive him of a minor piece that is likely to prove quite influential in his central and queenside strategy. White therefore decides that it is worth spending two tempi to keep the bishop.

11...♗h3 12 ♗h1 f5 13 ♕c2

An interesting choice. One might have been tempted to put the queen on b3, especially now that the a2-g8 diagonal has been weakened by Black's previous move. However, Chernin is planning the move ♘d5, and in that case, his queen will be well-placed on the c-file if Black exchanges the knight. After White recaptures by cxd5, his queen will exert pressure down the c-file against the backward pawn on c7. Of course, Black is not obliged to exchange on d5, but if he does not, he will have to live with the powerful knight on d5, attacking c7 and constantly

threatening to jump into the weakened squares e7 and f6.

13...g5 *(D)*

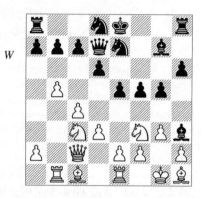

Black presses on with his kingside initiative, in marked contrast to Maximov's play against Dragomaretsky. The critical moment of the game is approaching, since such kingside attacks can be extremely dangerous to face, and accurate play is required of White. However, one thing he should always bear in mind is that, although his primary theatre of attack is the queenside, Black's own king is also weakened by the advances ...f5 and ...g5. In many such positions, in the event of accurate play from White, he can break through on the queenside or in the centre, and then switch the attack to Black's weakened king. This even occurred in Dragomaretsky-Maximov, and we shall see another example here.

14 ♘d5 ♘g6 15 ♘d2 *(D)*

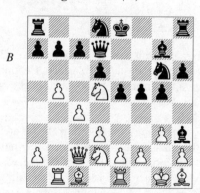

This move is another thematic manoeuvre in such positions. If his knight goes to f3 in these structures, White frequently plays a later ♘d2, to unmask his bishop down the long diagonal. In addition, the knight on d2 stands ready to hop into the central squares, such as e4, if Black plays ...f4, as he usually needs to do to further his kingside attack.

15...0-0 16 c5

White's play follows his logical plan. Now he has ideas of cxd6, followed by penetrating down the c-file, or b6, undermining Black's central and queenside structure. In some cases, a breakthrough with c6 may also be possible.

16...c6 *(D)*

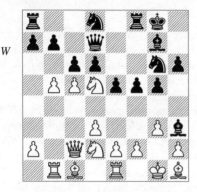

Always the critical reply to c5 in such positions. If White's knight has to retreat, Black will follow up with ...d5, when White has nothing, so White needs to have something special ready in reply to ...c6.

17 bxc6 bxc6 18 cxd6!

This is White's big idea, and a very typical sacrifice in such positions. For his piece, White gets two pawns, undermines Black's queenside and central structure and establishes a powerful passed pawn on d6, which can be supported by such moves as ♗a3 and ♘c4. He will follow up by trying to break through down the open queenside files with his major pieces. Black has no choice but to accept the piece, since 18...♕xd6 simply leaves White with all of his structural advantages and initiative, at no material cost.

18...cxd5 19 ♗xd5+ ♘f7 20 ♗a3!

This is the point of White's play, making it into a real sacrifice. By contrast, 20 ♗xa8 ♖xa8 would re-establish approximate material equality, but lose the initiative and give Black good counterchances against White's weakened king position.

20...♖ac8 21 ♘c4 *(D)*

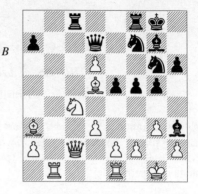

21...f4?

The decisive mistake. Black hurries to reintroduce his marooned light-squared bishop into the central action, but in the meantime, White breaks through down the b-file. A better defensive try was 21...♖b8, although after 22 ♖b3, planning ♖eb1, and meeting 22...♖xb3 with 23 ♕xb3, White would retain excellent compensation for his material.

22 ♖b7 ♕f5 *(D)*

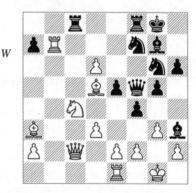

23 d7

The d-pawn ensures the regaining of a decisive amount of material.

23...fxg3 24 hxg3 ♖cd8

Black is tied hand and foot.

25 ♘d6 ♕f6 26 ♘e4 ♕f5 27 ♘d6 ♕f6 28 ♘e4 ♕f5

The repetition of moves gains White some time on the clock, as well as reminding Black who is boss (always a useful thing to do in such positions!). Now it is time to cash in.

29 ♗xf8 ♗xf8 30 ♕c7 ♗e7 31 ♘d6 ♗xd6 32 ♕xd8+ 1-0

Game 27
Ulf Andersson – Yasser Seirawan
Phillips & Drew, London 1982
English Opening, Hedgehog System

In *50ECL*, we examined the game Uhlmann-Bönsch (Game 41), a classic example of Black's counter-attacking plan in the Hedgehog. Here, we see the reverse side of the coin, as the Swedish grandmaster Ulf Andersson manages to spike (pun intended) Black's guns, and exploit White's space advantage in superb style.

1 ♘f3 ♘f6 2 c4 c5 3 g3 b6 4 ♗g2 ♗b7 5 0-0 e6 6 ♘c3 ♗e7 7 d4 cxd4 8 ♕xd4 d6 (D)

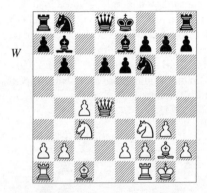

Thus, Black establishes the Hedgehog formation. He will follow up by developing his pieces on the first two ranks, behind the row of pawns on the third rank, and wait for a convenient moment to break out with ...b5 or ...d5.

9 ♗g5

In Uhlmann-Bönsch, we saw White adopt the more ambitious plan of e4, followed by ♕e3 and ♘d4. By taking the centre in such fashion, White hopes to be able to convert his space advantage into an attack on the kingside with an eventual f4. However, as that game showed, Black has plenty of dynamic counter-chances, and White must be very careful that advancing his pawns does not weaken his position, and lay him open to a devastating counter-attack.

Andersson's approach is altogether different, and involves a very deep plan. He intends to exchange bishop for knight on f6, and then bring his knight quickly to e4, with early pressure on the d6-pawn. This will usually force Black to exchange by ...♗xe4. After this, White will try to exploit the weakness of the c6-square, by

eventually bringing his remaining knight, via d4, into the c6 outpost. This may seem like an elaborate and long-winded plan, but in this game, we see it demonstrated with crystal clarity.

One interesting aspect of White's plan is that it involves the exchange of a couple of pairs of minor pieces. On the face of it, this seems illogical, because in the Hedgehog, White has more space. When one has a space advantage, the classical strategy books all tell us that we should avoid exchanges, which only help relieve the defender of his cramp. However, the Hedgehog is rather different from the normal cramped position. The flexibility of Black's position, with the row of pawns on the third rank, means that he has a great deal of dynamic potential (as we saw very clearly in Uhlmann-Bönsch), and the space restriction is not usually so onerous for him. The exchanges which occur in this game actually have the effect of reducing Black's dynamic potential.

9...a6 10 ♗xf6 ♗xf6 11 ♕f4 0-0

Black could seize the chance to cripple White's queenside pawns by 11...♗xc3, but after 12 bxc3, the weakness of the black d6-pawn is more important than the weakness of White's pawns on the c-file.

12 ♖fd1 ♗e7 13 ♘e4 (D)

All part of White's plan, as outlined above. Now 13...d5 14 cxd5 would leave Black in trouble on the d-file, so his next move is forced.

13...♗xe4 14 ♕xe4

Thus, White has achieved his first aim, in forcing the exchange of Black's important light-squared bishop. One can easily see that the c6-square is a significant weakness in Black's position, and he needs to be careful to ensure that the white knight does not some day land on

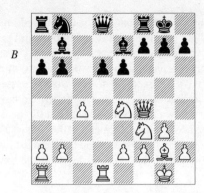

this square. Having said that, White has only a small advantage, but it is of a rather different type from that usually reached in the Hedgehog. Here the position is much less dynamic than in Uhlmann-Bönsch, and White is not planning a kingside demonstration with moves such as e4 and f4. Instead, he will manoeuvre carefully, trying to exploit his queenside chances. This, in turn, will make it more difficult for Black to strike out with ...b5 or ...d5, moves which are usually only good if the white position is over-extended.

14...♖a7 15 ♘d4

The knight immediately directs its sights on the c6-square.

15...♖c7 16 b3 ♖c5 *(D)*

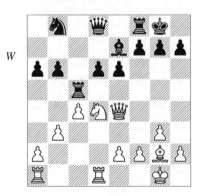

Black threatens 17...b5 but White immediately stops this. Note that the weakness of the c6-square is already tying down Black's knight, which is reluctant to leave b8 because of the unpleasant reply ♘c6.

17 a4 ♕c7

In all such positions, it is important to examine the freeing break ...d5, which, if playable tactically, would usually solve most of Black's problems. Here, however, 17...d5 is not good

because of 18 ♕g4 followed by 19 cxd5, and Black will be left with a weakness on d5. After the move in the game, however, 18...d5 is a real threat.

18 ♕b1! *(D)*

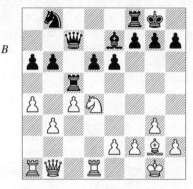

A very typical manoeuvre for this line, and the start of the next link in White's plan. The immediate point is to meet the threat of 18...d5, which would now simply result in an isolated pawn appearing after 19 cxd5. However, there is also a much deeper and more subtle purpose to the move. As we shall see, it is all part of White's plan to get his knight into c6.

18...♖c8

Here, Black had his last chance to exchange off the white knight with 18...♗f6 followed by 19...♗xd4. This would remove once and for all the Damocletian threat of a later ♘c6, and would thus force a complete change of plan from White. However, the drawback is that the bishop would be sorely missed as a defender of the d6-pawn, and White would be able to switch to a plan of putting his major pieces on the d-file, tying Black down to his weakness. Even so, this may be an improvement on the game, but at this stage, one suspects that Seirawan had not divined his opponent's full plan.

19 ♖a2!

Another step in the white plan. The rook is on its way to c2, to defend the c4-pawn more securely, and in the process, by unpinning his knight, White ensures that Black will no longer be able to force an exchange by ...♗f6 followed by ...♗xd4.

19...♗f8 20 e3

By contrast with Uhlmann-Bönsch, the white e-pawn makes only this modest one-step advance, keeping everything defended in the centre, and leaving open the long diagonal for his bishop on g2.

20...♕e7

Black is reduced to marking time, waiting to see what White plans to do. White's set-up, with the exchange of Black's f6-knight and b7-bishop, has prevented Black from achieving a satisfactory ...d5 break, whilst the excellently-placed white knight on d4 not only eyes c6, but also shuts down the ...b5 break.

21 ♖c2! g6 *(D)*

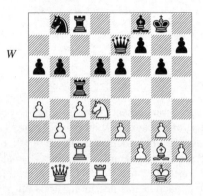

22 ♕a2!!

Finally revealing the true underlying point of his last few moves. The queen joins the rook in over-protecting the c4-pawn. White now intends to follow up with b4 and b5, after which his knight will finally be able to hop into c6. Black's only attempt to prevent this plan is to play 22...a5, but this ugly move donates White's knight the b5-square, from where it exerts pressure on the weak d6-pawn. After 23 ♖cd2 (but not immediately 23 ♘b5?, allowing 23...d5! because of the pin on the c-file – always watch for tactics!) and 24 ♘b5, the d6-pawn is a goner.

Probably the best defence, as suggested by Russian GM Sergei Shipov, was 22...♗g7, when Black can still eliminate the knight after 23 b4 ♖5c7 24 b5 ♗xd4!, etc. However, White is not forced to rush, and, as Shipov himself recommended, can continue to strengthen his position by 23 ♖dc1, defending the c2-rook and stopping tactics along the c-file. In that case, White would retain some positional advantage.

22...♕g5?! 23 h4 ♕f6 24 b4 ♖5c7 25 b5 a5

Opening the a-file would just play into White's hands.

26 ♘c6

Thus, White's plan has been fulfilled, and his knight occupies an extremely powerful position in the heart of the black position. Unfortunately, exchanging it off would result, after 26...♘xc6 27 bxc6, in a very strong passed pawn appearing on c6, and White would have pressure down the open b-file against the weakness on b6. Seirawan decides that the cure would be worse than the disease, and that he must live with the intrusive knight, at least for the time being.

26...♘d7 *(D)*

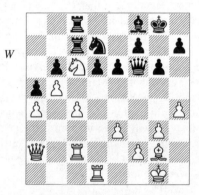

White, in his turn, must now form a new plan to strengthen his position. Although he has achieved his first aim of getting the knight to c6, the game is far from won yet.

27 ♖cd2 ♘c5 28 ♕c2 ♕g7 29 f4! *(D)*

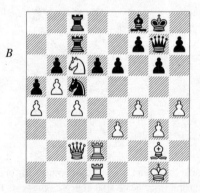

Finally, White begins to expand in the centre and on the kingside. This is ultimately the same plan that Uhlmann adopted, but of course, Andersson's preparations have been much more thorough and effective. Rather than play e4 and f4 as soon as he has developed his pieces, Andersson has first played an elaborate plan of queenside action, and only turns to expansion on the other flank when he has tied Black down and prevented any counterplay.

29...♔h8 30 ♗f3 ♖e8 31 ♔g2?!

Andersson continues to prepare his next actions quietly, but in view of Black's next move, the more energetic 31 g4 may have been stronger.

31...f5!

Seirawan understands that passive play is likely to prove hopeless, so he fights back in the centre, although this does involve creating weaknesses. If he sits tight, White can play for e4-e5, to break through in the centre, or push the pawn to g5, followed by a later h5. Black would have no counterplay, so White could take his time in finding the most effective plan.

32 e4 e5! 33 fxe5 dxe5 *(D)*

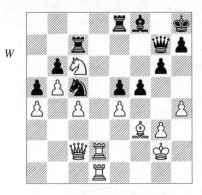

Black has managed to rid himself of the backward pawn on d6, and given his rooks a little more scope, but on the other hand, the open d-file allows White to penetrate Black's position quickly. The game now becomes much sharper.

34 ♖d8 ♖xd8 35 ♖xd8 fxe4 36 ♗xe4 ♕f6

Now Black hopes to create counterplay by 37...♖f7.

37 ♗d5!

The bishop takes up a secure position in the centre, and also eyes the black king.

37...♔g7

The liquidation 37...♖xc6 38 ♖xf8+ ♕xf8 39 bxc6 would eliminate the active white rook, but the resulting passed pawn on c6 would be very strong.

38 ♖e8

Now the e5-pawn cannot be defended, since 38...♗d6 39 ♖g8+ results in his king being chased to extinction on h5. Seirawan therefore jettisons the pawn, in the search for activity.

38...e4 39 ♗xe4 ♖f7 40 ♕e2 ♘xa4

Over the past 10 moves, Seirawan has fought back well and broken the shackles. Now his a-pawn may offer counterplay in the endgame, and White's king remains vulnerable.

41 ♗f3 ♖d7 42 ♗g4 ♖d6 43 ♘e5 ♘c5 44 ♖a8 *(D)*

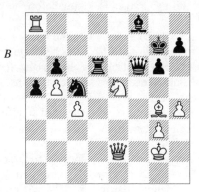

44...♖d8?

A mistake, which negates all of his previous excellent fight-back. The computer defence 44...♕e7 was much tougher, when the seemingly powerful 45 ♕b2 can be met by 45...♘e4, and nothing decisive is visible for White.

45 ♖a7+ ♔g8 46 ♗f3!

Now the bishop returns to d5, with decisive threats against the black king.

46...♗g7

Or 46...♖e8 47 ♗d5+ ♔h8 48 ♖f7! ♖xe5 (48...♕xe5 49 ♖xf8+ is winning for White) 49 ♖xf8+ ♔g7 50 ♖g8+ ♔h6 51 ♕d2+ and White wins.

47 ♗d5+ ♖xd5

Clearly forced, but also hopeless.

48 ♘g4! ♕d8 49 cxd5 ♕xd5+ 50 ♔h2 ♘e4 51 ♖e7 1-0

Despite White's loss of control between moves 30-40, a classic demonstration of his middlegame plan in this line.

Game 28
Predrag Nikolić – Dragan Paunović
Yugoslav Ch, Herceg Novi 1983
Queen's Gambit, Semi-Slav Defence

The various Sicilian Defence examples with Black playing ...e5 have shown how a player can sometimes accept a backward pawn in order to gain more space and control key squares. The present game is another example of this. Nikolić saddles himself with a backward pawn on d4, and gives Black a powerful-looking outpost on d5, but he has realized that Black will not be able to exploit these factors in time. More important is the burying of his pieces on the queenside, and White breaks through to the black king before his opponent can free himself.

1 ♘f3 ♘f6 2 c4 e6 3 ♘c3 d5 4 d4

By transposition, we have reached a Queen's Gambit Declined. Black now chooses the Semi-Slav Variation, one of his sharpest options.

4...c6 5 ♗g5

And White in turn selects the most ambitious reply. 5 e3 can lead to the Meran Variation.

5...h6 *(D)*

For many years, this was considered inferior, and Black usually preferred the ultra-sharp Botvinnik Variation, starting 5...dxc4. After the main line follow-up 6 e4 b5 7 e5 h6 8 ♗h4 g5 9 ♘xg5 hxg5 (9...♘d5 is another wild sideline) 10 ♗xg5 ♘bd7, we reach a highly unbalanced position. White will regain his piece, with a mass of kingside pawns, but Black has a strong pawn-majority on the queenside. In recent years, this line has been analysed and tested so deeply, that many innovations now occur well after move 30. Either due to a feeling that the Botvinnik favours White, or a desire to avoid heavy theory, over the past ten years or so, Black has increasingly often chosen the text-move, which is usually called the Moscow Variation.

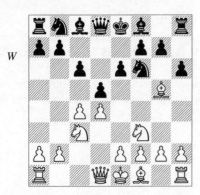

6 ♗xf6

The point of Black's move-order is that after 6 ♗h4, he can avoid the Botvinnik Variation by playing 6...dxc4 7 e4 g5! 8 ♗g3 b5, when Black has avoided the temporary piece sacrifice on g5. However, this is a perfectly reasonable gambit for White, who has a strong pawn-centre to compensate for Black's queenside superiority. Indeed, at the time of writing, 6 ♗h4 is regarded as the best try for an advantage, but this was not theory's verdict at the time the present game was played, and Nikolić instead chooses a quieter continuation.

6...♕xf6 7 e3

Having taken on f6, the move White would like to play is 7 e4, seizing the centre, but then 7...dxe4 8 ♘xe4 ♗b4+ is a little inconvenient. He therefore usually develops more quietly with e3, ♗d3 and 0-0, before advancing in the centre.

7...♘d7 8 ♗d3 ♕d8

Paunović realizes that he cannot stop the e4 advance in the long run, and will have at some stage to lose a tempo with his queen, so he retreats her to d8 immediately. At the time of this game, the Moscow Variation was not very well explored, and Black's best set-up was not yet clear. Nowadays, the most usual reply is 8...dxc4 9 ♗xc4, and now the slightly odd-looking 9...g6. Black puts the bishop on g7, where it exerts pressure on White's potentially weak d4-pawn. The slight weakening of Black's dark squares on the kingside is not usually so important, given that White does not have a dark-squared bishop. Theory suggests that chances are roughly equal in the resulting position. Paunović chooses a more passive set-up.

9 0-0 ♗e7 10 e4 dxe4 11 ♘xe4 0-0 *(D)*

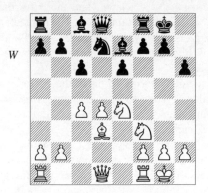

This pawn-structure is one which often arises from Slav and Semi-Slav positions, but also many other openings, including the Catalan, some lines of the Caro-Kann, and even some French Defence variations. White enjoys more space in the centre, and has prospects of a kingside attack. However, Black's position is very solid and has no real weaknesses, and in this example, he also has two bishops. If he can develop his pieces and prevent his king from coming under fire, he will have good prospects.

One thing White always has to be careful about is that his d4-pawn does not prove weak. A classic example of this occurred in an old game of Alekhine's, which is worth looking at briefly: 1 ♘f3 d5 2 d4 c6 3 e3 ♗f5 4 ♗d3 e6 5 0-0 ♘d7 6 c4 ♘gf6 7 ♕c2 ♗xd3 8 ♕xd3 ♘e4 9 ♘fd2 ♘df6 10 ♘c3 ♘xd2 11 ♗xd2 ♗e7 12 e4 dxe4 13 ♘xe4 0-0 14 ♗c3 ♕c7 15 ♖ad1 ♖ad8 16 ♖d2 ♕f4 17 ♘xf6+ ♗xf6 18 ♖fd1 ♖d7 19 ♕g3 ♕f5 20 f4 ♖fd8 *(D)*.

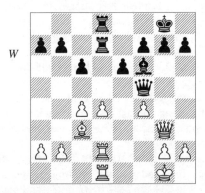

It is clear that White's kingside initiative has come to nothing, and his d4-pawn is seriously weak. Black won after the further moves

21 ♕e3 h5 22 b4? b5! 23 ♕f3 bxc4 24 ♕xc6 ♕xf4 25 ♕xc4 e5 26 ♕e2 exd4 27 ♖d3 dxc3 28 ♖xd7 ♖xd7 29 ♖xd7 ♗d4+ 30 ♔h1 ♕c1+ 0-1 Kmoch-Alekhine, Kecskemet 1927.

12 ♕e2 b6

One very important difference between the game position and the Kmoch-Alekhine game above, is that Alekhine had managed to exchange off his light-squared bishop. Although this meant that he did not have the bishop-pair, he also avoided having the rather passive bishop which Paunović has in this game. A significant part of Nikolić's subsequent strategy is based on the position of this bishop. Paunović's last move aims to develop the bishop to b7, with a view to a later ...c5, but Nikolić anticipates this and prevents it. The immediate 12...c5 may therefore be preferable.

13 ♖ad1 ♗b7 14 ♗b1

Now the pressure on the d-file means that the immediate 14...c5 just leads to a weak pawn on that square after 15 dxc5.

14...♕c7 15 ♖fe1 ♖fe8?!

Black's play hereabouts is rather stereotyped, and he soon allows White a lethal bind. Nikolić later suggested the disruptive 15...♗b4 as an improvement.

16 ♕c2 g6?! *(D)*

And this move severely weakens the kingside. If Black's h-pawn were still on h7, it would not be so bad, but with that pawn already on h6, the g6-pawn becomes too much of a target. Black should prefer the Steinitzian 16...♘f8, avoiding weakening pawn moves in front of his king.

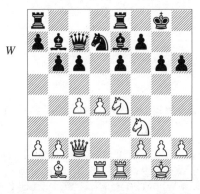

After the text-move, Black is threatening 17...c5, which would open the long diagonal for his bishop, and give his pieces some freedom.

However, Nikolić now produces an excellent positional decision, which underlines White's advantage.

17 c5!

This is an important move in such structures. White radically prevents Black's freeing move ...c5, and shuts in the bishop on b7, thereby depriving Black of most of his counterplay. The obvious drawback of playing c5 is that White gives his opponent a nice central outpost on d5. However, Nikolić has realized that this factor is of less importance in this position. The other point which Nikolić had to foresee is that Black does not have the tactical response 17...e5, undermining the c5-pawn. This fails to 18 ♘d6! (18 ♘xe5 ♘xe5 19 dxe5 ♕xe5 20 ♘d6 is less convincing, in view of 20...♕xe1+ 21 ♖xe1 ♗xd6) 18...♗xd6 19 cxd6 ♕xd6 20 dxe5 ♕e7 21 e6!, when Black's kingside is fatally weakened.

17...♖ad8

The obvious course is to direct the knight to the d5-square, but this allows White's knight into e5, and in view of the weakened black kingside, this knight is even stronger than its black counterpart; e.g., 17...♘f6 18 ♘e5 ♘d5? loses at once, to 19 ♘d6! ♗xd6 20 cxd6 ♕xd6 21 ♘xf7!, etc.

18 h4! *(D)*

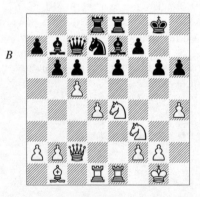

Immediately targeting the weakened black king.

18...h5

The alternative is 18...f5, when Nikolić gives 19 ♘g3 ♗f6 (19...bxc5 20 ♖xe6 is also very strong for White) 20 h5 g5 21 ♕c4, when both e6 and f5 are attacked.

19 b4

Securing the c5-pawn, and ensuring that Black will have no counterplay. The immediate 19 ♘eg5 is met by 19...♗xg5 20 ♘xg5 ♘f6, when White has nothing decisive.

19...a5

Desperately trying to break the chains, but this allows White to proceed aggressively on the kingside.

20 ♘eg5!

The simple 20 a3 would have maintained his grip, but Nikolić has spotted the tactical weakness of Black's last move. The threats now are 21 ♘xf7, 21 ♘xe6 and 21 ♖xe6, so Black is forced to part with his dark-squared bishop, leaving terrible weaknesses on d6 and g6.

20...♗xg5 21 ♘xg5 ♘f8 *(D)*

Nikolić's point is that 21...♘f6 is now met by 22 cxb6!, deflecting the queen, and after 22...♕xb6, 23 ♘xf7 is decisive.

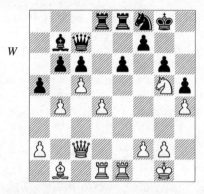

22 ♘e4

Black's last move has shored up his g6-square, thus meeting sacrificial threats against f7 or e6, but now White switches his attention to the weak dark squares.

22...♘h7 23 ♘d6 ♖e7 24 bxa5 bxa5 25 ♖e5

Threatening 26 ♖xh5.

25...♘f6 26 ♖g5 ♗c8 27 ♖d3

Bringing up the last reserves. Black is helpless against this accumulation of overwhelming force against his king.

27...♘e8 28 ♖dg3 ♖xd6 29 ♖xg6+ fxg6 1-0

Black resigned without waiting to see 30 ♕xg6+ ♘g7 31 ♕h7+ ♔f8 32 ♕h8+ and mate in two.

4 Thematic Endings

This chapter ties in, in some ways, with aspects of Chapter 2, on opening play. Game 12 in that chapter illustrated the effectiveness of having a well-understood middlegame plan that arises naturally from the opening. In this chapter, we shall look at several examples where a certain type of endgame arises naturally from a given opening. There are some opening variations in which a major part of the player's strategy is to head for a particular endgame structure, where he will enjoy certain advantages. By studying and understanding the endgame concerned, the player can enjoy great practical advantages, and such variations can be very good point-scorers.

One particular aspect of playing such endgame-oriented openings is that the player's losing chances tend to be minimized. By heading for a slightly superior ending, the player is able to give himself some chances to win the game, whilst at the same time, 'keeping the draw in hand'. This approach can be very effective in tournament and match play, and players such as Ulf Andersson have made a healthy living over the years by adopting such an approach.

Game 29
Zoltan Ribli – Anatoly Karpov
Amsterdam 1980
Catalan Opening

Here, we see a typical Catalan ending. The cleared c- and d-files, and the slightly weakened black queenside pawns, mean that White frequently enjoys a healthy positional advantage in such endings. Ribli gives a textbook demonstration of this.

1 d4 ♘f6 2 c4 e6 3 g3

The Catalan Opening, so-called because it was first adopted by Tartakower at the tournament in Barcelona in 1929. This combination of Réti's Opening and Queen's Gambit has become extremely popular at GM level in the past 50 years. White's plan, as in the English Opening, is to exert pressure on the central light squares. One characteristic feature of the opening is that White frequently welcomes simplification, on the basis that in the resultant endgame his Catalan bishop will prove very powerful on the long diagonal, raking Black's queenside.

3...d5 4 ♗g2 ♗e7

Black has a number of defensive systems available, but broadly speaking, they can be divided into two groups: those where Black captures on c4, and tries to free his position by a later ...c5, and those where he holds the long diagonal and centre solidly, with the move ...c6. As will be seen, Karpov chooses a variant of the first strategy, first developing his kingside, and then capturing on c4. In *50ECL* (Game 27), we saw Reshevsky play the immediate 4...dxc4, leading to similar positions to the present game.

5 ♘f3 0-0 6 0-0 dxc4 7 ♕c2 *(D)*

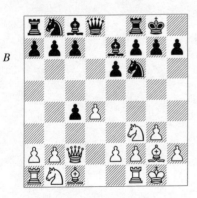

White first regains his pawn. Black cannot retain the pawn in view of 7...b5 8 a4 c6 9 axb5 cxb5 10 ♘g5, winning material.

7...a6 8 ♕xc4

This is an important decision, which will have a profound influence on the further course of the game. White decides to allow Black to expand on the queenside and develop his bishop to b7, thereby solving one of Black's principal problems in the Open Catalan, namely how to develop his queen's bishop. Very often, this piece proves difficult to activate, because of the pressure from White's Catalan bishop on the long diagonal. However, the price Black pays for this is the weakening of his queenside pawns. In the first instance, his c-pawn remains backward, and if he is unable to achieve the advance ...c5, he can be left with a serious long-term weakness on the c-file. The second problem, which will be seen in this game, is that even after achieving ...c5, Black's pawns on a6 and b5 can prove weak later in the game. One of White's main strategies in such positions is to simplify to an endgame, hoping to exploit the weakness of these pawns, and this is exactly the strategy we shall see employed by Ribli in the present game.

White's alternative plan is to stop Black's queenside expansion by 8 a4, when Black usually develops his bishop by 8...♗d7 9 ♕xc4 ♗c6. Although White has a certain space advantage, he has weakened his b4-square, which Black can often exploit by ...a5 and ...♘a6-b4, whilst Black's position is very solid and has no real weaknesses. The choice between 8 ♕xc4 and 8 a4 is largely a matter of taste, but most strong GMs tend to prefer the former.

8...b5 9 ♕c2 ♗b7 10 ♗f4

A popular alternative here is 10 ♗d2, threatening the unpleasant pin by 11 ♗a5. Black usually reacts to this by playing 10...♘c6, after which White tries to show that the knight is misplaced on c6, where it obstructs Black's c-pawn. Ribli prefers a different plan, attacking the c7-pawn immediately.

10...♘d5 11 ♘c3 *(D)*

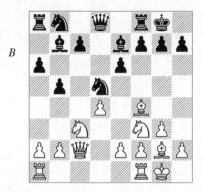

B

This is another common theme in the Catalan. At first sight, it may look strange to allow ...♘xf4, giving Black the bishop-pair, and breaking up White's kingside pawn-structure. However, the resulting structure often offers White good kingside play, with a plan such as ♘e5, ♗f3, ♔h1 and ♖g1. Another idea is to make the f5 advance, undoubling White's pawns and freeing the way for the d-pawn to advance to d5.

11...♘xf4 12 gxf4 ♘d7

Black cannot yet free his position by 12...c5?, in view of the tactic 13 dxc5 ♗xc5? 14 ♘g5, winning. This is already the second such tactical trick on the long diagonal that we have seen in this game, and it is a typical theme in Catalan positions.

13 ♖fd1 ♕c8 14 ♘e4!

Having defended the b7-bishop, Black is now ready to break out with ...c5. White cannot directly prevent this, so he adopts the next stage of his endgame-oriented strategy. The text-move prepares to ensure that White can play various exchanges on c5, leading to an endgame in which he will be able to claim a small advantage, based on the exposed black queenside pawns. Ribli's last move was actually an innovation at the time of his game, previous games having seen 14 f5 exf5 15 ♕xf5 ♘f6, with equal chances.

14...c5

Black has to play this, as otherwise 15 ♖ac1 will follow.

15 dxc5 ♘xc5 16 ♘xc5 ♕xc5 17 ♕xc5 ♗xc5 *(D)*

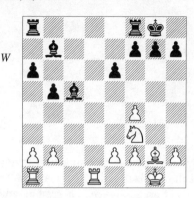

W

This is the type of endgame position White has been envisaging. To the uninitiated, it may look very drawish, but in fact White has a small but clear edge. The black pawns on a6 and b5 could well prove vulnerable, and White's rooks will occupy good positions on the two open files. Admittedly, Black has the two bishops, but that will not be the case for long, as we shall see. The other point about such a position is that White can play on a risk-free basis, with some winning chances, and very few chances of losing. Psychologically, it is not very pleasant for Black, knowing that he must just defend and defend, hoping for half a point, with few, if any, chances of actually winning the game.

18 ♖ac1 ♖fc8 19 ♘e5!

An excellent move, which ensures White a definite pull. As we have pointed out before, both in this book and in *50ECL*, when the opponent has the two bishops, a standard strategy for the other side is to exchange his remaining bishop for its opposite number.

19...♗xg2 20 ♔xg2 f6

Slightly weakening Black's structure, especially the e6-pawn, but the knight exerts unpleasant pressure from its current location. It attacks f7, and prevents Black from centralizing his king (20...♔f8?? 21 ♘d7+). In addition, Black needs to do something to fight for the c- and d-files. For example, if 20...♖c7, White can penetrate immediately by 21 ♘d3 ♗b6 (21...♖ac8?? leads to mate on the back rank after the double exchange on c5) 22 ♖xc7 ♗xc7 23 ♖c1, when White's rook will come down the c-file to c6.

21 ♘f3 ♗f8 22 e3 g6 23 b3 *(D)*

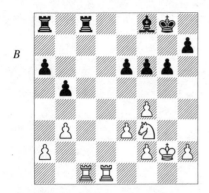

This weakens the dark squares a3 and b4, which allows Black's bishop to make a bit of a nuisance of itself, but White is keen to remove some pawns from the second rank, so he can play ♖xc8 and ♖d7, without the reply ...♗c2 causing too much damage.

23...♗b4 24 h3 ♔f8 25 ♘d4 ♔f7 26 a4!

As in the previous note, White needs to remove his queenside pawns from the second rank, so as to reduce Black's chances for counterplay and activate his own rook. Although one of Black's potentially weak queenside pawns is exchanged off, the remaining pawn on a6 is a clear target, as also is the e6-pawn.

26...bxa4 27 bxa4 ♗c5?!

Maybe Black should prefer 27...a5 here, but Karpov was probably reluctant to give White's knight the outpost on b5.

28 ♖c4 ♗a3 29 ♖xc8 ♖xc8 30 ♖b1 ♖c4

Black is close to a draw around this point, but does not quite manage to kill off White's initiative. 30...♖c7 is answered by 31 ♖b8, when the threats of both 32 ♖a8 and 32 ♖h8 are awkward to meet.

31 ♖b7+ ♔e7 32 ♖a7 e5

This is now forced, as otherwise the a-pawn is lost without compensation.

33 fxe5 fxe5 34 ♘f3 ♖xa4 35 ♘xe5+ ♔f6 36 ♘c6

With the elimination of White's last queenside pawn, the position looks very drawish, but Black in fact still has significant problems, since he cannot defend avoid the loss of a pawn. White's rook and knight are very active and co-operate well together, harassing Black's king, whilst the passed e-pawn will become a threat.

36...♗c5 37 ♖xh7 ♖a2 38 ♔f3 a5

"Passed pawns must be pushed!" Advancing the a-pawn is Black's only hope of counterplay.

39 h4 a4 40 ♔e4! *(D)*

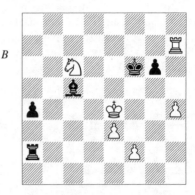

This is decisive, the main point being that 40...♖xf2 is impossible because of 41 ♘d8, when Black has no defence to 42 ♖f7+, either mating or winning a rook. This mating construction is worth noting, as it is typical for endings of ♖+♘ vs ♖+♗. A rook and a knight, working together against an exposed enemy king, can frequently conjure up mating threats. A good way to develop one's awareness of such endgame tactics is to spend time regularly, looking at endgame studies. Not only are they the source of enormous aesthetic pleasure, they can also teach a great deal about the capabilities of the various pieces.

40...♗f8 41 ♖a7 ♗d6?!

41...♖xf2 was a more stubborn defence. Presumably Karpov rejected it because of 42 ♘e5, which threatens both 43 ♘g4+ and 43 ♖f7+, and appears to win a piece. However, after 42...♖b2! it turns out that 43 ♖f7+ ♔e6 44 ♖xf8 does not win a piece after all, because of 44...♖b4+, regaining it. White would probably have to settle for answering 41...♖xf2 with 42 ♖xa4, but Black would have better drawing chances than in the game.

42 f4 ♖h2 43 ♖a6! ♔f7

If 43...♖xh4, then 44 ♘e5 ♔e6 45 ♘c4 wins a piece.

44 ♘e5+

Now White settles for a transition into a theoretically winning rook ending, with two pawns against one and his king occupying a very active position.

44...♗xe5 45 ♔xe5 ♔g7 46 ♖a7+ ♔h6 47 ♖xa4 ♖xh4 48 ♔f6 ♖h5 49 e4 ♖h4 50 e5 ♖h5 51 e6 ♖f5+ 52 ♔e7 ♔g7 53 ♔d6 ♖f8 54 ♖a7+ ♔f6 55 ♖d7 1-0

Game 30
Wolfgang Uhlmann – Svetozar Gligorić
Hastings 1970/1
King's Indian Defence, Averbakh System

In the previous game, Ribli-Karpov, we saw an example of a player choosing an opening variation in which achieving a certain outline endgame was a major part of his strategic plan. This is an even more striking example.

1 d4 ♞f6 2 c4 g6 3 ♞c3 ♝g7 4 e4 d6 5 ♝e2 0-0 6 ♝g5

This variation with ♝e2 and ♝g5 is named after the Russian grandmaster Averbakh, and become highly popular around the late 1960s and early 1970s, being played with great success by both Polugaevsky and Uhlmann. There are various ways that the game can develop, depending on how Black responds. The variation in this game was played extensively for a few years, until White's technique in the ensuing endgame had become so refined that King's Indian practitioners became fed up with suffering in it, and looked for new paths.

6...c5

Nowadays, the most popular move is 6...♞a6, retaining flexibility with Black's pawn-structure.

7 d5 e6 8 ♕d2 exd5 9 exd5 *(D)*

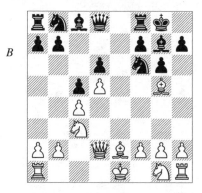

B

This recapture is the key to White's plan in this variation. Rather than take with the c-pawn, reaching a Modern Benoni structure where Black would be well-placed, White adopts a symmetrical pawn-formation. Such positions, with one open file, are often very drawish, as the rooks tend to come off on the open file, and the position simplifies heavily. In this particular

line, however, Polugaevsky realized that even after the exchange of queens and rooks, the endgame can be very difficult for Black. White's basic strategy is therefore to develop his pieces, encourage Black to exchange pieces, and head for a minor-piece endgame.

9...♖e8 10 ♞f3 ♝g4

This move leads to the conceding of the bishop-pair, but as explained in the context of Game 13, Black's rather cramped position means that it is difficult to do without this exchange. If the bishop stays on the board, it does not really have a decent square, since on f5 it can be hunted down by h3 and g4, or ♞h4, whilst on d7, it would cause congestion by occupying the square intended for Black's queen's knight.

11 0-0 ♞bd7 12 h3 ♝xf3 13 ♝xf3 a6 14 a4 *(D)*

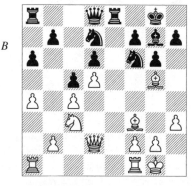

B

White has several small advantages here, i.e. more space, the two bishops, and a weak black pawn on d6. Thanks to the symmetrical pawn-formation, Black does not really have any active plan, and it is hard for him to do anything else except bring his rooks to the e-file. If he does not do so, White will occupy the open file himself.

14...♕e7 15 ♖ae1 ♕f8 16 ♗d1 ♖xe1 17 ♖xe1 ♖e8 18 ♖xe8 ♕xe8 19 ♗f4 ♕e7 20 ♕e2 ♔f8 21 ♕xe7+ ♔xe7 (D)

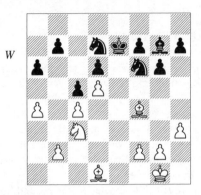

W

White has ruthlessly exchanged down to his desired endgame. It may not look as though he has much advantage, but in practice, White won a whole series of endgames of this type around this period. Indeed, Uhlmann himself had learnt the hard way about the difficulties facing Black in such positions. A few months prior to this game, he had reached the following position after 24 moves, as Black against Polugaevsky, at Amsterdam 1970:

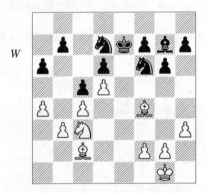

W

The position is almost identical to that in Uhlmann-Gligorić. Against Polugaevsky, Uhlmann defended stoutly, but was remorselessly ground down in almost identical fashion to that in which he now proceeds to beat Gligorić. The moral of the story is clear – if you lose a game, learn from it!

22 a5!

A vital move to underscore White's advantage. Now Black's pawns on a6 and b7 are fixed on light squares, and will forever be vulnerable to White's unopposed light-squared bishop

penetrating Black's position to c8. Indeed, this is exactly what happened in Polugaevsky-Uhlmann. Another idea for White is to play b4, when an exchange on b4 will allow his other bishop to attack d6 along the a3-f8 diagonal. We shall see this later in the present game. Of course, Black could always break out with ...b6, but this would leave him with a weak, isolated pawn on a6.

22...♘e8 23 ♗d2

Black was threatening to cripple White's queenside pawns by 23...♗xc3.

23...h5

This move is directed against the typical kingside space-clamping move g4, which would certainly have followed, if permitted. Nonetheless, White still has designs on a kingside squeeze to complement his queenside play.

24 ♔f1 ♗d4 25 b3 ♘g7 26 ♗c2 ♘e8 27 ♘e2 ♗b2 28 f3 ♘g7 29 ♔f2

White is in no hurry, as Black has no real counterplay. In such situations, it pays to improve one's position gradually, not revealing one's hand until absolutely necessary.

29...♗f6 30 ♘c3 ♗d4+ 31 ♔e2 f5 32 f4!

Fixing Black's kingside pawns on light squares. Now g6 is especially vulnerable, and White can gradually prepare to break the kingside open with g4. This plan, too, was not new to Uhlmann – it was precisely what happened in his game with Polugaevsky!

32...♘e8 33 ♗d3 (D)

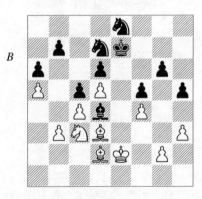

B

33...♗xc3!?

A radical decision. Gligorić grants White the 'whole' bishop-pair, hoping to entrench his knights on good squares, such as e4. This was widely criticized by various commentators after the game, but it is far from clear that it was such a bad decision. Uhlmann, against Poluga-evsky, had kept his bishop, but the white knight proved at least as strong.

34 ♗xc3 ♘ef6 35 ♗e1 ♔f7 36 ♔e3 ♔e7 37 ♗c2 ♔f7 38 b4! *(D)*

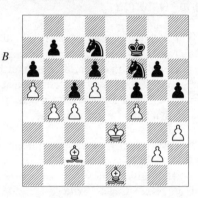

After much slow manoeuvring, White finally makes his first planned pawn-break.

38...cxb4

If Black does not capture on b4, White is always able to do so himself on c5, and Black must also reckon with the possibility of b5, followed by either b6, or bxa6 and ♗a4-c6-b7.

39 ♗xb4 ♘c5

Now we see the point of Black's thinking at move 33. His knights can occupy c5 and d7. With only one minor piece able to attack c5, it is not obvious how White can break down the blockade.

40 ♔d4 ♘fd7 41 ♗d1! *(D)*

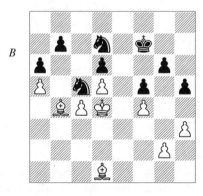

Two weaknesses! In classic style, White sets about opening a second front on the kingside.

41...♔e7

He cannot stop White's next move, because 41...h4 would lose a pawn after 42 ♗e1.

42 g4 hxg4 43 hxg4 ♔f6 44 ♔e3 b6

This too was criticized by some commentators, and even accused of being the losing move, but the position is already beyond salvation. After a waiting move, such as 44...♔f7, Marić demonstrated that White wins by 45 gxf5 gxf5 46 ♗h5+ ♔e7 47 ♗g6 ♔f6 48 ♗h7, when 49 ♗c3+ is a threat, and 48...♘e4 49 ♗a3 leaves Black no defence against 50 ♗b2+.

45 gxf5 gxf5 *(D)*

46 ♗xc5!

Every annotator of such endings points out that the advantage of having two bishops is that one can exchange one of them for a knight at an appropriate moment – and you wouldn't expect me to do anything different, would you? In all seriousness, though, it is truly amazing how often such a timely exchange proves to be the key moment in such endings.

46...♘xc5

This loses a pawn, but after 46...bxc5 47 ♗a4 ♘b8 (47...♘f8 48 ♗c6 ♘g6 49 ♗b7 wins for White – see note to move 22!) 48 ♔f3 ♔g6 49 ♔g3, and the white king will penetrate to g5 and win the f5-pawn; e.g., 49...♔f6 50 ♔h4 ♔g6 51 ♗c6! ♔h6 52 ♗e8 with zugzwang.

47 axb6 a5 48 ♗c2 ♔e7

There is no counterplay from 48...a4 because of 49 ♗xa4! ♘xa4 50 b7 winning. The rest poses no problems to White.

49 ♔d2 ♔d8 50 ♗xf5 ♘a4 51 b7 ♔c7 52 ♗c8 ♘c5 53 f5 ♘e4+ 54 ♔c2 ♔b8 55 ♔b3 ♘d2+ 56 ♔a4 ♘xc4 57 f6 ♘e5 58 ♔xa5 1-0

Game 31
David Howell – Vladimir Kramnik
Exhibition game, London 2002
Ruy Lopez (Spanish), Berlin Defence

In most of the endgame-oriented opening variations, it is White who is looking to force the ending, but in this next example, it is Black. This defence to the Ruy Lopez has become extremely popular in recent years, after Kramnik's success with it against Kasparov in their world championship match in 2000. The present game was an exhibition game, played when David Howell was just 12 years of age, so you may feel it is a little cruel of me to showcase it here. However, it happens to be an exceptionally clear example of Black's strategy, so I hope that David will forgive me.

1 e4 e5 2 ♘f3 ♘c6 3 ♗b5 ♘f6

The characteristic move of the Berlin Defence. Highly popular in the early years of the 20th century, it was then largely eclipsed by 3...a6, but has reappeared at GM level in recent years, in the form seen in this game.

4 0-0 ♘xe4 5 d4 ♘d6 (D)

This knight move is the key to the Berlin's revival. Although known a hundred years ago (it was played several times by Pillsbury, as well as Lasker and Tarrasch), the move was never the most popular method of play for Black. Instead, 5...♗e7 was the usual move, leading to a standard position after 6 ♕e2 ♘d6 7 ♗xc6 bxc6 8 dxe5 ♘b7. Although this line remains unrefuted, nowadays it is regarded as slightly passive and inferior, and attention has shifted to the text-move, which virtually forces an early queen exchange.

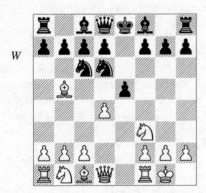

6 ♗xc6

Instead of this exchange, White can avoid the endgame by the temporary piece sacrifice 6 dxe5 ♘xb5 7 a4, regaining the piece. However, this is not considered to promise White anything

after 7...♘bd4! (other moves are inferior) 8 ♘xd4 ♘xd4 9 ♕xd4 d5, and so the text-move is overwhelmingly the most popular choice.

6...dxc6 7 dxe5 ♘f5 8 ♕xd8+

A common inaccuracy at club level is 8 ♕e2?!, trying to avoid the queen exchange. After 8...♘d4! 9 ♘xd4 ♕xd4 10 ♖d1 ♗g4! Black forces off the queens anyway, and in more favourable circumstances than the game, since his king has not lost the right to castle.

8...♔xd8 (D)

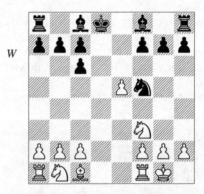

This is the main starting position for this variation, and is worth considering in detail, since it is a deceptive position. In particular, it is worth comparing it with the Exchange Variation of the Spanish, which arises after 1 e4 e5 2 ♘f3 ♘c6 3 ♗b5 a6 4 ♗xc6 dxc6. In the Exchange, if White follows up with d4, and the pawns are exchanged, we get a very similar structure to the game, but with some important differences.

White's main strategy in the Exchange Variation is to exploit his superior pawn-formation. He has a healthy 4 vs 3 pawn-majority on the kingside, which in due course can expect to produce a passed pawn. Black, on the other hand, has a 4 vs 3 majority on the other flank, but the doubled c-pawns mean that his majority cannot force a passed pawn. In principle, therefore, the structure should favour White in the endgame, and his main plan in such positions is to exchange queens and try to exploit his structural advantage in the ending. Black's main compensation for his inferior pawn-structure is his bishop-pair, which offers him the chance of active counterplay.

In the Berlin case, White has achieved the normal pawn-structure advantage, and has already got the queens off. In addition, Black's king is stuck in the centre and cannot castle, and although the absence of queens makes this less significant than would normally be the case in a middlegame situation, he still has some problems to overcome in order to complete his development and activate his rooks. On the face of it, therefore, White should have a much-improved version of the Exchange Spanish. So why is this not the case?

The answer all lies in one seemingly insignificant factor, namely the position of White's e-pawn. In the Exchange Variation, this pawn would normally be on e4, whereas in the Berlin, it is on e5. Tiny though this factor may appear, it is hugely significant. On e5, the pawn is fixed on a dark square, obstructing the path of White's remaining bishop. In addition, Black has use of the f5-square, which is frequently an excellent outpost for his knight or light-squared bishop. Often, the d5-square is also available to Black's pieces. Although these factors may not sound too important, they are the key to rendering Black's position playable. In fact, the whole line is an excellent example of the old adage that "pawns don't move backwards". If White could play the move 9 e5-e4 in this position, I don't think one would find too many grandmasters keen to play this line with Black!

The subtlety of this whole position is such that it has foxed many grandmasters. Although the queens are off, the position still resembles a middlegame, rather more than an endgame. If Black can overcome his development problems, get his king out of trouble and activate his rooks, he will have very good prospects, not only of equalizing, but even of taking over the

initiative and playing for a win. Consequently, White needs to play energetically over the next few moves to exploit his superior development and prevent Black from solving his short-term problems.

9 ♘c3 ♚e8 (D)

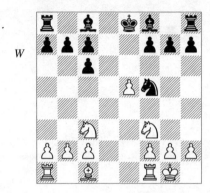

This is already a significant decision by Black. He has two main options with his king. The text-move is one, and the other is to put the king on c8 and later b7. The latter takes longer to achieve, but if Black can manage it, he is likely to have a good game. On e8, the king is still rather clumsily placed, and prevents the h8-rook from getting into the game, but on the other hand, the other rook can come to d8 quickly, to oppose White's short-term pressure on the d-file.

10 b3 ♗b4 11 ♗b2?! (D)

This move is very natural, but is almost certainly an error. As noted above, the white pawn on e5 obstructs the operation of his remaining bishop. One of Black's most common plans in this variation is to exchange his dark-squared bishop for the knight on c3, producing an opposite-coloured bishop ending. In such endings, White's queenside pawns frequently prove vulnerable to Black light-squared bishop, which can emerge via f5-c2, and attack the white pawns from behind. By contrast, White's bishop usually has much more trouble doing the same to Black's queenside pawns, because the e5-pawn gets in its way. We shall see this scenario demonstrated later in the present game.

Rather than allow the exchange on c3, White should prefer 11 ♘e4, retaining pieces and hoping to use his knights to create active play in the centre, for example, with a later e6 thrust. As noted earlier, White's advantages in his position are more of a middlegame nature (superior development, centralized enemy king, etc.), and so he needs to pursue an initiative-based, active plan, if he is to avoid drifting into an inferior position.

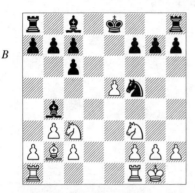

11...♗xc3! 12 ♗xc3 c5

Having exchanged his dark-squared bishop, Black arranges his pawns on dark squares. His ultimate strategy is to achieve a position where he has his pawns on something like a5, b6, c7 and c5, whilst White's queenside pawns are on a4, b3 and c4. A later ...♗f5-c2 will then leave the white pawns highly vulnerable.

13 ♖ad1 h6

A common move in such positions, and a complement to Black's last move. He prepares ...♗e6, without allowing the bishop to be exchanged off by either ♘d4 or ♘g5. It is notable how difficult it is for White to achieve any active play in this position, following the exchange on c3. In fact, he already stands somewhat worse, as it is difficult to oppose the black plan outlined in the previous note.

14 h3 ♗e6 15 ♗b2 b6 16 ♖d2 *(D)*

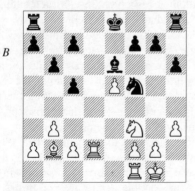

16...♘e7!

As in any position, strategic plans must always be balanced with tactical alertness. Black would like to continue 16...♔e7, but here that would be a blunder in view of 17 g4, winning a pawn. Kramnik therefore re-routes the knight to c6 first. Note that although White can double rooks on the d-file, it does not bring him any dividends, since the entry squares d6, d7 and d8 are all covered.

17 c4

This helps to fix the pawns on light squares, which Black wishes to see anyway, but if White does not play this, he has to worry about the enemy knight coming in to d5, and also a potential ...c4 break, dissolving Black's doubled pawns.

17...♘c6 18 ♗c3 ♔e7 19 ♖fd1 *(D)*

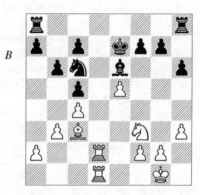

19...a5!

A thematic advance in such positions. Black threatens 20...a4, after which he would have the permanent threat of penetrating down the a-file. White cannot really allow this, so his next move is forced.

20 a4

Now Black has the queenside pawn-structure that he wants. A subsequent ...♗f5-c2 will cause White great problems defending his b3-pawn.

20...♖ad8

With progress on the a-file stopped, the black rooks have little to do, so exchanging them off on the d-file is the logical continuation. In a pure minor-piece ending, Black will have more freedom to manoeuvre.

21 ♖xd8 ♖xd8 22 ♖xd8 ♔xd8 23 ♔f1 ♗f5 24 ♘e1 *(D)*

The first passive step, necessary to prevent ...♗c2. For the remainder of the game, White will be forced to take account of this threat at every move.

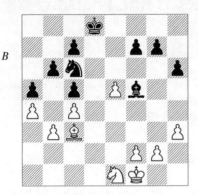

24...g5!

Artificially isolating White's e-pawn, which can no longer be supported by f4. The threat now is simply 25...♔e7 and 26...♔e6, winning the pawn. In such a structure, one can see very clearly how much White suffers from his pawn being on e5, rather than e4.

25 ♔e2 ♔e7 26 ♔e3 ♔e6 27 f4 g4?!

A strange decision. The obvious, and thematic, continuation is 27...gxf4+ 28 ♔xf4 ♘e7, when White must already lose the e5-pawn. After the text-move, Black has to win the game over again.

28 hxg4 ♗xg4 29 ♘f3 ♗f5 30 ♘d2 ♘e7 31 ♔f3 h5 32 ♘e4 ♗g4+ 33 ♔f2 (D)

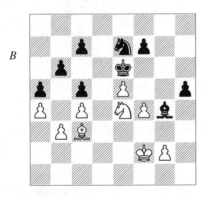

33...♘f5

At the risk of labouring the point, I would emphasize again the excellent use Black's pieces make of the f5-square. Despite the inaccuracy at move 27, Black retains a clear advantage, with the vulnerable queenside pawns tying down White's pieces. The only question is whether White can hold the kingside.

34 ♘g5+ ♔e7 35 ♘e4 ♗d1 36 ♘d2 ♔e6 37 ♔e1 ♗c2 38 ♔e2 ♘h4 39 g3 ♘g6 40 ♔f3 ♗d1+ 41 ♔e4 ♗c2+ 42 ♔f3 ♔f5 (D)

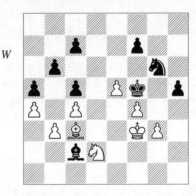

Now the answer is clear. Black will play ...♗d1+, forcing his king to g4. Then he will bring the knight via e7, back to the beloved f5-square, after which White's pawn on g3 will be indefensible. Note how helpless his bishop has been throughout the ending. Rather than watch this scenario unfold, Howell prefers to jettison the b-pawn, but after this, the position is hopeless, since the a4- and c4-pawns are too weak.

43 ♘f1 ♗d1+

But not, of course, 43...♗xb3?? 44 ♘e3+ ♔e6 45 f5+, winning a piece. Do not hurry, and look out for every tactical resource!

44 ♔f2 ♗xb3 45 ♘e3+ ♔e4 46 f5 ♘xe5 47 ♗xe5 ♔xe5 48 ♘d5 ♗xc4 49 ♘xc7 ♗b3 (D)

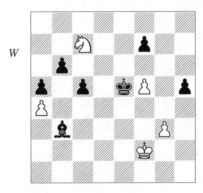

The position is clearly now hopeless, and the remaining moves require no comment.

50 ♘a8 ♗xa4 51 ♘xb6 ♗b5 52 ♔e3 a4 53 ♔d2 ♔xf5 54 ♔c3 ♔g4 55 ♘d5 ♔xg3 56 ♘f6 h4 57 ♘e4+ ♔g2 58 ♘xc5 h3 59 ♘e4 h2 60 ♘d2 h1♕ 61 ♔b4 ♕e1 62 ♔xb5 ♕xd2 63 ♔xa4 f5 0-1

Game 32
Alexandra Kosteniuk – Peter Heine Nielsen
Hastings 2002/3
Caro-Kann Defence, Classical Variation

In the main line of the 4...♗f5 Caro-Kann, White usually advances his kingside pawns in the opening and early middlegame. Although this can prove very strong, there is also the danger that his position will later become over-extended, especially if the queens come off. The present game is an illustration of this.

1 e4 c6

The Caro-Kann is one of Black's most solid and respected defences to 1 e4. Black prepares to stake a foothold in the centre by 2...d5, in similar fashion to the French Defence, but without blocking in his light-squared bishop.

2 d4 d5 3 ♘d2 dxe4 4 ♘xe4 ♗f5

Black can also play both 4...♘d7 and even 4...♘f6 here, but the text-move is the classical continuation. Black develops his bishop outside the pawn-chain, prior to playing ...e6. Despite some 80 years of regular use at master level, White has never succeeded in demonstrating more than a small plus in this line. The only slight drawback for Black is that he has relatively few winning chances, which makes the line suitable for use against strong opponents, but less so against lower-rated opposition, or in other situations where Black needs to play for a win. The main way in which Black can win such positions is when White overstretches, and this is what we see in the present game.

5 ♘g3 ♗g6 6 h4 *(D)*

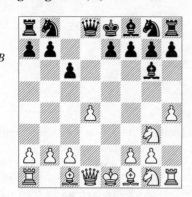

The advance of the white h-pawn is the standard plan in such positions. White forces a slight weakening of the enemy kingside, and gains space.

6...h6 7 ♘f3 ♘d7 8 h5 ♗h7 9 ♗d3 ♗xd3 10 ♕xd3 e6

This move is the start of a relatively modern interpretation of the defence. For many years, the move 10...♕c7 was regarded as best here, to prevent White's bishop from taking up an active position on the h2-b8 diagonal.

11 ♗f4 *(D)*

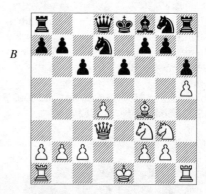

11...♘gf6!?

This continues a relatively unusual plan. In many modern games, Black prefers 11...♕a5+ here, after which 12 ♗d2 ♕c7 returns to positions usually reached after 10...♕c7 11 ♗d2. White cannot very well answer 11...♕a5+ with 12 c3, since then White would be unable to castle queenside, because the pawn at a2 would be hanging.

Nielsen's plan is rather different. He intends to allow the bishop to remain on the h2-b8 diagonal, and to post his queen on a5 only after White has castled queenside.

12 0-0-0 ♗e7 13 c4 *(D)*

This move is to some extent a consequence of Black's strategy of allowing ♗f4. White slightly exposes her king, but gains space and takes control of the d5-square. Without this move, she would always have to reckon with a later ...♞d5, hitting the bishop on f4.

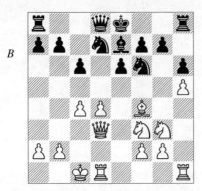

13...0-0!?

This is an integral part of the modern interpretation of this variation. For most of the past 80 years, Black almost invariably castled queenside in this line, since with the position of the respective h-pawns, it was thought much too risky to castle short. White appears to have a ready-made attack with g4-g5, opening lines in front of Black's king, whereas Black's counter on the other flank seems much slower.

However, over the last decade or so, castling kingside has become *de rigeur* for Black in the 4...♝f5 Caro-Kann. The truth is that White's kingside pieces, notably the knight on g3, are rather clumsily placed, and get in the way of his pawns. In order to start his pawn-storm, White will usually have to play ♞e4, which will allow Black to exchange a pair of minor pieces, and thus ease his slightly cramped position. Furthermore, the black kingside is easier to defend than at first appears, and meanwhile, he can often open lines on the other wing, either by ...c5 and ...cxd4, opening the c-file, or even by a pawn sacrifice ...b5, seeking to open the b-file as well.

The result is that the positions are often much sharper and more double-edged than is the case after ...0-0-0 by Black. In the latter case, he usually stands slightly worse in a quiet position, where a draw is usually all he can hope for. After opposite-side castling, however, the game is more unbalanced, and Black can hope to play for more than just half a point.

14 ♔b1 ♛a5 *(D)*

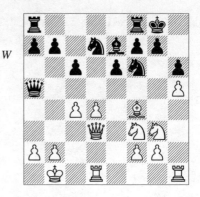

15 ♞e5

This soon leads to multiple exchanges, after which White's hopes of a kingside attack evaporate. The alternative is 15 ♞e4, when taking the h-pawn is not good: 15...♞xh5 16 ♝d2 ♛f5 17 g4! ♛xg4 18 ♖dg1 and White will soon win material. Instead, however, Black can play the solid 15...♞xe4 16 ♛xe4 ♞f6 17 ♛c2 ♖ad8, with a sound position. 18 g4 is a reasonable way to tear open lines on the kingside, although after 18...♞xg4 White must choose 19 c5, with enough play for the pawn, since 19 ♖dg1? allows 19...♛f5!, when the queens come off.

15...♖ad8

The vis-à-vis of queen and rook along the d-file sets up veiled tactical threats after the break 16...c5, which induces White to spend another tempo getting her queen off the d-file.

16 ♛e2 ♖fe8 17 ♞e4 *(D)*

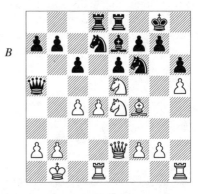

It is hard to see any other constructive plan for White, but now the exchanges lead to a position where she has no hope of a successful kingside attack.

17...♞xe4 18 ♛xe4 ♞xe5 19 dxe5

19 ♝xe5 c5 also gives Black comfortable equality.

19...♖xd1+ 20 ♖xd1 ♖d8 21 ♖xd8+ ♕xd8 (D)

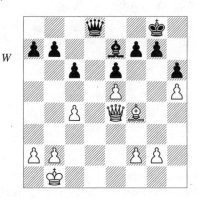

By means of multiple exchanges, Black has equalized easily. After 22 ♔c2, a draw would be by far the most likely result, but already, White is the one who must exercise slightly the greater care. Her h5-pawn can easily prove vulnerable in such an ending, whilst her bishop is a little worse than its opposite number, because of the pawn fixed on e5. At present, these are very minor factors, but it does not take too many inaccuracies from White, before they start to take on greater significance.

22 ♕e2?

This is hard to understand, allowing Black's queen to take up a dominant position in the centre.

22...♕d4 23 ♗d2 b5!

White was threatening to dislodge the queen by means of 24 ♗c3, so Black exploits the momentary tactical vulnerability of the bishop on d2 to secure for his queen the powerful central post d5.

24 cxb5 cxb5 (D)

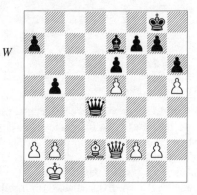

25 f4

This puts another pawn on the same colour squares as White's bishop, but in the long run, it can scarcely be avoided. Black can attack the e5-pawn by ...♗d8-c7, and if White defends the pawn with ♗c3, the advance ...a5 and ...b4 will later threaten to drive the bishop away.

25...b4 26 ♕e3 ♕d5 27 g4 a5 (D)

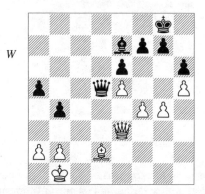

In just five moves, White's position has become seriously unpleasant. Her kingside pawns remain a permanent source of weakness, her king is exposed, and the powerfully centralized black queen is impossible to drive away. Worst of all, White has no active plan, and can only wait to see how Black will strengthen his position.

28 ♗c1 ♕d1

Exploiting the weakness of the g4-pawn to activate his own queen still further, whilst simultaneously driving its opposite number more passive.

29 ♕g3 ♕e2 30 a3

If White does nothing, 30...a4 will follow, with threats of both 31...a3 and 31...b3.

30...♕e4+ 31 ♔a1 ♕c4 32 ♕e3?!

This allows the black bishop in with tempo. 32 ♔b1 is slightly more stubborn, although White's position remains critical.

32...♗c5 33 ♕d2 ♗d4 34 ♔b1 (D)

34...bxa3 35 ♕xa5

This ultimately loses a pawn, but 35 bxa3 was hopeless after 35...♕b3+ 36 ♗b2 ♗xb2 37 ♕xb2 ♕d1+, followed by 38...♕xg4. The resulting queen endgame, a pawn down and with weaknesses on e5 and g4, would be indefensible.

35...♗xb2 36 ♕d8+

Once again, a pawn is lost on the kingside after 36 ♗xb2 ♕d3+ 37 ♔a2 axb2 38 ♔xb2

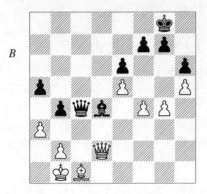

B

♕e2+ and 39...♕xg4. Note how in all these variations, it is White's over-extended kingside pawns which ultimately cost her dearly. This is typical of Black's strategy in this opening.

36...♔h7 37 ♗xb2 ♕e4+ 38 ♔a2 axb2 39 ♕d1 g6!

White's defensive idea was 39...♕xf4 40 ♕d3+ g6 41 hxg6+, when 41...fxg6 allows some counterplay against the exposed black king. Even this position may well be winning for Black, but Nielsen prefers to restrict White's counterplay. Now 40 hxg6+ can be met by 40...♔xg6. The white kingside pawns cannot be defended anyway.

40 ♔xb2 ♕b4+! *(D)*

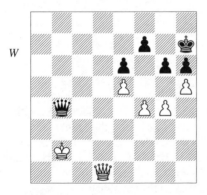

W

This too is a small, but neat, point of good technique. Before taking on f4, Black slightly worsens the position of White's king. Since 41 ♔c2 ♕a4+! would result in the f4-pawn falling with check, White is forced to put her king on the a-file, where it is one file further away from the action than at present. This is typical of the endgame lesson we emphasized many times in *50ECL* – do not hurry; seize every little advantage!

41 ♔a2 ♕xf4

White's position is lost, since in addition to the pawn minus, her king is offside and her pawns are weak.

42 ♕e2 ♔g7 43 ♔b3 ♕d4!

Another patient move. The queen still attacks e5 and g4, tying down the white queen, and also keeping White's king from coming to c3.

44 ♔a2 ♕b4 45 ♔a1

Forced, since 45 ♕d1 or 45 ♕f3 would lose another pawn after 45...♕a5+.

45...♕b3

Zugzwang. Now 46 ♕e4 drops a pawn to 46...gxh5 47 gxh5 ♕d1+, so White cannot avoid the pawn exchange on g6, which allows Black's king into the game.

46 hxg6 ♔xg6 47 ♕e4+ ♔g5

White has no checks, and in the meantime 48...♕d1+ will pick up the g-pawn.

48 ♕h7 ♕c3+ 49 ♔a2 ♕xe5 50 ♕g8+ ♔h4 51 ♕xf7 ♕e3! *(D)*

51...♔xg4 52 ♕g6+ would allow White to exchange a pair of pawns. The resulting ♕+♙ vs ♕ ending is actually winning for Black, but Nielsen sees no need even to allow White that much. With White's king trapped on the first two ranks, Black will sooner or later be able to force a queen exchange or win the g-pawn for nothing.

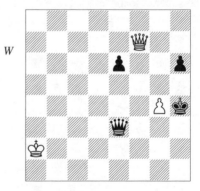

W

52 ♕h5+ ♔g3 53 ♔b2 e5 54 ♔c2 e4 55 ♔d1 ♕g1+ 56 ♔e2 ♕f2+

Avoiding the last trap: 56...♕h2+?! 57 ♔e3 ♕xh5?? (57...♕h3 still wins, but it is much harder work than it should have been) 58 gxh5, when the pawn ending is drawn.

57 ♔d1 e3 0-1

Beautifully precise technique by Nielsen, and a nice example of how White's position can prove over-extended in this opening variation.

Game 33
Evgeny Sveshnikov – Igor Novikov
USSR Rapid Cup, Tallinn 1988
Sicilian Defence, 2 c3

A key feature of the present game is White's queenside pawn-majority. Right out of the opening, White obtains a 3 vs 2 pawn-majority on the queenside, and, following an early queen exchange, he obtains a decisive advantage.

1 e4 c5 2 c3

Thanks partly to the efforts of Sveshnikov himself, this has become just about the most popular way for White to avoid the main lines of the Sicilian. The modest-looking pawn move is a very logical response to 1...c5, in the sense that Black's first move seeks to prevent White from establishing a classical two-pawn centre by 2 d4. White's move 2 c3 simply renews this positional threat.

2...d5

This is one of the two most popular ways to meet 2 c3. Black takes advantage of the fact that the pawn on c3 means that White cannot later attack Black's queen with ♘c3. The alternative is 2...♘f6, which Sveshnikov has always maintained is superior to the text-move, although not all authorities would agree.

3 exd5 ♕xd5 4 d4 *(D)*

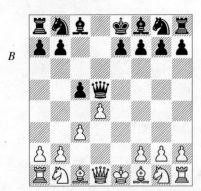

Already at this very early stage, one can discern the basis of White's strategy. If the pawns on d4 and c5 are exchanged for one another, White will be left with a 3 vs 2 majority on the queenside. Such a majority is frequently an advantage in the endgame, primarily because if both sides castle on the kingside, the queenside majority is more distant, and offers the chance

of an outside passed pawn. Consequently, White's strategy in this variation is frequently based on striving for an endgame, relying on his queenside pawn-majority. This plan is seen to perfection in this game.

4...e6

Black can also delay this move and develop his bishop to g4, which is a slightly more active set-up.

5 ♘a3 *(D)*

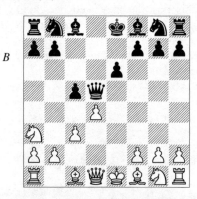

On the face of it, this looks like rather a clumsy way to develop the knight, and a condemnation of White's second move. However, with the black queen on d5, it is a very common idea, since the knight can often jump to b5, threatening an invasion on c7.

5...♘f6?!

As the sequel shows, this is not the most accurate, and allows White to force the endgame he wants. 5...♘c6 was better, preventing White from capturing on d4 with the queen, and preparing to answer 6 ♘b5 with 6...♕d8.

6 ♗e3

Creating the threat of 7 dxc5, and thereby forcing Black to clarify the central pawn position.

6...cxd4 7 ♘b5

See the note to move 5. White has no intention of allowing an IQP structure by 7 cxd4, when his knight really would be badly posted on a3. Instead, the knight attacks Black's queenside with gain of tempo.

7...♘a6!? (D)

Here, the knight is badly placed, and remains stuck on the edge of the board for a long time to come. Sveshnikov suggests as superior 7...♕d8 8 ♕xd4 ♘d5, offering a pawn to avoid the ending that arises in the game. After the further moves 9 ♘xa7 ♗d7 10 ♘b5 ♕a5 11 ♕d3 ♘c6, he claims that Black has compensation for the pawn, although I am not entirely convinced.

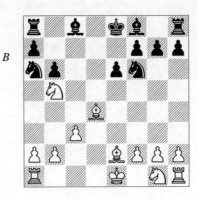

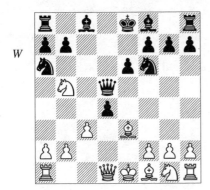

8 ♕xd4!

Continuing his strategy of seeking to reach an ending, where the queenside majority will give him the advantage.

8...♕xd4

Black would prefer not to make this exchange himself, but to force White to do so by 8...♗c5, with the idea of 9 ♕xd5 ♘xd5, when the knight on d5 covers c7. However, as was shown by the game Sveshnikov-Osnos, Rostov-on-Don 1993, 8...♗c5?? is a blunder, because of 9 ♕xc5!. After the further moves 9...♕xc5 (or 9...♘xc5 10 ♘c7+ ♔d8 11 ♘xd5 and Black loses a piece) 10 ♗xc5 ♘xc5 11 ♘c7+ ♔d8 12 ♘xa8, White was a rook up, and although the knight on a8 may not get out alive, White will emerge with at least an exchange extra.

9 ♗xd4 b6 10 ♗e2 (D)

White has reached exactly the type of endgame he wanted. He has his 3 vs 2 majority on the queenside, and the knight on b5 exerts very uncomfortable pressure against Black's position, tying down both the knight on a6 and the rook on a8. White already has a small but

definite advantage, and Black must defend very carefully. Another important point is that such a passive defence in a slightly inferior ending is certainly not the reason most players choose the Sicilian Defence. Thus, White's opening choice is likely to be highly unpleasant for the average Sicilian player from a psychological perspective.

10...♗b7 11 ♗f3 ♗xf3 12 ♘xf3 ♘d5

Preparing to activate his own pawn-majority on the kingside, and to drive the white bishop from its strong central post by means of ...f6 and ...e5.

13 0-0 f6 14 c4 (D)

14...e5 was now a threat.

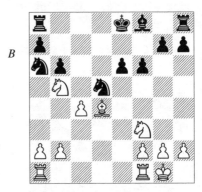

14...♘db4 15 ♗c3 ♘c6 16 ♘fd4 ♘xd4 17 ♗xd4 ♔f7!?

Sveshnikov recommends 17...♗c5 18 ♗xc5 bxc5, although it is not very pleasant for Black to have to accept broken queenside pawns. Sveshnikov then gives 19 ♖fd1 ♔e7 20 ♖d6 as slightly better for White, whilst 19 f4 is also interesting, as the e6-pawn remains backward and potentially vulnerable.

18 ♖fd1 ♗e7 19 ♗e3 ♖hd8 20 ♖xd8 ♗xd8 21 ♖d1 ♔e7 22 a3 (D)

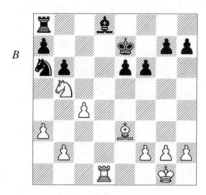

One thing which is very striking about this game is how naturally and easily White's position can be played. He has not had to find a single difficult move so far, yet he has a clear advantage, and Black is really struggling to untangle. One of the main reasons for this is that Sveshnikov has had a very clear plan right from the first few moves, and moreover, that he had analysed and played similar positions many times before. Such experience and erudition is an enormous help in playing any position.

22...♘c7 23 ♘d4!

Putting his finger on the tender spot in Black's position. Although Black has finally shifted the knight from b5, the c6-square is extremely hard to defend, and from there, the knight still attacks the a7-pawn, thus tying down Black's rook.

23...♚e8 24 ♘c6 ♗e7 25 b4 ♘a6 26 ♚f1 ♘b8 *(D)*

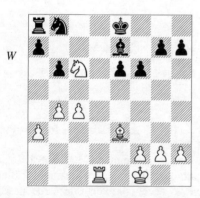

The white knight is finally evicted, but at the cost of Black's two remaining pieces standing back on their original squares. Meanwhile,

White's pieces are both active, and his pawn-majority on the queenside is already rolling.

27 ♘xe7 ♚xe7 28 c5 b5 *(D)*

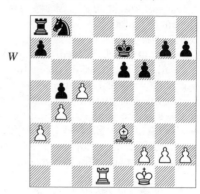

The majority has already yielded a protected passed pawn.

29 ♖d6 ♘d7 30 ♖a6 ♘b8 31 ♖d6 ♘d7 32 ♖c6 *(D)*

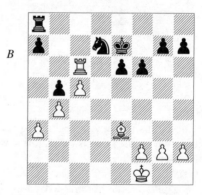

32...a5

Now White wins quickly, but Black's position was extremely difficult, as he cannot prevent White's rook from invading on c7. The only way to avoid immediate collapse is 32...a6, with the idea of meeting 33 ♖c7 with 33...♚d8 34 ♖b7 ♖c8. However, after 32...a6, the black rook is tied to the a6-pawn, and White can simply strengthen his position by 33 ♚e2, or perhaps first 33 f4. Black is totally passive and must inevitably lose in the long run.

33 ♖c7 ♚d8 34 ♖b7

Now there is no defence to 35 c6, since 34...♖c8 is answered by 35 bxa5.

34...axb4 35 c6 ♘e5 36 ♖xg7 1-0

5 Other Aspects of Strategy

This chapter looks at a number of different aspects of strategy. These include battles between bishops and knights, play on squares of a certain colour, the use of the principle of two weaknesses, etc. Some of these topics were dealt with in *50ECL*, but in this volume, we concentrate on different aspects of the subject.

The first two games look at the perennial problem of the bishop-pair. In Game 34, Black brilliantly tames the enemy bishops, but in Game 35, White's subtle strategy sees the bishops triumph completely. Game 36 is a beautiful example of the principle of two weaknesses, as White switches the attack from one flank to the other and back again, until the defences are overwhelmed.

In the opening stage of Game 37, Black manages to shut several enemy pieces out of the game, and the struggle revolves around White's attempts to free these pieces, and Black's determination to keep them bottled up. Black's strategy succeeds, thanks to a fine positional exchange sacrifice. Game 38 illustrates a positional pawn sacrifice to keep the initiative, whilst in Game 39, Black suffers from an offside knight, which never manages to return to the game in time.

Games 40-42 involve a strategy of concentrating play on squares of a certain colour, whilst Game 43 illustrates several strategic themes, including play on both flanks and excellent use of the king as a strong piece in the middlegame.

Game 34
Bobby Fischer – Wolfgang Uhlmann
Buenos Aires 1960
French Defence, Winawer Variation

This game sees a classic struggle between bishops and knights. Black concedes the bishop-pair in the opening, and the middlegame turns into a battle between White's attempts to open the position, and Black's to keep it closed. At the critical moment, Fischer errs, and allows a brilliant positional pawn sacrifice, after which Black takes over the initiative.

1 e4 e6 2 d4 d5 3 ♘c3 ♗b4

This move characterizes the Winawer Variation. Black pins the enemy knight, thereby exerting pressure on the e4-pawn. He hopes to induce White to close the centre by 4 e5, after which Black's subsequent strategy will be to exchange bishop for knight on c3, doubling White's pawns. The resulting middlegame battle will revolve around White's two bishops, and his attempts to open the position so as to use them to maximum effect. Black, meanwhile, tries to keep the position closed, and use his knights effectively.

Fischer himself famously declared that he did not believe the Winawer to be sound, "because it is anti-positional and weakens the kingside". By anti-positional, he meant that Black establishes his central pawns on light squares, and then exchanges off his dark-squared bishop. This leaves his dark squares very weak, and it is true that many games have been lost by Black in such positions as a result of the white queen's bishop slicing through Black's position, often along the a3-f8 diagonal.

4 e5 c5 5 a3 ♗xc3+ 6 bxc3 ♘e7 *(D)*

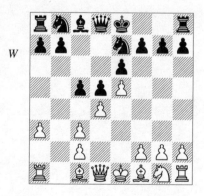

7 ♘f3

The sharpest and most dangerous try for White is 7 ♕g4, immediately attacking the g7-square, which has been weakened by the absence of Black's king's bishop. Given Fischer's comment about the Winawer weakening Black's kingside, one might have expected him to choose this line, but he prefers a more positional approach. At the time this game was played, Black usually met 7 ♕g4 with 7...♕c7, sacrificing his entire kingside after 8 ♕xg7 ♖g8 9 ♕xh7 cxd4 10 ♘e2 ♘bc6. The resulting very sharp position remained controversial for many years, but with Black generally scoring well in practice. However, over the past decade or so, possibly under the influence of computer-assisted analysis, most grandmasters have come to the view that this line should favour White, and nowadays Black usually meets 7 ♕g4 with 7...0-0. In this line, though, he has to be prepared to face a dangerous onslaught on his king, and Black seems to be under pressure in these lines, judging by the latest theoretical developments. All in all, the Winawer generally is out of fashion at top GM level, and Black usually prefers the less ambitious lines with 3...♘f6.

7...♗d7 8 a4

Black's last move, an Uhlmann speciality, threatened 8...♗a4, when the bishop would tie down White to the defence of c2, and also prevent him from playing a4 and ♗a3. The latter is a very common idea for White in these positions, trying to activate his dark-squared bishop.

8...♕a5 9 ♕d2 ♘bc6 10 ♗d3 c4 *(D)*

This is a crucial decision, very typical of such Winawer structures. Black commits himself wholly to the strategy of closing the position, to thwart the activity of the enemy bishops. However, in doing so, he puts yet another pawn on a

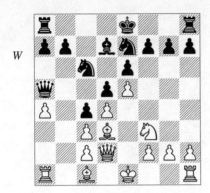

light square, thus weakening his dark squares even further. In particular, White's bishop will now have a splendid diagonal from a3 to f8.

11 ♗e2 f6 12 ♗a3 ♘g6 13 0-0-0!

Offering a pawn, so as to open the centre for his bishops.

13...0-0-0 (D)

Black declines the offer, and continues with his strategy of keeping the position closed. Instead, after 13...fxe5?! 14 ♘xe5 ♘gxe5 15 dxe5 ♘xe5? 16 ♕g5 ♘g6?! 17 ♗h5, White creates decisive threats.

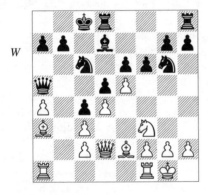

14 ♗d6 ♘ce7

Another thematic Winawer manoeuvre. The knight heads towards f5, hoping to drive the strong bishop away from d6, and at the same time Black's d7-bishop takes aim at the a4-pawn. In many Winawer positions, Black grabs this pawn, and hopes that his queenside pawns will eventually decide the ending, if he can repulse the threats on the other side of the board.

15 ♘h4!

The start of a deep plan. Fischer sees that his bishop will be chased away from d6, so he prepares an even more effective diagonal for it – that from h2 to b8.

15...♖de8 (D)

Black could of course help himself to the a4-pawn immediately by 15...♗xa4, but this runs the risk that the bishop may well be shut out of play for a long time. Because of the pin on the a-file, it will be hard for Black to avoid playing ...b5 to support the bishop, but then the bishop will be cut off from the rest of its forces. For this reason, Black usually hesitates to take the a4-pawn too soon in such positions, preferring to await a better moment later in the game.

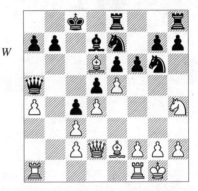

16 ♘xg6! hxg6 17 exf6 gxf6 18 h3!

This is the culmination of Fischer's plan, begun at move 15. Now his bishop has the retreat ♗h2, remaining on a very strong diagonal, pointing towards the black king.

18...♘f5 19 ♗h2 g5 (D)

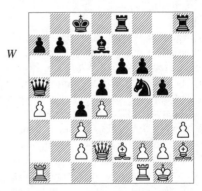

20 f4?

Thus far, Fischer has played very well, and obtained rather the better position, but this move spoils things, thanks to Black's superb 21st move. He should play more slowly with a move such as 20 ♖fe1, when his excellent dark-squared bishop and the exposed black king would give him some advantage.

20...♞d6!

Immediately putting his finger on the major drawback of White's last move, namely the weakening of the e4-square. Now 21 fxg5 would be met by 21...♞e4, followed by capturing on c3.

21 ♗f3 (D)

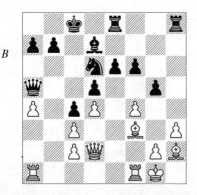

Now, however, the e4-square is covered, and White is threatening to take on g5. Capturing on f4 is horrible, and it appears that White is going to get his way, and succeed in opening the position further for his bishops. In fact, White's whole opening strategy seems on the verge of being crowned with success, as his unopposed dark-squared bishop looks set to wreak havoc in the black camp. However, Uhlmann finds a splendid response, which turns the position on its head.

21...g4!!

The refutation of White's 20th move, and entirely thematic for the Winawer. Black must fight against the activity of White's bishops, especially the dark-squared one, and Uhlmann's pawn sacrifice does exactly that. For his pawn, Black will nail the f4-pawn to the spot, thereby in turn burying the bishop on h2, where it is hopelessly blocked by its own pawn. The fact that White also gets a protected passed pawn on g5 is of no consequence, since the pawn is not supported by its pieces, and therefore can go nowhere.

22 hxg4

22 ♗xg4? ♞e4 23 ♕e3 f5 24 ♗f3 ♕xc3 is much better for Black.

22...f5!

The key follow-up, fixing the f4-pawn in place.

23 g5 ♖e7 (D)

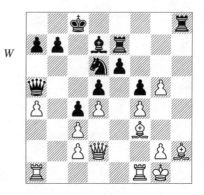

Looking at this position, we can see how the pawn sacrifice has transformed the situation. Both of White's bishops are crippled, and he has no active play at all. The backward pawn on e6 and the hole on e5 are of no use to White, since Black can easily shield them by playing his knight into e4. Meanwhile, White's queenside pawns remain very weak, and Black also has the open h-file, along which his rooks threaten to penetrate towards the enemy king. White's position is entirely passive, and he can only wait to see how Black will strengthen his position. Despite all this, however, the blocked nature of the position means that White still has good chances to hold the position, providing he is prepared to defend passively, but it is clear that Black's strategy of taming the white bishop-pair has triumphed.

24 ♗g3 ♗e8 25 ♕e3 ♞e4 26 ♗xe4 dxe4 (D)

Not, of course, 26...fxe4??, which would be an appalling positional blunder, allowing White to free his entombed bishop by 27 f5. White's hopes are now connected with the blocked nature of the position and the opposite-coloured bishops, which may enable him to draw.

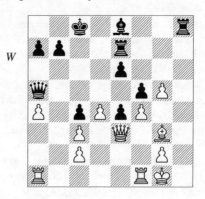

27 ♔f2

Here and on the next move, White could consider returning the pawn by 27 d5, so as to free some dark squares for his pieces. Fischer, who was always a great materialist, prefers to cling on to his booty, but does not obtain any counterplay.

27...♖eh7 28 ♖fb1 ♕d5

Putting an end to any d5 ideas.

29 ♕e1?

A serious mistake, after which White is struggling to hold. If he maintains the blockade, it is not easy for Black to make progress. A move such as 29 a5, getting the pawn off a vulnerable square, looks sensible.

29...♖h1! *(D)*

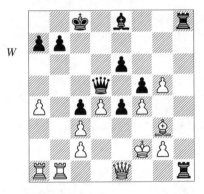

W

30 ♕xh1?

Compounding his previous error, after which he is lost. He had to return the queen to e3, although after 30 ♕e3 ♖xb1 31 ♖xb1 ♗xa4 32 ♖a1 b5, Black is clearly better.

30...e3+!

The point of Black's play. Now the long light-square diagonal is opened decisively.

31 ♔g1

31 ♔xe3 ♕e4+ 32 ♔f2 (32 ♔d2? loses to 32...♖xh1 33 ♖xh1 ♕xg2+) 32...♖xh1 33 ♖xh1 ♗c6! 34 ♖h2 ♕xc2+ 35 ♔g1 ♕xc3 is easily winning for Black.

31...♖xh1+ 32 ♔xh1 e2! 33 ♖b5? *(D)*

Fischer evidently decided that passive defence was hopeless, and so tried something

desperate. However, passive defence by 33 a5 would still force Black to demonstrate precisely how he will break down White's resistance.

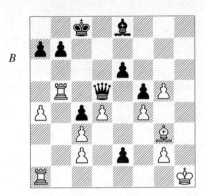

B

33...♗xb5 34 axb5 ♕xb5!

Trading the passed e-pawn for a passed pawn on the a-file. The latter is far more dangerous, because the bad bishop on g3 cannot assist his rook in combating the a-pawn.

35 ♖e1 a5 36 ♖xe2 a4! 37 ♖xe6 a3 38 g6 ♕d7! *(D)*

Avoiding the final trick: after 38...a2?? 39 g7 a1♕+ 40 ♔h2 White actually wins, because the g-pawn cannot be stopped. Never relax, even in the most overwhelming position!

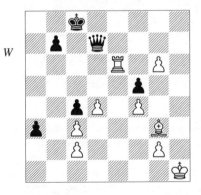

W

39 ♖e5 b6 40 ♗h4 a2 41 ♖e1 ♕g7 42 ♖a1 ♕xg6 0-1

After 43 ♖xa2 ♕h5 44 g3 ♕f3+ 45 ♔h2 ♕xc3 46 ♗f6 b5 the queenside pawns decide.

Game 35
Iosif Dorfman – David Bronstein
USSR Ch, Erevan 1975
Old Indian Defence

This game is a splendid example of how to exploit the bishop-pair. As discussed earlier, one important principle is to make maximum use of the unopposed bishop, which is what Dorfman does here. Black has no light-squared bishop, so the basis of White's middlegame plan is to exert pressure on the light squares in Black's position.

1 c4 e5 2 ᐃc3 d6

A slightly unusual move, which has been played quite extensively by Smyslov.

3 ᐃf3

White can also play 3 g3 and 3 d4.

3...ᐃg4

This early development of the bishop is one of the points of Black's second move.

4 d4 *(D)*

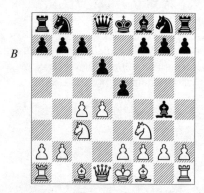

4...ᐃd7

Bronstein supports the centre, reaching a kind of Old Indian Defence, but with his queen's bishop outside the pawn-chain. 4...ᐃxf3 is an important alternative, when White must decide how to recapture. Both options have their merits, with 5 gxf3 being the more aggressive. In general, the exchange on f3 looks a little suspect positionally, since Black has already committed his centre pawns to the dark squares d6 and e5. This means that his central light squares are not well protected by his pawns, and so exchanging off his light-squared bishop is likely to prove rather risky. The early exchange on f3 fits in much better with a c6-d5-e6 pawn-formation, when his pawns would cover the light squares and blunt the effects of White's bishop on g2.

5 g3 ᐃgf6

Here, too, Black could capture on f3, but the same considerations as in the previous note apply.

6 ᐃg2 ᐃe7 7 0-0 0-0 8 h3

White forces his opponent's bishop to declare its intentions.

8...ᐃxf3

The retreat 8...ᐃh5 is also possible, but then 9 ᐃh4, threatening to come to f5, is a little better for White.

9 ᐃxf3 exd4 10 ᐃxd4 c6 11 b3 ᐃe8 12 ᐃb2 ᐃc5 *(D)*

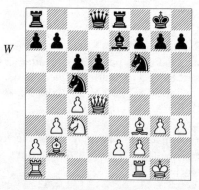

Summing up the results of the opening, we can see that White has emerged with more space and the bishop-pair. Black's position is solid, and his only weakness is the pawn on d6, which is not so easy to attack. Black's main problem is that he stands rather passively, and it is difficult to find an active plan, so he will need to await developments, and see how White sets about strengthening his position.

13 ᐃab1!

As Nimzowitsch never tired of pointing out, one of the most important positional principles in chess is prophylaxis. At every point in the game, a player should ask himself what his opponent wants, and whether there is an effective way of preventing it. Many players make the mistake of thinking that prophylaxis is a purely negative, defensive thing, but this is not the case. Good prophylaxis involves not only preventing the opponent's ideas, but doing so in a way that contributes positively to one's own plans.

In this position, the obvious, 'natural' continuation for White is 13 ♖fd1, perhaps followed by 14 ♗g2. However, Dorfman asks himself what Black wishes to do in reply, and he sees that Black threatens 13...a5 and ...a4; for example, 13 ♖fd1 a5 14 ♗g2 a4 15 b4 a3!. Dorfman therefore anticipates this by removing his bishop from b2. In so doing, he puts his rook on the b-file, and as we shall see later on, this is more than just a defensive measure.

13...a5 14 ♗a1 ♗f8

Now 14...a4 would be ineffective because of 15 b4, when Black no longer has 15...a3.

15 ♗g2

Having neutralized Black's immediate threat, White completes his development.

15...♕c7 16 ♖fd1 ♖e6 (*D*)

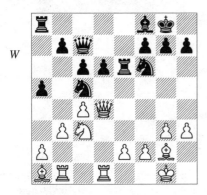

17 e3!

An important decision, and an indication of White's longer-term strategic plan. As noted above, Black's position is very solid, with his d6-pawn, his only weakness, very well defended. It is clear that White cannot entertain any hope of bringing serious pressure to bear on this pawn in the near future, so another plan is needed. Since he has the two bishops, it is logical that his plan should be connected with making the most of this asset. As we have noted elsewhere, one of the main strategic principles

in exploiting the bishop-pair is to make maximum use of the unopposed bishop.

In this instance, that means the light-squared bishop, and so White's plan is connected with developing play on the light squares. For this reason, he plays the pawn to e3, rather than e4, since he wishes to keep open the long light-square diagonal. His further plan is to weaken Black's position on the light squares. There are two possible ways to do this. The first is by a queenside pawn advance with b4-b5, attacking the c6-pawn. In this case, the white rook on b1 will be very well placed, and so now we see that White's prophylactic measure at move 13 also contained a positive idea. However, the immediate queenside pawn advance is not possible, since 17 a3 is met by 17...a4 18 b4 ♞b3. The second, and more subtle, way to weaken Black's light squares is to attack the pawn on a5, in the hope of inducing the move ...b6, which will weaken c6 and the whole long diagonal. This is the plan initiated by White's 17th move.

17...♖d8 18 ♞e2

The knight heads towards f4, whilst unmasking the bishop on the long diagonal and making way for the queen to attack the a5-pawn from d2.

18...♖ee8 19 ♕d2 ♞fe4 20 ♕c2 ♕e7 (*D*)

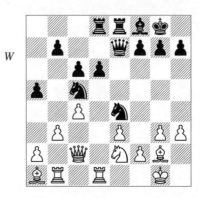

For the time being, it seems that Black is holding his own well, with his knights actively placed in the centre. In order to make progress, White needs to drive them back, but if he can do so, the long-term prospects are with him, thanks to his bishop-pair and extra space. Dorfman's play is very logical and systematic.

21 ♞f4 f5 22 ♞d3

This challenges the knight on c5, which Bronstein prefers to retain, rather than exchange off.

22...♘d7 23 ♔h2 (D)

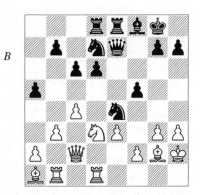

Now White begins a systematic plan to expel the other knight from e4, by the move f3. The text-move prepares this by defending g3, and on the next move, the rook defends e3, so that this pawn will not be hanging after the enemy knight moves away. White can afford such slow and methodical manoeuvres, because Black has no active counterplay.

23...♕f7 24 ♖e1 ♗e7 25 f3 ♘ec5 26 ♘f2

Previously, White was happy to exchange a pair of knights, but now Black's position feels rather cramped and uncoordinated, and so White avoids an exchange that might free Black's position somewhat. This is a good example of the need to be flexible, and adapt to changing circumstances during a game.

26...♕g6 27 ♕d2 ♖a8 28 ♖bd1 ♘f6 (D)

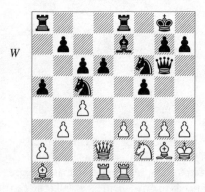

It is clear that White has made a fair amount of progress over the past 8-10 moves, but it is still surprising how quickly Black's position collapses.

29 ♗c3!

This far-from-obvious move forms part of White's strategy of weakening his opponent on the light squares.

29...b6?

A tactical oversight, after which his position collapses like a house of cards. He had to play 29...a4, although after 30 b4 ♘cd7 31 f4, White is ready to hit the light squares further with 32 b5.

30 ♗xf6! ♕xf6 31 f4

Suddenly, it transpires that Black cannot defend the c6-pawn, since after 31...♖ac8 White has the tactic 32 ♗xc6 ♖xc6 33 ♕d5+, winning the exchange. Of course, this immediate disaster is the result of Black's tactical oversight on move 29, but nonetheless, it is entirely logical, being a consequence of White's strategy of weakening the enemy light squares and maximizing the strength of his unopposed light-squared bishop.

31...d5 32 cxd5 ♖ad8 33 ♕c2

White has won a pawn for nothing.

33...cxd5 34 ♖xd5 ♖xd5 35 ♗xd5+ ♔h8 36 e4 (D)

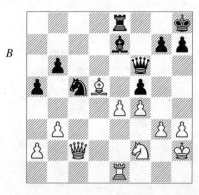

Ridding himself of his backward e-pawn, and further exposing Black's light squares.

36...fxe4 37 ♗xe4 ♗d6

Taking on e4 would submit to a fatal pin on the e-file after 37...♘xe4 38 ♕xe4.

38 ♖d1 g5?!

An act of desperation which hastens the end, but Black's position is lost anyway.

39 ♘g4 ♕g7 40 ♗g2 ♖d8 41 fxg5 ♕c7

On 41...♕xg5, 42 ♕c3+ wins.

42 ♕c3+ ♕g7 43 ♘e5 1-0

Game 36
Shakhriyar Mamedyarov – Mikhail Brodsky
Russian Clubs Ch, Dagomys 2006
Queen's Pawn Opening

The principle of two weaknesses is one of the most important in chess, and here Mamedyarov gives a splendid demonstration of its effectiveness. After an initial build-up on the queenside, he switches the attack to the other flank, and eventually overwhelms Black's defences with a series of switches between kingside and queenside.

1 d4 ♘f6 2 ♘f3 e6 3 e3

This move indicates already that White is seeking a quiet opening, and is not concerned with fighting for a substantial opening advantage per se. Instead, he just plans to develop his pieces in sound fashion and await developments in the middlegame. In the first instance, White plans ♗d3 and 0-0. The main drawback to his set-up is that he locks in his queen's bishop behind the pawn-chain. There are two broad ways to follow up for White. The first is to play c3 and ♘bd2, aiming to advance e4 in the centre, which will liberate the queen's bishop along the c1-h6 diagonal. This plan is the so-called Colle System, developed and widely practised by the Belgian master Edgar Colle, and is a particular favourite with many club players.

The alternative plan is the Zukertort formation, where White leaves the c-pawn at home for a time, and develops the queen's bishop on the long diagonal, by b3 and ♗b2. Although the bishop's diagonal is currently blocked by the pawn on d4, this pawn is frequently exchanged (e.g. when Black plays ...c5, and White exchanges by dxc5). Practice has shown that the two bishops on d3 and b2, often referred to as 'Horwitz bishops', can become very dangerous in the middlegame, as they target the black king.

All in all, White's set-up is relatively quiet, but should not be under-estimated.

3...b6 4 ♗d3 ♗b7 5 0-0 g6!? *(D)*

This is a somewhat odd-looking move, by traditional standards. With his pawn already on e6, one would expect Black to develop the king's bishop on e7. Instead, the combination of ...e6 and ...g6 leaves the dark squares around Black's king (notably the f6-square) weakened, and for this reason, such a combination of pawn moves is not generally recommended.

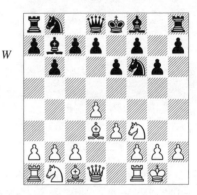

However, the player with Black in this game is a grandmaster, and of course understands the risks of combining ...e6 and ...g6. The reason for his choice is reflected in the previous note. White's Horwitz bishops on d3 and b2 can often exert uncomfortable pressure on Black's kingside in the subsequent middlegame, as the central pawns become exchanged and lines open. By fianchettoing his king's bishop, Black hopes to neutralize the Horwitz bishops. Thus, the d3-bishop has its diagonal firmly blocked by Black's pawn on g6, whilst the other white bishop on b2 will be neutralized by Black's opposite number on g7. Although the dark squares, such as f6, have been weakened, Black reasons that it will be relatively hard for White to exploit these, given that he has already shut in his own dark-squared bishop by the move 3 e3.

6 c4!

One of the biggest differences between lesser players and grandmasters is the latter's flexibility. Many club players have a tendency to form a plan of play, and then blindly stick to it, almost regardless of what their opponent does. However, good chess is all about responding to one's opponent's moves and ideas, and the ability to adjust one's plans appropriately is essential.

In this case, as explained in the previous note, Black's 5th move is designed to neutralize the standard Colle and Zukertort set-ups, by blunting the effects of White's bishops on the kingside. Mamedyarov therefore switches plans, and starts a plan of playing on the queenside, taking advantage of the fact that Black's king's bishop is about to leave the a3-f8 diagonal.

6...♗g7 7 ♘c3 d5 8 cxd5 exd5 9 b4! *(D)*

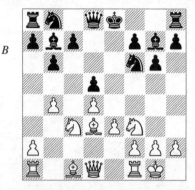

This is the point of White's idea. With the black king's bishop on g7, this move becomes tactically possible, and in conjunction with the exchange of pawns on d5, it is also positionally desirable. White anticipates that Black will want to play a subsequent ...c5, so as to rid himself of a potential backward pawn on c7, and to put more pressure on White's centre. Mamedyarov fights against this plan by making it difficult for Black to get in the move ...c5, which would now lose a pawn. Furthermore, even if Black were able to regain the pawn, he would be left with an isolated pawn on d5, which would be likely to prove weak.

9...0-0 10 a4 ♖e8 11 ♕b3 a6 12 ♗a3 ♘bd7 13 b5

This move fixes the c7-pawn as a backward pawn on the half-open c-file, and ensures that White will always be able to answer a subsequent ...c5 by taking *en passant*, leaving Black with a weak pawn on d5.

13...axb5 14 axb5

Now White plans to bring a rook to the c-file, to exert pressure on the backward c7-pawn.

14...♗f8?!

A very questionable decision, exchanging off the bishop that defends the weakened dark squares around Black's king. Presumably, Brodsky's reasoning was that his bishop is not very active on g7, since its long diagonal is securely blocked by White's d4-pawn. The normal way to activate the bishop would be to hit the d4-pawn by advancing ...c5, but as we have already seen, White is ready to answer that move by bxc6 (*en passant*). Brodsky therefore decides that his bishop on g7 is never likely to develop much activity, and so he seeks to exchange it off. However, this runs the risk that the kingside dark-square weaknesses will later come back to haunt Black. Although this may not seem likely at present, we shall see that this is precisely what happens later in the game.

Instead of the text-move, Black should seek to drum up some counterplay on the kingside, so as to distract White from exploiting his advantage on the queenside. Counterplay is almost always better than passive defence, so Black should prefer 14...♘e4, with the tactical point that White cannot capture on d5, because of 15 ♘xd5? ♘dc5!, when Black solves all of his problems.

15 ♖fc1 ♗xa3 16 ♖xa3 ♖xa3 17 ♕xa3 ♕a8 18 ♕b4 ♖c8 19 h3 ♕a7 *(D)*

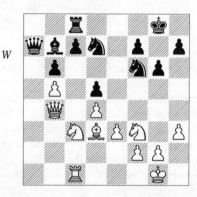

Black has erected some reasonably solid barriers on the queenside, and although the pawns on d5 and c7 remain weak, it is very difficult to see how White can directly increase the pressure on them. This is a very typical situation in chess. One player creates a target, attacks it, and his opponent defends it. Once there is no effective way to increase the pressure on that target, the first player has to find another way to increase his advantage. Just as in warfare, the classic method is to open up a second front.

20 g4!

An absolutely standard method of play in such positions. Almost all of Black's pieces are on the queenside, where they are tied down defending his weaknesses there. Mamedyarov therefore starts action on the kingside, so as to exploit the superior mobility of his pieces. With his cramped and passive position, Black will find it extremely difficult to funnel pieces across to the kingside for defensive purposes. In addition, the exchange of bishops on move 15 has weakened the dark squares around Black's king, and so White already has targets on that wing.

20...♖a8?! 21 ♘e2 ♕b8

Black's last move was presumably aimed at seeking a queen exchange by 21...♕a3, but now that would just lose the pawn on c7. Black is therefore forced to remain passive, and the only effect of his 20th move has been to shut the rook off from the kingside, where it is likely to be needed for the defence.

22 g5

See the note to move 20. Now White has already taken control of the weak dark squares f6 and h6, and Black is missing his dark-squared bishop.

22...♘e8 23 ♘f4 ♕d8 24 h4 ♘f8 25 ♗f1

A move with several points. Firstly, it prepares to bring the bishop to a more active post on either h3 or g2 (from the latter square, it bears down on the weak d5-pawn). Secondly, it frees the d3-square, which White may wish to use to transfer his knight from f4 to d3 and then, b4 or e5. Thirdly, it shields the white king against checks on the back rank, which may come in handy in some variations, if his rook ever leaves the back rank.

25...♖a5 26 ♘e5 h6?!

One of Steinitz's fundamental defensive principles was that the defender should try not to make pawn moves in the area of the board where he stands worse. Of course, like all such rules of thumb, there are many exceptions, but nonetheless, this is a good rule to bear in mind. In this case, Black was clearly tired of conducting a purely passive defence, with no counterplay, where White can strengthen his position in his own time. He therefore tries to stir things up, so as to complicate White's task, but this is achieved only at the high cost of weakening his kingside.

27 gxh6 ♘h7

Unfortunately, the obvious 27...♕xh4 loses at once to the nice tactical blow 28 ♕xf8+!, followed by 29 ♘(either)xg6+. Indeed, it may

even be that this is the tactical point that Black overlooked when playing his previous move.

28 h5 g5 29 ♘fg6! ♘d6

Accepting the Trojan horse loses quickly, after 29...fxg6 30 hxg6 ♘hf6 31 h7+ ♔g7 32 h8♕+!, etc.

30 ♕c3! *(D)*

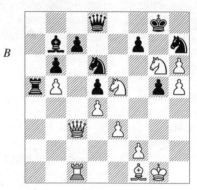

Another instructive switch of targets. Having first switched his focus from the weak queenside pawns to the kingside, Mamedyarov now reminds Black that the c7 weakness is still there. Once again, taking on g6 loses, this time simply to 31 ♕xc7. Black is therefore forced to return his knight to the passive position on e8, from which it has just come.

30...♘e8 31 ♘c6 ♗xc6 32 ♕xc6 ♘hf6

The knight on g6 continues its charmed life. This time, 32...fxg6 loses most simply to 33 ♕e6+! ♔h8 (33...♔f8 34 hxg6 ♕f6 35 g7+ wins for White) 34 ♕f7.

33 ♘e5 ♕e7 34 ♗d3 ♖a3 35 h7+

The simplest way to win. White exchanges the doubled h-pawn for the key d5-pawn. Black cannot decline, as 35...♔g7 36 h6+ is hopeless.

35...♘xh7 36 ♗xh7+ ♔xh7 37 ♕xd5

Thus, White's constantly switching attack has finally annexed the artificially isolated d5-pawn, which has been in White's gunsights ever since move 13.

37...♘d6 38 ♘c4 ♘xc4 39 ♖xc4 ♔h8 40 ♕f5 ♖a8 41 ♖c6

The attack returns to the black king.

41...♔g7 42 h6+ ♔h8 43 ♖xc7 1-0

Appropriately enough, one final switch from kingside to queenside removes the long-time target on c7 and ends the game. Black resigned in view of 43...♕xc7 44 ♕f6+, mating – yet another switch back to the kingside!

Game 37
Terry Bennett – Raymond Keene
English Counties Ch 1970
Modern Defence, Classical Variation

The theme of this game is excluding enemy pieces from the action. We saw an example of this strategy in Miles-Smyslov, examined in *50ECL* (Game 13). Here, White gets several queenside pieces stuck out of play. Black sacrifices an exchange in order to maintain the blockade over the key central square, and by the time White liberates his queenside material, his king has fallen under a decisive attack.

1 e4 g6 2 d4 ♗g7 3 ♘c3 d6 4 ♘f3 a6

Black continues his provocative strategy of playing around the edges of the board, rather than occupying the centre. White could hold back the intended ...b5 advance by playing 5 a4, but he prefers to continue developing.

5 h3

This move prepares to develop the bishop to e3, without allowing it to be molested by a later ...♘g4 from Black.

5...b5 6 ♗e3 ♗b7 7 ♗d3 ♘d7 8 a4

White lures Black's pawns forward, hoping to be able to show that they are weak.

8...b4 9 ♘e2 ♘gf6 10 ♘g3 0-0 11 0-0 c5 12 c3 *(D)*

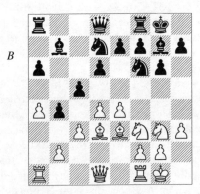

12...c4!?

The start of an interesting plan. Black takes the pressure off the white pawn-centre, but in return, he hopes to bury White's rook and bishop on the queenside.

13 ♗b1

The alternative was 13 ♗xc4, but this leaves Black with a comfortable game after 13...♘xe4. He would have succeeded in exchanging his flank pawn on the c-file for White's valuable e-pawn, thus securing a slight preponderance in the centre. Such delayed central actions are the dream of every Modern Defence or hypermodern player. Instead, Bennett takes up the challenge, and allows Black to shut in the white queenside pieces. Everything will now depend on whether Black is able to maintain the c4-b3 pawn duo. If he can, White will be to all practical purposes a rook and piece down. On the other hand, Black has relaxed the pressure on White's centre, and if White can undermine the c4- and b3-pawns, he will emerge with the better game.

13...b3 14 ♘d2 ♕c7 15 ♕e2 ♖ac8

White consistently attacks the vital c4-pawn, and Black defends it.

16 f4 e5 *(D)*

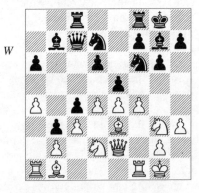

This is another vital move for Black. Even with the c4-b3 pawn duo in place, White can still liberate his queenside pieces if he can play e5 and then f5. In that case, his bishop on b1 would be taking part in the attack on Black's king. In order to keep the b1-bishop, and hence the a1-rook, bottled up, Black needs to keep the white e4-pawn in place.

17 ♕f2?

Thus far, White has played logically enough, but this move is a cardinal mistake, after which Black obtains the advantage. White absolutely had to play 17 a5!, ensuring that his rook has access to a4, from where it can add to the pressure on c4. In addition, Black would be prevented from bringing his bishop to a6, defending the c4-pawn. In that case, the position would have been unclear. Now Black himself seizes the chance to play his pawn to a5, after which the white rook and bishop on a1 and b1 are condemned to a lengthy spell of imprisonment.

17...a5! 18 ♘f3

Now that he no has way to increase the pressure against c4, White's only other method of relieving the siege is to eliminate Black's e5-pawn, and play e5 himself, thereby allowing his b1-bishop out. Hence, White increases the pressure on e5, and prepares exchanges in the centre. However, Black has anticipated White's plan, and has prepared a surprise in reply.

18...♖fe8!

This appears to lose material, but is part of Black's idea. He could instead have sought to maintain control of e5 by 18...♘e8, but the text-move is more dynamic.

19 dxe5 dxe5 20 fxe5 ♘xe5 21 ♘xe5 ♖xe5!

This exchange sacrifice is the key to Black's idea. Actually, it is now forced, since 21...♕xe5? would lose a piece after 22 ♗d4.

22 ♗f4 (D)

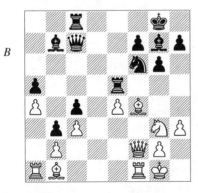

22...♖ce8! 23 ♗xe5 ♖xe5

Black has given up a whole exchange, and does not even have one pawn for it. However, he has maintained the blockade on White's e4-pawn, and so long as that is the case, White is playing without his bishop on b1 and his rook

on a1. Black is effectively two pieces up. Throw in the weakness of White's dark squares, and it is clear that White is lost, unless he can shake off the blockade.

Such positional exchange sacrifices, based on the concept of blockade, derive their themes from Nimzowitsch, and were a favourite device of Tigran Petrosian. As usual with any sacrifice, what matters is not the actual material-count on the board, but the number of pieces which are active in the area of the board where the play is taking place.

24 ♖d1 h5 25 ♕d2 ♖e8 26 ♕d6 ♕c8 27 e5

White has finally lifted the blockade on e5, but his e-pawn is soon lost and Black's pieces jump out on the weak dark squares in White's camp. By the time the reinforcements on a1 and b1 get into the fight, it is already too late.

27...♘h7 28 ♗e4 ♗xe5 (D)

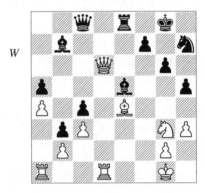

29 ♗xb7?

The only hope of defending successfully was 29 ♕b6, although even then, after 29...♗xe4 30 ♘xe4 ♗c7 31 ♕d4?! (31 ♘f6+ is better) 31...♕e6, Black has tremendous compensation for his exchange – a pawn, complete domination of the dark squares, and an exposed white king.

29...♕xb7 30 ♕d5 ♕b6+

Black could have won back a whole piece, with a winning endgame, by 30...♕xd5 31 ♖xd5 ♗xg3, but prefers to win the material in an even more effective way.

31 ♔h2 ♕e3 32 ♕f3 ♕xf3 33 gxf3 h4 34 ♔g2 ♗xg3 35 ♖ab1

Rather a strange move, but the position is lost. White cannot defend his second rank against the enemy rook's invasion, because 35 ♖d2 is refuted by 35...♗f4!.

35...♖e2+ 0-1

Game 38
Vladimir Kramnik – Rafael Vaganian
Horgen 1995
Queen's Indian Defence, Petrosian System

Positional sacrifices to seize the initiative are a common theme in grandmaster play. Here, we see Kramnik sacrifice a pawn for purely positional considerations. The resulting initiative enables him to prevent his opponent from mobilizing his forces adequately, and White's initiative grows decisively.

1 ♘f3 ♘f6 2 d4 e6 3 c4 b6 4 a3 *(D)*

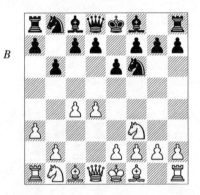

This strange-looking move is generally attributed to Petrosian, who initially popularized it, but it was played over 70 years ago by Sultan Khan, the remarkable Indian talent. Its modern popularity is primarily due to Kasparov, who used it extensively in his youth, and did much to mould it into one of the most aggressive replies to the Queen's Indian.

"Aggressive?", I hear you ask. Well, yes, actually it is. The modest-looking pawn move challenges Black's strategic aims in the Queen's Indian quite radically. Black's main strategic idea is to control the e4-square, preventing White from establishing his pawn on that square, and thus dominating the centre. The purpose of 4 a3 is to prevent Black from pinning a white knight on c3, and thus White can follow up with 5 ♘c3, threatening 6 d5, shutting off the long diagonal of Black's bishop. This is a threat that Black has to take seriously.

4...♗b7

Black has tried other moves here, notably 4...♗a6, but the text-move is the main line.

5 ♘c3

Now Black must make a decision. If he plays passively with 5...♗e7?, White's idea can be seen in full relief. He plays 6 d5!, shutting out the bishop on b7, and following up with 7 e4, taking a dominating share of the centre. Note that if the pawn were not on a3, Black could meet 6 d5 with the pin 6...♗b4, when White cannot maintain his d5-pawn in view of the pressure against it (7 e4 would be answered by 7...♘xe4).

5...♘e4?!

This was reasonably popular for several years, but has now gone out of favour. The usual move is 5...d5, radically preventing White's threatened 6 d5.

6 ♘xe4 ♗xe4 *(D)*

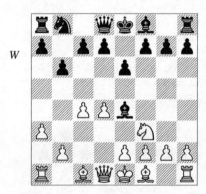

7 e3

A quiet approach. The main reason for the decline in popularity of 5...♘e4 is 7 ♘d2, with the idea of 7...♗b7 8 e4, when White's strong pawn-centre is generally considered to give him the advantage.

7...♗e7 8 ♗d3 d5

Vaganian plays to hold the e4 point, although this involves some weakening of his pawn-structure. 8...♗b7 is a rather passive alternative which allows White to take over the centre with 9 e4.

9 ♗xe4 dxe4 10 ♘d2 f5 11 f3

This is the problem with Black's chosen set-up. The e4-pawn cannot be defended directly, and 11...exf3 is bad in view of 12 ♕xf3, when Black has serious weaknesses on the light squares and in the centre. A later e4 by White would open up the e-file against the weak backward pawn on e6. Vaganian appreciates all of this, of course, and has planned a tactical method of defending his e4-pawn.

11...♗d6!

Here it is. Now 12 fxe4? is impossible because of 12...♕h4+ (13 g3? ♗xg3+), and the latter remains a threat anyway.

12 ♕a4+! (D)

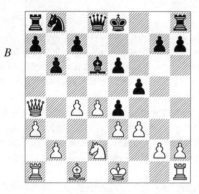

An excellent intermediary check. Beginners are always taught not to bring out their queen before developing their other pieces, but there are many exceptions to this. In this case, the check on a4 forces some concession from Black. Interposing the queen on d7 loses a pawn after the exchange of queens, followed by capturing on e4. 12...♘d7 looks natural, but after 13 0-0 ♕h4 14 f4, Black would be unable to castle, because of the undefended knight. Vaganian therefore blocks the check with the pawn, but this also leaves his knight on b8 tied down to the defence of the c6-pawn.

12...c6 13 0-0

Now he again threatens to take on e4, and it is still unfavourable for Black himself to exchange on f3. He therefore follows up with his intended kingside aggression.

13...♕h4 14 f4

Forced, but now Black has managed to relieve the pressure on his e4-pawn.

14...0-0 (D)

Summing up the results of the opening, it seems that Black has roughly equalized. His

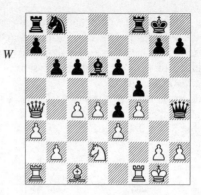

knight on b8 is tied down, but White has no obvious way to make progress on the queenside, whilst Black has the idea of attacking White's king with ...♖f6-h6. Routine play by White, such as 15 b4, would not give him anything, but Kramnik seizes the initiative with an excellent long-range positional pawn sacrifice.

15 c5! bxc5

Black has little choice but to accept. Note that the attempt to decline the pawn and leave White with a bad bishop, obstructed by his own pawns, after 15...b5, fails to 16 ♕b3, when Black loses the e6-pawn.

16 ♘c4 ♕e7 17 dxc5 ♗xc5 18 b4 ♗d6 (D)

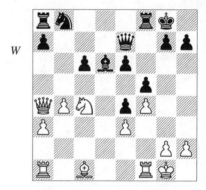

19 ♗b2!

The last few moves have been almost forced, and we can now see the first results of White's pawn sacrifice. Both his knight and bishop have taken up excellent, active posts, and his rooks are ready to occupy the open c- and d-files. As well as a serious weakness at e5, Black's knight remains tied to the defence of the c6-pawn, and all the while the knight remains on b8, the a8-rook is shut out of the game. It is clear that White's minor material investment has brought him more than enough positional compensation.

Note that White could have won the exchange by 19 ♘b6. However, after 19...axb6 20 ♕xa8 e5!, Black has excellent counterplay. Kramnik prefers to maintain the pressure.

19...♗c7 20 ♖fd1 c5

Ridding himself of the c6-weakness is the only way to develop his knight.

21 bxc5 ♕xc5 22 ♖ac1 ♕e7 *(D)*

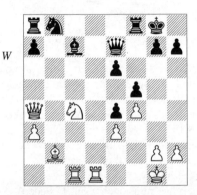

White has achieved maximum mobilization, and now needs to find a way to prosecute his initiative.

23 ♕b5!

A subtle move, threatening to win material with 24 ♕b7.

23...♗b6 24 a4 *(D)*

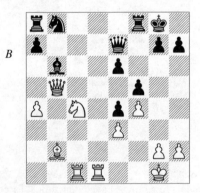

Once again declining to grab material, and preferring to step up the pressure. Black still cannot develop his queenside.

24...♗c5 25 ♗d4 ♗xd4

Yet again, Black cannot develop the queenside by 25...♘d7, in view of 26 ♗xg7!.

26 ♖xd4 a6 27 ♕b6 ♖a7 28 ♘d6 ♖d7 *(D)*

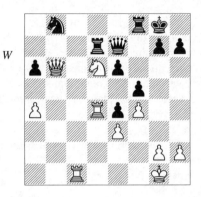

29 ♖c8!

Another instructive and non-standard decision. In general, the side with the initiative does not want to exchange pieces, since his pieces are usually more active than their enemy counterparts. However, every such rule of thumb has its exceptions, and concrete calculation frequently shows that the best move is one which apparently contradicts such general rules of thumb. Here, the tactical weakness of Black's knight on b8 is the key.

29...♖xc8

Forced, since 29...♖dd8 loses to 30 ♘xf5! discovering an attack on the d8-rook.

30 ♘xc8 ♕a3

The knight on b8 cannot be defended, so a counterattack is the only hope. The alternative route was 30...♕h4, threatening mate on e1, but this loses to 31 g3 ♕h5 32 ♕xb8 ♖xd4 33 ♘d6+ and mates. After the text-move, the attack on e3 leaves White no time to capture on b8, but instead, he can harvest Black's kingside pawns with check.

31 ♕xe6+ ♔f8 32 ♕xf5+ ♔e8

Or 32...♖f7 33 ♖d8#.

33 ♕e6+ ♔d8

If 33...♔f8, then simply 34 ♖xd7, and Black soon runs out of checks; e.g., 34...♕xe3+ 35 ♔f1 ♕c1+ (35...♕xf4+ 36 ♔e2) 36 ♔e2 ♕c2+ 37 ♖d2 and the checks are finished.

34 ♕b6+ ♔e8 35 ♘d6+ 1-0

After 35...♔e7, 36 ♖xe4+ ♔f6 (36...♔f8 37 ♖e8#) 37 ♘c4+ wins the queen.

Game 39
Andor Lilienthal – Mikhail Botvinnik
USSR Ch, Moscow 1940
Queen's Indian Defence, 4 g3 ♗b7

Tarrasch famously declared that if one piece stands badly, then the entire position is bad. In the present game, Black ends up with a knight offside on a6, which proves very difficult to get back in the game. With his opponent's pieces tied up on the queenside, Lilienthal employs our favourite strategic device of opening a second front, and breaks through decisively.

1 d4 ♘f6 2 c4 e6 3 ♘f3 b6 4 g3 ♗b7

The players choose the classical main line of the Queen's Indian, deploying his bishop on the long diagonal, to fight for the e4-square. Nowadays, the more combative 4...♗a6 is generally preferred.

5 ♗g2 ♗e7 6 0-0 0-0 7 ♘c3 ♘e4

The most natural move. The older continuation 7...d5 is now rather discredited, but if Black wishes to avoid the main line, he can do so with Sergei Tiviakov's interesting idea, 7...♘a6.

8 ♕c2 ♘xc3 9 ♕xc3 d6 *(D)*

This move more or less commits Black to playing ...f5 next move. An alternative strategy is 9...c5, whilst the old line 9...♗e4 is also playable.

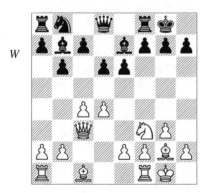

10 ♕c2 f5

White was threatening 11 ♘g5, winning material, so it was already too late for 10...c5. In view of the additional positional threat of 11 e4, taking control of the centre, the text-move is practically forced. The pawn-structure now has the contours of a Dutch Defence, but whereas in the Dutch proper, it is difficult for Black to fianchetto his light-squared bishop without running into an early d5 advance, here his problem

bishop has already found a good diagonal. In principle, therefore, Black should be doing satisfactorily in this position, and indeed theory considers that if White has any advantage, it is fairly small.

11 ♘e1 *(D)*

This is a thematic manoeuvre introduced by Rubinstein back in the 1920s. The exchange of bishops looks a little illogical in that it weakens White's king position, but it also weakens Black's light squares on the queenside, and reduces his hold over e4. Just as in similar Dutch Defence positions, White would like to achieve the advance e4, when a subsequent pawn exchange on e4 would expose the weak black pawn on e6.

11...♘c6?

It is a good general rule of thumb in queen's pawn openings that one should be very careful about playing the knight to c6 (or c3) in front of one's unmoved c-pawn. Here too, it proves a bad idea. Botvinnik was probably keen to complicate the fight, rather than accepting a slightly worse position after either 11...♕c8 12 e4 ♘d7 or 11...♗xg2 12 ♘xg2, followed by e4. However, both of these lines would have been better than the text-move, which results in the knight being driven around the board, and eventually ending up on a very bad square at a6. Ultimately, this offside knight proves to be the main cause of Black's defeat.

12 d5! exd5 13 cxd5

The structural change has already given White a clear positional advantage. He has pressure down the open c-file, against the backward pawn, and also the possibility of a later ♘d4, eyeing the weakness at e6.

13...♘b4?! (D)

Another mistake, and a good example of how a tactical miscalculation can result in a positional error. As Lilienthal himself explained, Botvinnik had missed White's next move.

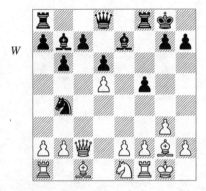

14 ♕d2!

This is the refutation of Black's play. Botvinnik's calculations had been based on the mistaken belief that White had to defend the d5-pawn with 14 ♕b3, after which Black can continue 14...a5 15 a3 ♘a6, and now White's queen obstructs his b-pawn. Black would have time to play 16...♘c5 and 17...a4, cementing his knight on c5 (16 ♕c2 ♘c5 17 b4? is impossible because of 17...axb4). Not only would the knight be actively placed there, but it would also shield the backward c7-pawn and defend the e6-square. As a result, Black would have a satisfactory position.

After the simple text-move, however, White is able to get in a3 and b4 before Black's knight can reach c5. Black is therefore left with an offside knight, and weaknesses on c7 and e6. This is a perfect illustration of a phenomenon which frequently arises – what appears to be bad positional play is actually the result simply of a tactical oversight. Botvinnik understood the position

only too well, and knew that if his knight got stuck on a6, he stood badly. However, when playing 11...♘c6, he believed that he could avoid this, and only after White's last move did he realize what he had done.

14...a5

The alternative was 14...c5 15 dxc6 ♘xc6, when White would also have a clear positional advantage, in view of the weaknesses of d5 and d6. Nevertheless, Botvinnik subsequently felt that this was what he should have played.

15 a3 ♘a6 16 b4! (D)

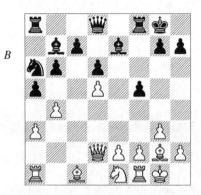

The point of 14 ♕d2. Now the knight is stuck badly offside, and remains so virtually until the end of the game.

16...♗f6 17 ♗b2 ♕d7 (D)

Exchanging pieces by 17...♗xb2 18 ♕xb2 ♕f6 would not bring Black any relief. After 19 ♕xf6 ♖xf6 20 ♘d3, White retains all the advantages of his position. Botvinnik prefers to keep the queens on the board, in the hope of being able to stir up complications later on.

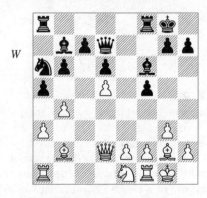

18 ♗xf6 ♖xf6 19 ♘d3

Lilienthal points out that grabbing a pawn by 19 bxa5? would be bad, in view of 19...♘c5!

with good play for Black. Instead, White pursues a consistent strategy of keeping the black knight bottled up on a6, and bringing pressure to bear down the c-file.

19...a4

Now 20 bxa5 really was a threat.

20 ♖ac1 ♕f7 (D)

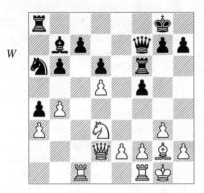

21 ♘f4

White's pieces gradually take up their best positions. From here, the knight defends the d5-pawn and attacks the weak square on e6.

21...♗c8 22 ♖c3 ♗d7 23 ♖fc1 h6 24 h4

Stopping any counterplay by 24...g5, which would now be met by 25 hxg5 hxg5 26 ♘e6, winning material.

24...♖a7 25 h5 ♖a8 (D)

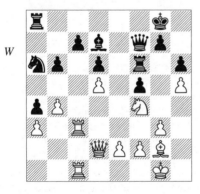

Black is bound hand and foot, and can undertake nothing active. Consequently, he waits to see how White will attempt to strengthen his position decisively.

26 ♖e3!

A perfect example of the principle of two weaknesses. With Black tied up and his pieces offside on the queenside, White switches his attack to the central files and the e6-square.

26...♔h7 27 ♖cc3 ♖b8 28 ♕d3 ♖a8 29 ♘g6

Finally cashing in some of his chips. The threat of 30 ♖e7 forces Black to give up the exchange.

29...♖xg6 30 hxg6+ ♔xg6

30...♕xg6 allows 31 ♖e7.

31 ♖e6+

Lilienthal points out that although this rook is immune, the immediate 31 g4, forcing exchanges, was even simpler.

31...♔h7 32 g4 (D)

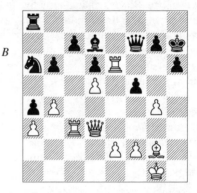

It is clear that Black's position is hopeless, and he now makes a last desperate effort to muddy the waters.

32...c5 33 b5 ♘c7 34 gxf5 ♘xb5

Lilienthal gives 34...♖e8 as a slightly more stubborn defence, and indicates that he intended to meet this with 35 ♕e4. However, although Lilienthal's move wins, it appears that 35 ♖xd6 is even simpler, as also is 35 f6+ g6 36 ♖xd6.

35 f6+ ♔g8 36 ♖c4 ♖e8 37 ♖g4

There are many roads to Rome at this point, with 37 ♖xe8+ being amongst the simplest. Lilienthal prefers to force open the position of the black king.

37...g5 38 ♖xe8+ ♗xe8 39 ♖e4 ♔f8 40 ♖e7 ♕g6 41 ♗e4 ♕h5 42 ♗f3 ♕g6 43 ♖xe8+! 1-0

After 43...♕xe8, 44 ♕h7 ♕f7 45 ♕xh6+ ♔g8 46 ♗h5 is decisive. A beautiful display by Lilienthal.

Game 40
Per Johansson – Steve Giddins
Gausdal 1995
Bogo-Indian Defence

Another common middlegame strategy is to aim one's play at squares of a particular colour. Certain openings give rise to pawn-structures in which such a one-colour strategy is particularly appropriate. In this game, Black selects a dark-square strategy right from the very opening. With the help of some positional errors from his opponent, he succeeds in establishing a crushing bind on the dark squares, which he then converts into victory by means of a tactical finish.

1 d4 e6 2 c4 ♘f6 3 ♘f3 ♗b4+

This is the characteristic move of the Bogo-Indian Defence, Black's main alternative to the Queen's Indian. The Bogo-Indian is very much a dark-square defence, at least in the form it is seen in this game. Black's basic plan is to exchange dark-squared bishops, and then place his central pawns on dark squares, by ...d6 and ...e5.

4 ♗d2 *(D)*

The alternative is 4 ♘bd2, aiming to secure the two bishops by a later a3. Black has several possible responses, including 4...b6, 4...d5, 4...c5 and 4...0-0, with the first two being the most reputable.

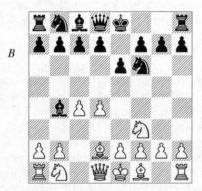

4...♕e7

Here, too, Black has alternatives, notably 4...a5, 4...c5 and 4...♗xd2+. The reason for avoiding the last of these moves is that White would answer 5 ♕xd2. As will become clear, Black's idea is to time the exchange on d2 at such a moment when White is obliged to recapture with the knight, which is less actively placed on d2 than it would be on c3.

5 g3 ♘c6 *(D)*

The key move in Black's anti-♕xd2 strategy. In queen's pawn openings, one is usually well advised to avoid playing ...♘c6 in front of the c-pawn, but this is one of the exceptions. That said, the knight move involves some loss of time, and attempts have also been made to make Black's position work after 5...0-0 6 ♗g2 ♗xd2+ 7 ♕xd2 d6. White is probably slightly better in both cases, but Black's position is always solid.

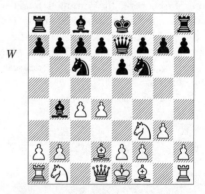

6 ♗g2

6 ♘c3 is also possible, and possibly a little stronger. Black's most consistent reply is to pursue his dark-square strategy by 6...♗xc3 7 ♗xc3 ♘e4 8 ♖c1 0-0 9 ♗g2 d6, although White is somewhat better after 10 d5. This is an example where the unfortunate position of the knight on c6 hurts Black a little.

6...♗xd2+ 7 ♘bxd2

The point of Black's 5th move is that this recapture is now forced, since 7 ♕xd2? ♘e4 8 ♕c2 ♕b4+ is awkward. White would be forced to accept a weak pawn-structure after 9 ♘c3 ♘xc3 10 ♕xc3 ♕xc3+ 11 bxc3, for which he has no real compensation.

7...d6 8 0-0 a5

The immediate 8...e5 is also possible, when White can continue 9 d5 ♘b8 10 b4. Black prefers to hold back the b4 advance for the time being.

9 e4 e5 10 d5 ♘b8 *(D)*

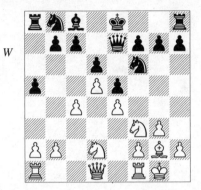

W

This is a basic position for this variation, and one which illustrates Black's opening strategy very clearly. Having exchanged off his dark-squared bishop, he arranges his central pawns on dark squares. His remaining bishop is unobstructed, and rather better than its opposite number, and Black has a rock-solid position with no weaknesses. However, he has less space, and is also temporarily behind in development, largely thanks to the time lost with his queen's knight. The latter is not such an important factor since the position is closed, but there is the danger that Black will be squeezed. White has the possibility of the pawn-levers b4 and c5 on the queenside, and f4 on the kingside, and Black must be ready to meet these. Overall, practice suggests that chances are approximately equal, and this is a position where the stronger player tends to win.

11 ♘e1

A standard manoeuvre. The knight will be ideally placed on d3, supporting a possible advance with b4 and c5, and also freeing the way for the f-pawn to advance.

11...0-0 12 ♘d3 ♘a6

Black holds up c5, and prepares to settle his knight on the c5-square. In this respect, 12...♘a6 is better than 12...♘bd7, since the latter square is needed for Black's bishop.

13 b3

There was no need for this preparatory move in this position, and White could have played simply 13 a3 and 14 b4.

13...c6

Again, typical for this structure. Black envisages playing ...♗d7 and putting a rook on the c-file.

14 a3 ♗g4!

A useful interpolation. The bishop is going to d7, but it is helpful first to provoke a slight weakening of White's position.

15 f3 *(D)*

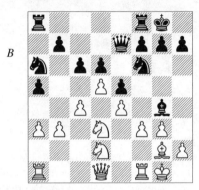

B

Now the dark squares in White's position are weakened, and the scope of his bishop reduced.

15...♗d7 16 ♖c1 ♖fc8 17 dxc6!?

A radical decision. White could have continued 17 b4, after which Black intended 17...cxd5 18 cxd5 ♗b5 with approximate equality. Instead, White prevents this, and seeks to expose the d5-square.

17...♗xc6

The alternative was 17...bxc6, when a common strategy for Black is to follow up with ...c5 and ...♘b8-c6-d4. However, in this position, White was planning to meet 17...bxc6 with the pawn sacrifice 18 c5!, when after 18...♘xc5 19 ♘xc5 dxc5 20 ♕c2, White will regain the pawn with pressure against c6. This is probably still playable for Black, who has counterplay along the b-file, but the text-move is more solid.

18 a4?!

White evidently did not wish to allow counterplay by 18...b5, but this fixing of the queenside comes at the high price of a further weakening of the dark squares in White's position. A move such as 18 ♗h3 looks preferable.

18...♘d7 19 ♘b1?!

White mistakenly believes that he can exploit the d5-square, but this proves not to be the case. If a white knight ever reaches that square, Black will be happy to exchange it off for his bishop, leaving Black with a classic knight vs bad bishop structure. White should have played 19 ♗h3, with the idea of trading bishop for knight. He will not get another chance.

19...♘dc5 20 ♘xc5 ♘xc5 21 ♘c3 (D)

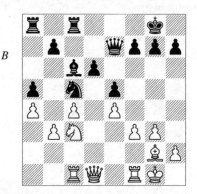

21...♖f8!

Preparing to open lines on the kingside with ...f5, and also setting up a transfer of his knight via e6 to d4, without allowing White to pin the knight by ♗h3. Although Black has a backward pawn on d6 and a hole on d5, these are difficult for White to exploit, as we have seen in similar Sicilian structures.

22 ♕c2

22 ♗h3 was still more to the point. It is rather ironic that White passed up a number of chances to play this move in much better circumstances than those in which he finally did play it.

22...♘e6 23 ♘e2 ♕c7

From here, the queen has the possibility of infiltrating on the weak dark squares, such as along the a7-g1 diagonal.

24 ♖fd1 ♖ad8 25 ♗h3?

As pointed out above, White chooses just about the worst possible moment to play this, although his position is already very difficult. A waiting move was in order, after which Black would probably play 25...g6 and follow up with ...f5. After the text-move, Black is able to achieve ...f5 in even more favourable circumstances, and his advantage rapidly becomes decisive.

25...♘g5 26 ♗g2

Forced.

26...f5 27 ♘c3 fxe4 28 ♘xe4

Allowing Black a 'clean' version of the knight vs bad bishop scenario, but even after 28 fxe4 ♕b6+, White's position is hopeless.

28...♗xe4! 29 fxe4 (D)

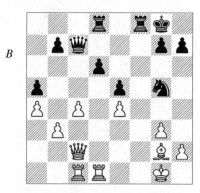

Just about Black's dream position for the Bogo-Indian. The total triumph of his dark-square strategy is clear, and it only remains to finish White off.

29...♘e6 30 ♕d3 ♕c5+ 31 ♔h1 ♘d4 32 ♖f1 b6 33 ♕e3 h6

There is no hurry. Black first removes any pin-pricks of white counterplay, such as ♕g5.

34 h3 ♖xf1+ 35 ♖xf1 ♖f8 36 ♖b1

The black rook on f8 is very powerful, but after the exchange of rooks, the ♕+♗ vs ♕+♘ ending would be hopeless for White.

36...♕a3 37 ♖d1 ♕b2 38 ♖d2

Allowing a neat finish.

38...♕c1+ 39 ♔h2 (D)

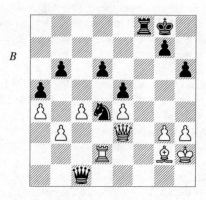

39...♖f3! 0-1

In view of 40 ♗xf3 ♕xd2+!.

Game 41
Tigran Petrosian – Florin Gheorghiu
Moscow 1967
English Opening, Reversed Sicilian

Here is another example of a colour-based strategy. Petrosian methodically weakens the light squares in his opponent's position, and soon establishes a winning bind.

1 c4

The English Opening is one of the main examples of a so-called 'flank opening'. Rather than advance one of his two central pawns, White adopts a more indirect strategy of development, aiming to control the centre from a distance, mainly with his pieces. The very first move of the English sets out White's stall quite clearly. By attacking the d5-square, White announces that he will focus his principal attention on the central light squares, usually by fianchettoing his king's bishop to the g2-square. We have already examined the game Chernin-Van der Sterren, which showed a typical example of White's queenside strategy in such positions.

1...e5

Black has many ways to meet the English. Gheorghiu's choice is in many ways the most principled of all, occupying the centre with a pawn in classical fashion. However, although undoubtedly fully sound, it does have the drawback of slightly weakening the central light squares, notably d5, thereby allowing White to pursue his typical plan.

2 ♘c3 ♘c6 3 ♘f3 ♘f6 4 g3 ♗b4

Another common and highly respected plan is 4...d5, leading after 5 cxd5 ♘xd5 to a position from the Dragon Sicilian, with colours reversed.

5 ♗g2 0-0 6 0-0 ♖e8 7 d3 *(D)*

7...h6

At the time this game was played, Gheorghiu's plan was quite common, but it has since gone out of fashion. The most usual line nowadays begins 6...e4 7 ♘g5 (or 7 ♘e1) 7...♗xc3, when White faces a fundamental choice of which way to recapture on c3. In either case, the struggle then usually revolves around White's attempts to make capital from his two bishops, which at present have relatively little scope, but

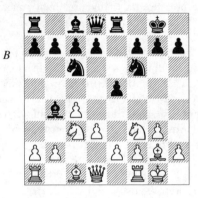

may become a potent force if the position later opens up.

Gheorghiu's move preserves his bishop, and stops White's positional threat of 8 ♗g5, pinning the f6-knight. Given that much of the struggle in this position revolves around the d5-square, the f6-knight is an important piece, and White will usually be happy to play ♗g5 and ♗xf6, removing it from the board. White's enhanced control over the squares d5 and e4 would then compensate for the surrender of the bishop.

8 ♘d5 ♗f8 9 ♘xf6+ ♕xf6 *(D)*

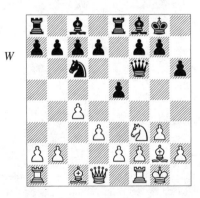

10 ♘d2

This move is typical for such English Opening positions, and is a continuation of White's standard plan of maximizing his influence over the central light squares. In the first place, White unmasks his fianchettoed bishop on g2, which now bears down on the long light-square diagonal. Secondly, White prepares to bring the knight, via e4, to c3, from where it will also attack the crucial squares d5 and e4. Note how consistently White plays. From as far back as move 1, he has conceived the general plan of putting pressure on the central light squares, and all of his moves since then have served that aim.

10...d6 11 ♘e4 ♕d8 12 ♘c3 ♗d7 13 b4!

White continues his standard English Opening plan. Having developed his minor pieces effectively, he initiates the typical queenside pawn advance. Note, however, that although he is following a standard plan, Petrosian is not stereotyped in executing that plan, but instead pays attention to the concrete features of the position. Thus, in 99% of cases, White's b4 advance is prepared by the move ♖b1. Here, however, Black's last move has undefended the b7-pawn, so White is able to advance 13 b4 without preparation. The exchange 13...♘xb4 14 ♗xb7 would favour White from a positional viewpoint, since he is better placed to exploit the open b-file.

13...♕c8 14 ♖b1

Black's last move defended b7, so 14...♘xb4 was now a threat.

14...♗h3 15 e4!? (D)

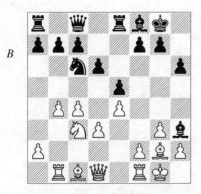

15...♗xg2?!

A most interesting moment. It may seem strange to criticize this exchange, since it is the logical consequence of Black's last two moves. In addition, it is generally favourable to exchange off the fianchettoed bishop in such

positions, since White's kingside is slightly weakened, and his bishop on g2 is an important piece in his overall strategy of exerting pressure on the central and queenside light squares. So what is the problem?

Well, the answer all revolves around White's previous move, 15 e4, which has changed the position quite radically. The move has blocked the long light-square diagonal, thus reducing the scope of White's bishop on g2. It is quite clear that the move 15 e4 anticipates the exchange of light-squared bishops. Petrosian has decided that once these bishops come off, his central pawns will be well placed on light squares. That way, they will control the central light squares, and will leave the road clear for his remaining bishop. In fact, arranging White's central pawns on c4, d3 and e4 is a common strategy in such positions, once the light-squared bishops have come off.

Here, however, the bishops have not actually come off the board yet, and Black should have reacted more subtly to his opponent's plans. Since it is clear that White is preparing for the exchange of bishops, Black should have adjusted to the changed situation, and instead retained light-squared bishops with 15...♗e6!. In the new situation, White's bishop on g2 is less effective than before, and the retention of the bishops now favours Black. This is a good example of the need for flexibility in chess. Consistency in strategy is excellent, as far as it goes, but one must always be ready to adjust to changes in the position. Here, the advance of White's pawn from e2 to e4 has actually changed the position quite substantially, and a new strategy is required of Black in order to respond to this. Instead, Gheorghiu blindly goes on with his original plan, thus playing into White's hands.

16 ♔xg2 g6 17 h4! ♗g7?

Another bad decision, which contributes further to the weakening of his light squares. It was essential to fight for these squares by 17...h5.

18 h5 g5 19 ♘d5

White's opening strategy has succeeded to a degree that he can scarcely have hoped for. He has seriously weakened the light squares in Black's position, and left him with a bad bishop on g7.

19...♘d4 20 ♘e3 f5!

The only hope. If Black plays passively, White will follow up with 21 &b2, followed by 22 &xd4, leaving Black with a strategically hopeless bad bishop vs knight position.

21 &b2 fxe4

Again, 21...f4? 22 &xd4 exd4 23 ♘f5 would be awful for Black.

22 dxe4 ♕e6 *(D)*

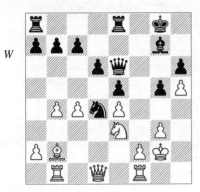

23 &c3

Now 23 &xd4 and 24 ♘f5 would lose the c4-pawn, so White must proceed more slowly. The text-move prepares the manoeuvre ♖b2-d2, when White would have the possibility of a positional exchange sacrifice on d4. Such sacrifices were one of Petrosian's most well-known visiting cards.

23...b5?

Gheorghiu of course understands that he has been comprehensively outplayed positionally, and as so often in such cases, he loses patience and tries to change the course of events by force. Unfortunately, such methods rarely work, and the cure frequently proves more deadly than the disease. In this case, the light squares in Black's camp are further weakened, and his queenside structure is destroyed. More patient defence by 23...c6 24 a4 a6, as suggested by the Soviet master Simagin, would still have left White with plenty of work to do to realize his positional advantage, although his task would be a great deal more pleasant than that facing the defender.

24 cxb5 ♕xa2

24...♘xb5 25 ♕d3 would not shake White's grip.

25 ♕d3 ♕e2

White's last move defended the e4-pawn, and thus threatened 26 &xd4 and 27 ♘f5. Simagin points out that the retreat 25...♕f7, trying to create counterplay against the f3- and h5-squares, would be met by 26 &xd4 exd4 27 ♘f5 ♕xh5 28 ♘xg7 ♔xg7 29 ♕xd4+, when Black's shattered pawn-structure and exposed king would be fatal disadvantages.

26 ♕xe2 ♘xe2 27 ♘d5 ♖ab8

Black does his best to seek counterplay against White's weak pawns. Instead, defending by 27...♖ac8 would be hopeless after 28 ♖a1. Note how useless Black's bishop on g7 remains in all these variations.

28 ♖fe1 ♘d4

28...♘xc3 29 ♘xc3 would be equally hopeless. With the text-move, Black at least hopes to be able to stir up some trouble with his passed d-pawn by, for example, a later ...d3, releasing his slumbering bishop from its prison.

29 &xd4 exd4 30 ♖bc1 ♖b7 *(D)*

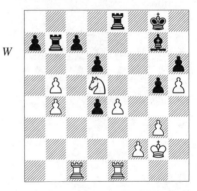

31 ♘xc7 ♖e5 32 ♖c6 g4 33 ♘d5 ♖xb5 34 ♖xd6 ♖b7

If instead 34...♖xh5, White wins by 35 ♖d8+ ♔h7 36 ♖d7 ♖e5 37 ♘f6+ ♔g6 38 ♘xg4, etc.

35 ♖g6 ♔h7 36 ♖xg4 ♖d7

After 36...♖xh5, 37 f4 is the simplest way to win.

37 ♖h1 ♖e6 38 ♖d1 ♖c6 39 ♖d2 &e5 40 f4 &h8 41 f5 1-0

Note how to the very end of the game, it was White's domination of the light squares which proved crucial – a fitting tribute to the excellence of his strategy, begun with his very first move.

Game 42
Magnus Carlsen – Giovanni Vescovi
Wijk aan Zee 2006
Sicilian Defence, Taimanov Variation

In this game, it is once again the weakness of a whole colour complex that decides events. Black ends up with serious weaknesses on the dark squares, and this, combined with White's pressure on the queenside, allows Carlsen to win in smooth positional style.

1 e4 c5 2 ᐠf3 e6 3 d4 cxd4 4 ᐠxd4 ᐠc6

This move characterizes the Taimanov Variation, named after the Russian GM and part-time concert pianist who did much to develop the variation in the 1960s and 1970s. Black plans relatively quick development of his queenside with an early ...b5, whilst retaining various options for kingside development, such as either ...ᐠf6 or ...ᐠge7. It has long been regarded as one of Black's soundest and most reliable Sicilian variations.

5 ᐠc3 a6 (D)

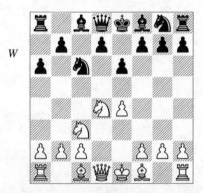

If Black is intending a set-up with ...a6, ...營c7 and ...ᐠf6, then he has an alternative move-order in the form of 5...營c7, which avoids White's next. However, this option is not available if Black is intending the 'pure' Taimanov treatment with ...ᐠge7, as the queen does not belong on the c7-square in that case, and moreover it would be exposed to tactics based on the weakness of the d6-square.

6 ᐠxc6

This exchange is not usually regarded as terribly effective in the Sicilian, since it strengthens the black pawn-centre and opens the b-file for his rooks. However, in this particular move-order, it renders ...a6 more or less a waste of a tempo and is one of the most troublesome lines for Black, thanks to the fact that White is able to probe the enemy kingside with 營g4. Nevertheless, such eminent Taimanov practitioners as Anand and Andersson have consistently defended the black side, and Black's game should by no means be regarded as necessarily inferior.

6...bxc6 (D)

The queenless middlegame after 6...dxc6?! 7 營xd8+ ⬦xd8 is not good for Black, as his king is a liability and his dark squares weak.

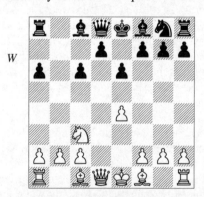

7 ᐠd3 d5 8 0-0 ᐠf6 9 ᐠe1 ᐠe7 10 e5 ᐠd7 11 營g4

This is White's key idea in this line. The attack on g7 is awkward for Black to meet, since 11...0-0? costs him the exchange after 12 ᐠh6. He is therefore forced to weaken the dark squares on the kingside with his next move.

11...g6 12 ᐠa4

This decentralization looks a little odd at first sight, but White wishes to play the move c4, attacking Black's pawn-centre and opening lines on the queenside.

12...營a5 13 ᐠh6 營b4

With his king trapped in the centre, it makes sense for Black to exchange queens, but this does not solve all of his problems.

14 ♕xb4 ♗xb4 15 c3 ♗f8?!

Up to this point, the game has been following established theory, but this is a new move, although probably not a very good one. Given that so many of Black's pawns are on light squares, his dark squares are potentially weak, and the exchange of dark-squared bishops is therefore in White's favour. In a game played some 24 years earlier (Hazai-Romanishin, Sochi 1982), Black preferred 15...♗a5, retaining the dark-squared bishop, and planning to bring it to c7, putting pressure on the white e5-pawn. That still does not fully solve Black's problems, but it looks a better try than the text-move.

16 ♗xf8 ♖xf8 17 c4! *(D)*

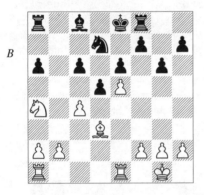

White has a lead in development, so it makes sense to open lines.

17...♔e7 18 cxd5 cxd5 19 ♖ac1 ♖a7?

This looks very natural, but turns out to be a significant mistake. As Magnus Carlsen himself pointed out, the apparent threat of 20 ♖c7 is not actually so strong, and Black should therefore have played 19...a5!, preventing White's next move. Then after 20 ♖c7, he can continue 20...♔d8, with the point that 21 ♖ec1? is met by 21...♘xe5 22 ♘b6? ♘xd3 winning. Consequently, White would have to answer 19...a5 with 20 f4, but then after 20...♖a7, we get a position similar to the game, but with Black's a-pawn on a5 instead of a6. This is a significant improvement on the game, since the pawn is much less vulnerable on a5, although White would still retain an edge.

20 b4! *(D)*

This is a very important, and typical, move. White fixes the weak pawn on a6, where it obstructs Black's bishop and is vulnerable to attack. Now, if Black plays 20...a5, White can

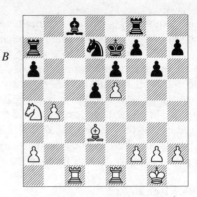

reply 21 b5, establishing a strong passed pawn. This same positional idea was used by Fischer in a very similar position, in one of his most famous games (Fischer-Petrosian, Candidates match (game 7), Buenos Aires 1971).

20...♗b7

Black's position is now extremely uncomfortable, with a bad bishop, a weakness on a6, and passive pieces. It is very difficult to find a constructive plan for him, and in the game, he is reduced to trying to exchange rooks along the c-file. As we shall see, this does not relieve his position very much. The only active possibility was to challenge the e5-pawn by 20...f6. Note that the obvious attempt to maintain the pawn-wedge by 21 f4? is then a mistake, since after 21...fxe5 22 fxe5, the e5-pawn is very weak, and White is tied to its defence. Instead, Carlsen intended to meet 20...f6 by 21 exf6+ ♘xf6 22 ♖c6! ♗d7 23 ♖b6, with a large advantage for White, since after 23...♗xa4 24 ♖exe6+, White will regain the piece and keep an extra pawn.

21 f4 ♖c8 22 ♖xc8 ♗xc8 23 ♖c1 ♔d8 24 ♔f2 *(D)*

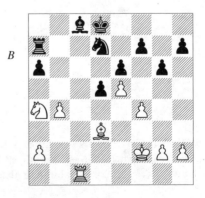

24...♘b8

Black continues his passive waiting tactics. As Carlsen points out, this was his last chance to play 24...f6, but after 25 exf6 ♘xf6 26 ♔e3, White retains excellent winning chances. The main point is that snatching the h-pawn by 26...♘g4+ 27 ♔d4 ♘xh2? is strongly met by 28 ♘b6! ♖c7 (28...♗d7 and 28...♗b7 are both answered by 29 ♖h1) 29 ♖xc7 ♔xc7 30 ♘xc8 ♔xc8 31 ♗xa6+ ♔c7 and now 32 ♗e2! traps the knight, after which Black's position is hopeless.

25 ♘c5 ♖c7 26 ♖c2

Defending the rook, and thus unpinning the knight on c5.

26...♘d7 27 ♘b3

The alternative was to allow the exchange on c5, but Carlsen felt that although a white pawn on c5 would be passed, it would be easily blockaded and could well prove more of a strength than a weakness. Instead, he is happy to allow the exchange of the last pair of rooks, since his rook does not have any obvious path by which to penetrate into Black's position. The minor-piece ending remains extremely difficult for Black.

27...♖xc2+ 28 ♗xc2 ♘b8 29 ♘d4 ♗d7? (D)

In such positions, it is usually vital to prevent White from establishing a clamp on the kingside by means of g4, g5, h4-h5-h6, etc. Consequently, Black should have played 29...h5, to stop White's next move.

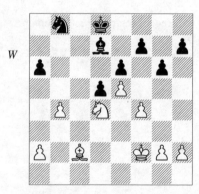

30 g4!

Now Black is lost. If he does nothing, White can establish his pawns on g5 and h6, after which he will have various breakthrough ideas,

based on f5, and sacrifices on g6. Such positions were examined in more detail in my book *101 Chess Endgame Tips*, notably in the context of the ending Miles-Mariotti, Tip 21. Vescovi decides to prevent 31 g5, but in so doing, he weakens his structure, and the h-pawn becomes a target.

30...h6 31 ♔e3 ♔c7 32 a4 ♔b6

Black could make things slightly more difficult by 32...♘c6, but this would not save the game. After 33 ♘xc6 ♗xc6 34 ♔d4, a combination of the threats of f5 and ♔c5 renders Black defenceless; e.g., 34...♔b6 35 h3 ♗d7 36 a5+ ♔c7 (or 36...♔b5 37 ♔c3, followed by 38 ♔b3 and 39 ♗d3+) 37 ♗d3 ♗c8 38 ♔c5 (zugzwang) 38...♗b7 (otherwise White's king enters on b6 or d6) 39 f5 gxf5 40 gxf5 exf5 (or 40...♗c8 41 f6 ♗b7 42 ♔g6!, winning) 41 ♗xf5, followed by ♗g4-f3, winning the d5-pawn.

33 a5+ ♔b7 34 ♗d3 ♗a4 35 ♗e2

The immediate 35 f5 wins more quickly.

35...♘d7 36 h4 ♘b8 37 f5 (D)

37...gxf5

37...♗d7 also loses to 38 fxg6 fxg6 39 g5!, when the g6-pawn is fixed as a new weakness. Then the principle of two weaknesses is seen in operation: Carlsen gives as a sample line 39...hxg5 40 hxg5 ♘c6 41 ♘xc6 ♗xc6 42 ♗d3 ♗e8. Now the black bishop is tied to one weakness, and the black king to the other. White wins simply by 43 ♔d4, followed by ♔c5-d6, etc.

38 gxf5 ♗d7 39 ♗h5 1-0

After 39...exf5 40 ♗xf7, the e-pawn costs Black a piece.

Game 43
Leonid Stein – Boris Spassky
USSR Ch, Erevan 1962
Ruy Lopez (Spanish), Smyslov Variation

This game illustrates a number of strategic ideas. Firstly, White combines queenside and kingside play, using the principle of two weaknesses. Secondly, his king takes an active part in the middle-game complications, an unusual thing, but very effective in the right circumstances. Finally, the game also illustrates the importance of concrete calculation, as Stein clinches the game thanks to accurate calculation of a long tactical variation.

1 e4 e5 2 ♘f3 ♘c6 3 ♗b5 a6 4 ♗a4 ♘f6 5 0-0 ♗e7 6 ♖e1 b5 7 ♗b3 0-0 8 c3 d6 9 h3 h6

The characteristic move of the Smyslov Variation, which enjoyed considerable popularity in the 1960s. Black prevents ♘g5, and so prepares ...♖e8 and ...♗f8, supporting his e5-pawn and deferring any decision about action on the queenside. Its popularity waned in the 1970s, not because of anything terribly wrong with the variation, but simply because players became more interested in the Breyer Variation with 9...♘b8. Later still, it was realized that ♘g5 is no great threat, and so Black started playing 9...♗b7 and 10...♖e8, the Zaitsev System, which is really an attempt to save a tempo on the Smyslov by dispensing with the move ...h6. Ironically, the wheel has now come full circle, and Ivan Sokolov, a great specialist on the black side of the Spanish, has been playing the Smyslov System regularly over the past couple of years.

10 d4 ♖e8 11 ♘bd2 ♗f8 12 ♘f1 ♗d7

Black has a major alternative in 12...♗b7. The bishop is somewhat more active on b7, but runs the risk of being shut out, after a subsequent d5 by White.

13 ♘g3 ♘a5

Having organized his other pieces as well as he can, Black cannot any longer manage without playing ...c5, to start some counterplay in the centre and on the queenside.

14 ♗c2 c5 15 d5 ♘c4 *(D)*

The fate of Black's queen's knight is just about the biggest single issue for Black in the Closed Spanish. The need to play ...c5 means that the knight inevitably has to move from c6, and the question is where it should go. In most variations, it goes to a5, which has the merit of

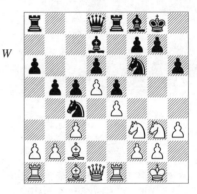

attacking White's 'Spanish' bishop, and thus gaining a tempo. However, on a5, the knight is frequently offside, especially after White closes the centre by playing d5. This is the main reason for the long-time popularity of the Breyer Variation, in which the knight retreats to b8 and then goes to d7, reinforcing the important e5-pawn.

In this position, with d5 already played, the knight has no real future on a5. Furthermore, White was potentially threatening 16 b3, which would leave the knight with only b7 as a retreat-square. From b7, the knight still has great difficulty finding a decent square, so Black pre-empts this by playing the knight to c4, and thence, to b6. The latter is certainly a better square than b7, but even so, Black frequently ends up playing the knight from b6 to d7, having taken four moves to do so (...♘a5-c4-b6-d7), rather than the two moves involved in the Breyer Variation.

16 ♘h2

A standard knight manoeuvre in such Spanish positions. With the pressure taken off his d4-square, White can remove the knight from f3. He has a variety of ideas – playing f4, bringing the knight to g4, and the queen to f3, to name but three.

16...a5?

This proves inaccurate after White's reply, which diverts the black bishop from d7, allowing White to post his knight on f5. 16...g6, defending f5, was a better idea, when Black could meet 17 b3 ♘b6 18 f4 with 18...exf4 19 ♗xf4 ♗c8, followed by ...♘bd7-e5.

17 a4! *(D)*

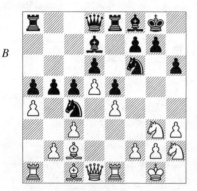

This queenside pawn-thrust is often the key to White's advantage in Spanish positions. Indeed, some have even argued that its effectiveness is an argument against 3...a6. I must even confess to having entertained such heretical thoughts myself, and I have wasted far too large a proportion of my adult life trying to make such moves as 3...♘f6, 3...d6 and 3...♘ge7 work for Black. Alas, I have to admit that Black's problems are even greater after these moves than after 3...a6.

There are a number of reasons why a timely a4 thrust can cause Black trouble. In many cases, it is the threat of opening the a-file, when White may be able to penetrate with his major pieces. On other occasions, an exchange of pawns on b5 may result in the b5-pawn being exposed to attack from White's pieces, with moves such as ♗d3 and ♕e2. If Black meets a4 by capturing, the isolated a6-pawn usually proves a significant weakness, whilst pushing on to b4 can often lead to the b-pawn becoming weak, and White having a valuable square at c4 for his pieces.

Here, the situation is a little different from normal, because Black's a-pawn is already on a5. This means that he cannot really avoid an isolated pawn on the a-file, except by blocking

the position with 17...b4. Then after 18 b3 ♘b6 19 c4, the queenside would be totally blocked, and Black would have no counterplay on that flank to offset White's kingside prospects. Spassky decides that he cannot afford this.

17...♘b6 18 axb5 ♗xb5 19 ♘f5!

This is the real point of White's 17th move. A knight on f5 is one of the classic Spanish themes, and frequently presages a winning kingside attack for White.

19...♗d7 20 g4! *(D)*

White wants to be able to recapture on f5 with the g-pawn, thus opening the g-file against Black's king. In the longer term, a kingside pawn-storm will follow. Note that in this position, White does not need to worry about the potential exposure of his own king resulting from this pawn advance. This is because the centre is blocked, and Black consequently has no chance to launch a central counterattack, such as would be likely in a Sicilian position, for example.

20...♘h7 21 ♔g2 ♗e7 22 ♘f3 ♘f8

Black is manoeuvring his knight to g6, in the hope that it will be less vulnerable to a g5 pawn advance.

23 h4 ♘g6

Stealing a pawn by 23...♗xf5 24 gxf5 ♗xh4 is suicidal. After 25 ♘xh4 ♕xh4 26 ♖h1 ♕f6 27 ♕g4 White has an overwhelming attack.

24 g5! h5 *(D)*

Up to now, the game has been dominated by positional considerations. Stein has handled this part of the game superbly, and by exploiting Black's minor inaccuracies, has built up a formidable attacking position. But in every game, the time comes when the player with the advantage has to go over to concrete action, which in

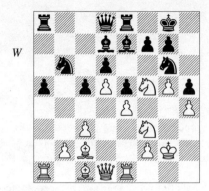

practice means calculating variations. For this reason, no matter how much a player may prefer and enjoy strategy and planning, and no matter how profound he may be in this area of the game, he will never achieve the successes that his strategic build-up deserves, unless he learns to calculate tactics and variations properly, and has sufficient imagination to find combinations and tactical ideas.

Fortunately, Leonid Stein most certainly did not suffer from any deficiency of imagination or tactical ability, as he now shows.

25 ♘h2!!

A move which could only be played by someone with great imagination, and great ability to calculate variations. At first sight, the move just loses two pawns, which would be reason enough for most players to reject it without further consideration. In order to play the move, Stein had to see at least as far as his 32nd move.

White is attacking the pawn on h5, which cannot be defended, so Black's reply is forced.

25...♗xf5 26 exf5 ♘xh4+ 27 ♔h3! (D)

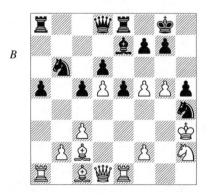

Another unusual feature of White's idea is that it involves the active use of his king in a

sharp middlegame situation. The h4-knight has no retreat, so Black must accept the second pawn.

27...♗xg5 28 ♗xg5 ♕xg5 29 ♖g1 ♕f6?

A critical moment. Another variation Stein had to foresee when playing 25 ♘h2!! was 29...♕f4, upon which he planned 30 ♕xh5 ♕xf2? 31 ♘g4! ♕xc2 32 ♘h6+, and mate in three. Perhaps Black's toughest defence was 29...♕h6, when after 30 ♔xh4 ♕f4+ 31 ♔h3 ♕xf2, Black has gained an important tempo over the previous variation (the white queen is still on d1). After 32 ♖g2 ♕f4 33 ♖g3!? (33 ♕xh5? ♘xd5 34 ♖ag1 ♕e3+ is a draw by perpetual), White's extra piece should outweigh Black's three pawns, but the position is still not entirely clear.

30 ♕xh5 ♘xd5 31 ♕xh4 ♘f4+ 32 ♔g4!

This was the move Stein had to see when he entered the complications by 25 ♘h2!!. If White had to play 32 ♔g3, Black would regain an exchange with 32...♘e2+ and emerge with rook and two pawns for two minor pieces. Now, on the other hand, it is a piece for two pawns, and in addition, Black cannot avoid the exchange of queens.

32...♕xh4+ 33 ♔xh4 (D)

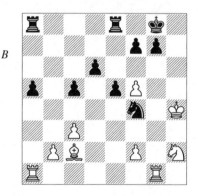

33...f6

If 33...d5, to prevent White's next move, then 34 ♘g4 ♔f8 35 f6 g6 36 ♖h1, and White will penetrate down the h-file.

34 c4

Now the black central pawn-mass loses its mobility, after which the remainder is easy.

34...♔f7 35 ♔g4 ♖ab8 36 ♖gb1 ♖h8 37 ♘f3 g6 38 ♘h4 gxf5+ 39 ♘xf5 ♔e6 40 ♖xa5 ♖bg8+ 41 ♔f3 ♖g5 42 ♘g3 f5 43 ♖a6 1-0

6 Endgame Themes

This penultimate chapter of the book looks at various endgame themes. As emphasized in *50ECL*, the endgame frequently has a slower tempo than the middlegame, and the principle 'do not hurry' is a highly important component of good endgame technique. This will be seen many times in the next few games.

As in *50ECL*, the games examined here cover various types of endgame, mostly differentiated by material. The first three games deal with minor-piece endgames. Game 45 is a superb example of how a knight can dominate a bishop, even in a relatively open position, whereas in Game 46, we see the World Champion give another typical demonstration of the strength of the two bishops.

In rook endings especially, the activity of the pieces is frequently a decisive factor, and this is illustrated in Game 47, where White loses an ending with equal material, just because his rook is so much less active than its opponent. Finally, in Game 48, we see a classic queen and pawn ending, lasting no fewer than 120 moves. Black methodical strategy, in the face of stiff resistance from White, makes this ending not only one of the great achievements by a British player in the 20th century, but also highly instructive.

Game 44
Tony Miles – Bent Larsen
Tilburg 1978
Queen's Indian Defence, 4 ♗f4

In this game, Black commits a serious error in the early middlegame, as a result of which he ends up with a seriously bad bishop on b7. Miles's subsequent strategy is to exchange pieces and reach a minor-piece ending where he is able to exploit the bad bishop.

1 d4 ♘f6 2 ♘f3 e6 3 c4 b6 4 ♗f4

An unusual move, which Miles played with great success for a year or two around 1978-9. White intends to play e3, but first develops the bishop to an active post outside the pawn-chain.

4...♗b7 5 e3 ♗e7 *(D)*

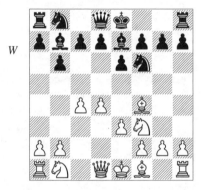

W

6 h3

As in similar London System positions, once Black has played his bishop to e7, he is threatening to hunt down the f4-bishop by means of 6...♘h5 (the immediate 5...♘h5 would have been met by 6 ♗g5). Spassky-Karpov, Montreal 1979 showed that this is a real positional threat; after 6 ♘c3?! ♘h5! 7 ♗g3 d6 8 ♗d3 ♘d7 9 0-0 g6 10 h3 ♘xg3 11 fxg3 0-0 12 ♖c1 ♗f6 13 ♖c2 ♗g7 Black had an excellent game, and went on to win a masterpiece. Miles therefore preserves the bishop from exchange.

6...0-0 7 ♘c3 d5 8 cxd5 exd5

An alternative plan is 8...♘xd5, not only keeping the long light-square diagonal open for the b7-bishop, but also seizing the chance to hassle White's bishop on f4. Miles had several games which went 9 ♘xd5 ♗xd5 10 ♗d3!? ♗b4+ 11 ♔e2, with unclear play.

9 ♗d3 ♘bd7 10 0-0 a6

The position reached is typical of many Queen's Indian and Queen's Gambit variations. Black has established a pawn outpost in the centre, on d5, and has developed his pieces soundly. White enjoys slightly more space, and his half-open c-file usually proves slightly easier to exploit than Black's half-open e-file. Black usually ends up playing ...c5, and the struggle then revolves around how the central pawn-formation will be clarified. Both sides must constantly assess the likely isolated or hanging pawn formations, which can arise after a pawn exchange on c5. Chances are probably a little better for White, but Black's game is perfectly playable.

11 ♘e5 ♖e8 12 ♕f3

The fact that White's bishop is actively developed on f4, rather than being confined behind its own pawn-chain on c1, means that White has better than usual chances of active play on the kingside.

12...♗d6 13 ♘g4 *(D)*

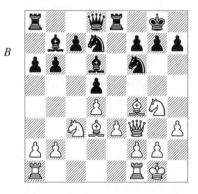

B

13...♘e4?

A very bad move, presumably based simply on an oversight. Black should exchange bishops on f4, when the position is slightly better for White, but no more than that.

14 &xd6 cxd6

This ugly recapture is unfortunately forced, since 14...&xd6 simply loses a pawn after 15 &xd5.

After the text-move, the position has changed radically. Rather than being roughly equal, White now has a clear advantage. However, it is important to understand precisely what this advantage consists of. The doubled pawns on the d-file are the basis of the advantage, but not so much because they themselves are weak. True, the d5-pawn is weak, and can be attacked by White's pieces, but Black can defend the pawn easily enough, whilst his d6-pawn is very hard to attack. The real advantage of White's position lies in the fact that the doubled d-pawns have no mobility, and obstruct Black's pieces, notably the bishop on b7. White's task is to combine pressure against d5 with threats to penetrate down the open c-file.

15 &fc1 &g5 16 &e2!

A move with two points, the obvious one being the threat of 17 &c7.

16...&ac8 17 &f4! *(D)*

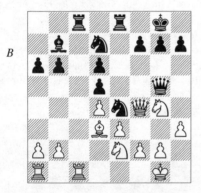

This is the other point of White's last move. In such positions, a queen exchange nearly always favours the stronger side, since his positional advantage can usually be exploited more easily in an endgame. The absence of queens reduces the defender's chances of creating counterplay. This is a typical example of what the Russians refer to as 'playing for two results' (i.e. a win or a draw). White's pressure may or may not be enough to win, but there is almost no chance of him losing, bar a one-move blunder. The most the defender can usually hope for in such endings is a draw, whereas in a middle-game position, there is usually more chance of

creating active play and thereby having some chances to win.

17...&xf4

For the reasons outlined in the previous note, 17...&e7 may have been a better practical chance, although the white queen is then well-placed on f4, eyeing the d6-pawn.

18 &xf4 g6 19 f3 &ef6 20 &xf6+ &xf6 21 &f2 &f8 *(D)*

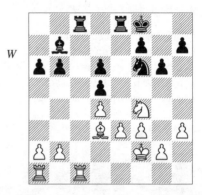

22 g4!

An absolutely typical plan in such positions. White annexes space on the kingside, threatens to drive away the knight which defends the d5-weakness, and also creates the possibility of opening lines on the kingside by a later h4-h5 (the principle of two weaknesses in action once again).

22...&e7

One recurring feature of the position is the possibility of Black trying to exchange all four rooks on the c-file. There are two points to mention here. Firstly, as we see later in the game, this does not necessarily relieve Black's position. Secondly, White's d3-bishop controls the important c2-square, and means that White can always retain a pair of rooks, even if this means abandoning the c-file to Black. All the while the bishop controls c2, and the rook c1, Black cannot penetrate along the c-file anyway. For the moment, the attempt to remove all the rooks would lose the d5-pawn, after 22...&xc1 23 &xc1 &c8? 24 &xc8+ &xc8 25 g5, etc.

23 h4 b5?! *(D)*

Putting another pawn on a light square is the last thing Black wants to do, but he has serious problems anyway. If he leaves the queenside pawns where they are, the a6-pawn is under permanent attack from White's d3-bishop. The more natural way to solve this problem is by 23...a5, but Larsen was probably concerned about the white knight coming round to b5, where it would exert unpleasant pressure on the d6-pawn and the c7-square. After the move played, he can at least meet White's potential threat of ♗c2-b3 by bringing his own knight to c4, via d7 and b6. So often in such positions, the defender has only a choice of evils, and it is extremely difficult to judge at any particular point which of those evils will prove to be the least significant.

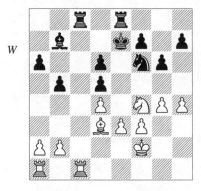

24 h5 ♘d7

The move 24...g5 would keep the h-file closed, but after 25 ♘e2 h6 26 ♘g3, the white knight reaches f5, where it is a veritable monster, attacking both d6 and h6.

25 ♖xc8 ♖xc8 26 ♖h1

See the note to Black's 22nd move. Although White has abandoned control of the open c-file, Black can do nothing with it, as the entry-squares in White's camp are all controlled.

26...♘f8

As mentioned above, one of the points of Black's 23rd move was to activate his knight by bringing it towards c4. Here, however, that is tactically impossible, because of 26...♘b6? 27 hxg6 hxg6 28 ♘xg6+!, winning a pawn.

27 hxg6 hxg6 28 ♔e2 ♔f6 29 ♔d2 ♔g7 (D) **30 ♖c1!**

Black has responded to the opening of the h-file by playing his king across to the kingside, to prevent White from penetrating down that file. In typical fashion, Miles therefore shifts his attention back to the queenside just at the

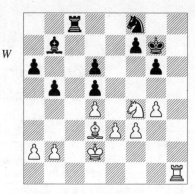

moment when the enemy king is furthest away, a perfect example of the principle of two weaknesses. Black cannot allow White's rook into c7, so he must exchange.

30...♖xc1 31 ♔xc1 ♘f6 32 ♔d2 b4

White's plan is to march his king in on the dark squares, by ♔c3-b4-a5, etc. Larsen tries to stop this by putting his pawns on dark squares, but to no avail. Note that if he tried to do so by 32...♗c6, planning to meet 33 ♔c3 by 33...a5, White would instead play 33 a4!. Then, whether Black exchanges pawns by 33...bxa4 34 ♗xa6, or allows 34 axb5, in either case, the white king will come in via c3 and b4, and win Black's remaining queenside pawn.

33 ♔c2 a5 34 ♗b5!

The final accuracy. 34 ♔b3? (do not hurry!) 34...♗c6! would prevent White from penetrating with his king. Instead, after the text-move, there is no defence to ♔b3-a4.

34...♘e6 35 ♘xe6 fxe6 36 ♔b3 ♔g5 37 ♔a4 e5 38 ♔xa5 exd4 39 exd4 ♔f4 40 ♗d7!

Neatly cutting off the enemy bishop. White needs only to calculate the finish.

40...♔e3 41 ♔b6 ♗a8 42 ♔a7

Sealing the fate of the unfortunate cleric, which has been staring at its prison walls on d5 and a6 for almost the entire game.

42...♔xd4 43 f4!

Do not hurry! The bishop is not going anywhere, so Miles secures his kingside pawns. Now a line such as 43...♔e4 44 f5 gxf5 45 gxf5 ♔e5 46 ♔xa8 d4 47 ♔b7 d3 48 ♗a4 ♔xf5 49 ♗d1, followed by 50 a4, is quite hopeless for Black.

1-0

Game 45
Erwin L'Ami – Shakhriyar Mamedyarov
World Junior Ch, Istanbul 2005
Ruy Lopez (Spanish), Exchange Variation

It is generally considered that bishops are superior to knights if the position is not blocked. However, the truth is rather more subtle. In particular, bishops suffer from one major disadvantage compared with knights, even in an open position: a bishop can only control squares of one colour, whereas a knight can access squares of both colours. The ending in this game illustrates this. Even though the position is not blocked, Black's knight finds excellent outposts on the light squares, which the bishop cannot cover.

1 e4 e5 2 ♘f3 ♘c6 3 ♗b5 a6 4 ♗xc6 dxc6 5 0-0

The Exchange Variation of the Spanish is one of White's most important options, to avoid the long and deeply-analysed main lines. First used regularly by Emanuel Lasker, its popularity leapt after it was taken up by Bobby Fischer, and it has remained a popular choice to this day.

The basic strategy of the Exchange Variation is to exploit White's superior pawn-structure in the endgame. After the move d4, and the exchange of pawns on d4, White will have a 4 vs 3 pawn-majority on the kingside, whilst Black's 4 vs 3 majority on the other wing is doubled, and cannot so easily produce a passed pawn. Black's compensation lies principally in his bishop-pair.

It is well-known that White cannot immediately win a pawn by 5 ♘xe5, owing to 5...♕d4, regaining it. Lasker's preferred handling of the line was to play 5 d4 immediately, but it was later shown that Black obtains good chances by 5...exd4 6 ♕xd4 ♕xd4 7 ♘xd4 ♗d7, followed by 8...0-0-0. When Fischer revived the Exchange Lopez in the mid-1960s, it was on the basis of the move 5 0-0, which delays d4 for a move, and forces Black to decide how to defend his e5-pawn. Fischer is often credited with having invented 5 0-0, but the move had been played regularly many years earlier by the Dutch master Barendregt.

5...♕d6 (D)

This looks a little odd, but is actually one of Black's most reputable choices here. The truth is that the various ways to defend the e5-pawn all have certain drawbacks. 5...♗g4 almost inevitably results in Black having to surrender the bishop-pair at some stage. 5...♗d6 avoids exchanges, but after 6 d4 exd4 7 ♕xd4, Black is forced into the move 7...f6, and most authorities consider that White stands somewhat better in the resulting position. The two most common replies are 5...f6 and the text-move. Although the queen looks badly-placed on d6, it facilitates queenside castling.

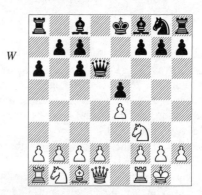

6 d4

Although this move is the cornerstone of White's usual strategy in the Exchange Variation, it is actually not terribly effective in this position, and theory prefers either 6 d3 or 6 ♘a3, in both cases hoping to harass the slightly exposed black queen by bringing a knight to c4.

6...exd4 7 ♘xd4

After 7 ♕xd4 ♕xd4 8 ♘xd4 ♗d7, White has no advantage, even though he has gained a tempo over Lasker's 5 d4.

We now have on the board the generic Exchange Lopez pawn-structure. In theory, if one removed all of the pieces from the board, leaving just kings and pawns, White should be winning the pawn ending, thanks to his healthy pawn-majority. Even that is not 100% clear (it is an interesting and instructive exercise to analyse the resulting ending in detail), but as it is, with a full board of pieces, Black should have good counterplay. His bishop-pair can become effective, and White must be careful not to advance his pawn to f4 prematurely, lest he have problems with the weakened e4-pawn. Rubinstein won several classic games as Black in just such a fashion.

7...♗d7 8 ♘c3 0-0-0 9 ♗e3 ♘f6 10 f3 ♕e5 11 ♘de2 ♗d6 12 ♗f4

Here, for example, 12 f4 ♕h5 would only weaken the e4-pawn, since 13 e5? ♘g4 is good for Black.

12...♕c5+ 13 ♔h1 ♗e6 14 ♕c1 ♗c4

Black's free and easy development has already enabled him to take the initiative.

15 ♕e3

Exchanging queens is usually part of White's agenda in the Exchange Variation, but here, it is more of a defensive measure, since the black queen is significantly more active than its white counterpart.

15...♕xe3 16 ♗xe3 ♗e5 17 ♖fe1 (D)

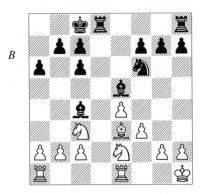

An instructive moment. Black now goes in for a superbly-judged liquidation, in which he gives up both of his bishops in order to cripple White's queenside pawns. Most important of all, though, is that he correctly judges that in the resulting position, his knight will be better than White's bishop.

17...♗xe2! 18 ♖xe2 ♗xc3! 19 bxc3 ♘e8!

The knight is heading for c4, from where it will be impossible to dislodge.

20 ♔g1 ♘d6

In order to illustrate the fine points on which the assessment of a position may depend, it is worth comparing this position with one reached by Lasker in one of his classic Exchange Spanish victories. The game Lasker-Janowski, match (game 3), Paris 1909 reached this position:

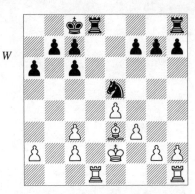

The similarity with the present game is striking, with the same material balance and pawn-structure. In both positions, the fact that White's queenside pawns are weakened is of relatively little importance in itself, since Black's queenside majority can still not create a passed pawn. The only way in which White's broken queenside pawns will matter is if Black is able to get his rook active and attack them, or if he can use the c4-square as an outpost for his knight.

In Lasker-Janowski, White was able to prevent both of these things from happening, and as a result, the position proved to be in White's favour. The game continued 15 ♖d4! (stopping ...♘c4) 15...b6 (15...b5!?) 16 f4 ♘d7 17 ♖hd1 c5 18 ♖4d3, and White had driven Black's pieces back successfully. The knight will not easily reach c4, and Black cannot activate his rooks against White's queenside weaknesses. Meanwhile, White has his usual advantage on the kingside, which he went on to convert into victory as follows: 18...♘b8 19 ♔f3 ♖de8 20 f5 f6 21 g4 ♖e7 22 ♗f4 ♖he8 23 ♖e3 ♘c6 24 g5 ♘a5 25 h4 ♘c4 26 ♖e2 ♖f7 27 ♖g1 ♔d7 28 h5 ♘d6 29 h6 fxg5 30 ♖xg5 g6 31 fxg6 hxg6 32 ♖xg6 ♖ef8 33 ♖g7 ♖xg7 34 hxg7 ♖g8 35 ♖g2 ♘e8 36 ♗e5 ♔e6 37 ♔f4 ♔f7 38 ♔f5 1-0.

Returning to L'Ami-Mamedyarov, we can see the difference. Unlike Lasker, L'Ami is unable to prevent the black knight from reaching c4, after which it is Black who assumes the initiative.

21 ♔f2 b6 22 ♔e1 c5 23 ♖d1 ♘b5

The knight first provokes some disruption in White's position, before taking up his intended post.

24 Xxd8+ Xxd8 25 &d2 &b7 26 Xe3 Qa3 27 &d1 Qc4 28 Xe2 a5 *(D)*

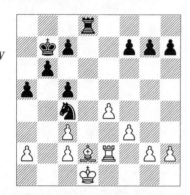

The difference from Lasker-Janowski is very clear. Black's pieces have taken up extremely active posts, and White is nowhere near exploiting his kingside majority. Any attempt to advance his pawns by f4 would just weaken the e4-pawn. Notice how the knight dominates the bishop, despite the fact that the position can hardly be described as being blocked. This is because the knight has an unassailable central outpost, on a light square, which the bishop cannot attack. Once again, the 'colour-blindness' of a single bishop is the key to its inferiority.

29 &c1 &c6 30 &f4 Xe8 31 &d1 b5 32 &c1 Xd8+ 33 &e1 a4

White's position is entirely passive, and he can only wait to see how Black will proceed. Mamedyarov handles the technical phase superbly, strengthening his position steadily, without ever relaxing his grip.

34 &f2 b4 35 cxb4

This move undoubles Black's pawns, so that now he too has a healthy pawn-majority. Unfortunately, White's hand is forced, since he cannot defend c3, and besides, allowing ...bxc3 would give Black the chance to penetrate with his rook along the open b-file.

35...cxb4 36 Xe1 &b5

Now that his queenside majority is straightened out, Black has the simple plan of creating a passed pawn on that side of the board. With his active pieces in support, such a passed pawn will prove far more dangerous than anything White may be able belatedly to create on the kingside.

37 &e2 c5 *(D)*

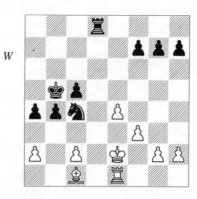

38 Xd1

White has to be able to include his king in the defence on the queenside, so this exchange is forced.

38...Xxd1 39 &xd1 Qa5 40 &b2 g6 41 &e2 Qc6 42 &e3 &c4 43 f4

White finally gets his kingside pawns going, but one can see at a glance how far behind he is in the race. We are now entering the phase of the game where positional build-up, based largely on general considerations, gives way to concrete calculation of variations.

43...f5!

Black continues the overriding theme of this game, which is the exploitation of the bishop's helplessness on the light squares. Now setting up a passed pawn by 44 e5 would be hopeless for White, because Black can blockade the pawn very easily on e6.

44 exf5 gxf5 45 g4!

The best chance. He must create some counterplay before Black's queenside pawns touch down.

45...a3 46 &h8 Qd4 47 gxf5

The pawn ending is hopeless after 47 &xd4 cxd4+ 48 &d2 fxg4; e.g., 49 f5 &d5 50 &d3 &e5 51 f6 &xf6 52 &xd4 &f5 53 &c4 h5 and Black's pawns are much quicker.

47...Qxf5+ 48 &e4 Qd6+! 49 &f3

One of the various tactical points calculated by Black is that White's king cannot come forward to support his passed pawn because of 49 &e5 Qf7+, winning the bishop.

49...&d5 50 &e5 Qf5 *(D)*

This position only serves to illustrate once again the impotence of a lone bishop, when faced with a blockade on squares of the opposite

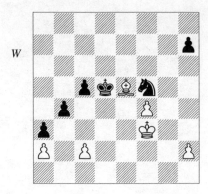

colour from those on which the bishop operates. Even though White has managed to create a passed pawn (something Black has not yet done), he can make nothing of it, because Black's king and knight cooperate to blockade the pawn, and White's king cannot relieve the blockade on its own.

51 &e2 c4?!

Hitherto, Mamedyarov's play has been majestic, but round about here, he commits a couple of inaccuracies, as a result of which the win almost slips away. The text-move does not yet spoil the position, but by weakening the b4-pawn, it does give White slightly more chance of counterplay. As Nunn has pointed out, there is no need to rush with this move, since it cannot be prevented anyhow, so Black would probably have done better to play 51...&e4, followed by the march of the h-pawn.

52 &d2 h5!

Commencing the final stage of the winning plan. White has managed to control the queenside threat, so Black adopts the classic strategy of going for a second weakness. He intends simply to win White's h-pawn.

53 &c1 h4 54 &c7 h3 55 &a5 (D)

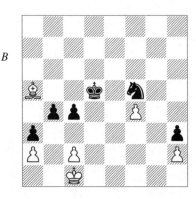

55...&d4?

This further inaccuracy should have destroyed all the fruits of Mamedyarov's previous play. There was a forced win at his point, as follows: 55...&e4! 56 &xb4 &f3 57 &d1 (White's only chance is to bring his king over to stop the h-pawn) 57...&g2 58 &e1. White's idea is to meet 58...&xh2? by 59 &f2, trapping the black king in front of its pawn, but after 58...&d4! White's only hope is to use his passed f-pawn to create counterplay with 59 f5!?. However, Black wins after 59...&xc2+ 60 &d1 (not 60 &d2, when Black can capture the bishop: 60...&xb4 61 f6 c3+! and his knight gets back to stop the f-pawn; e.g., 62 &d1 c2+ 63 &c1 &d3+, followed by 64...&e5) 60...&e3+! (but now not 60...&xb4? 61 f6 and White's pawn queens), and now:

a) 61 &e2 &xf5 62 &xa3 &g3+! 63 &e1 &xh2 64 &f2 &e4+ 65 &e1 &g3 and the h-pawn queens.

b) White can try to save a tempo by 61 &e1, so that after 61...&xf5 62 &xa3, Black does not have 62...&g3+. However, 62...&d4 63 &d6 &f3+ now comes with check, and Black wins by a tempo after 64 &e2 (or 64 &d1, when the same variation results in the h-pawn queening with check) 64...&xh2 65 a4 &f1 66 a5 &g3+ and again the h-pawn queens.

These variations are a good illustration of the fine line which exists between a win and a draw in many endgames. Even after outplaying his opponent so impressively, and building up what looks like an easily winning position, the actual win requires very accurate play and deep calculation, and in the final analysis, Black wins only by the odd tempo.

56 f5?

Missing his first drawing chance. After 56 &xb4! &f3 57 &d1, White appears to be hanging on; for example, 57...&xh2 58 &e2 &g4 59 &f3 &e3 60 &g3 &xc2 61 &d2 and White holds.

The text-move fails because the f-pawn isn't a big enough distraction for Black to justify the time spent on its advance.

56...b3 57 cxb3 cxb3 58 &b1 b2 59 &b4 &xf5?

This switch of targets was intended to be the key to Black's winning plan, but it should not suffice. He could instead have won by 59...&f3!

60 ♗xa3 ♘xh2 61 f6 (otherwise the h-pawn promotes immediately) 61...♔e6 62 f7 ♔xf7 63 ♗d6 ♘f1 64 ♔xb2 (64 a4 ♘d2+ and 64 ♗c7 ♔e6 65 a4 ♘d2+ 66 ♔xb2 ♘c4+ 67 ♔c3 ♘d6 are also hopeless for White) 64...♔e6 65 ♗c7 ♔f5 66 a4 ♔g4 67 a5 ♘g3.

60 ♗xa3 ♘d4 61 ♗xb2?

The decisive mistake, after which the ending is again lost for White. The b-pawn is not going anywhere, and capturing it just represents the loss of a tempo. White can draw by getting his bishop on the h2-b8 diagonal to stop the black h-pawn: 61 ♗b4! ♘f3 62 ♗a5! ♘xh2 63 ♗c7 ♘g4 (threatening 64...♘e5, shutting out the bishop) 64 ♗g3! ♔e4 65 a4! (starting counterplay) 65...♔f3 66 ♗b8 ♔e4 67 ♗g3, and Black can make no progress.

61...♘f3 62 ♗c1 ♔e4! *(D)*

Preventing the bishop from getting to f4, to stop the black h-pawn.

63 ♗a3

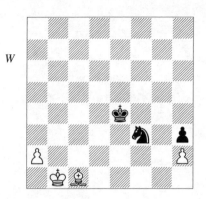

Another line Mamedyarov had to see was 63 a4 ♘xh2 64 a5 ♘f3 65 a6 ♘d2+!!, when after 66 ♗xd2 h2, the black pawn queens with check, whilst if the knight is declined by, e.g., 66 ♔c2, then after 66...♘c4 the knight reaches b6, stopping the a-pawn.

63...♘xh2 64 ♗d6 ♘f1 0-1

There is no defence to 65...♔f3 and 66...♘g3, when the h-pawn queens.

Game 46
Vladimir Kramnik – Peter Leko
Dortmund 2006
Nimzo-Indian Defence, Classical Variation

In this game, we see a typical example of a two-bishops ending. White enjoys the slight advantage of the bishop-pair in a position with a symmetrical pawn-structure. Despite Black's tenacious defence, White retains an edge, and a final error from Black, late in the endgame, seals his fate.

1 d4 ♘f6 2 c4 e6 3 ♘c3 ♗b4
This move characterizes the Nimzo-Indian Defence, one of Black's most reputable defences to 1 d4. By pinning the enemy knight on c3, Black begins a fight for control of the e4-square. A fundamental part of his strategy is to be prepared to exchange his bishop for the knight, thereby conceding the bishop-pair. If White has to recapture with the pawn, his queenside pawns will be doubled and will often provide a source of counterplay for Black. In this game, Kramnik chooses with his next move to protect the knight with his queen, thereby ensuring he can meet a subsequent ...♗xc3+ with ♕xc3, keeping his pawns intact. The drawback to this is that he loses some time, and Black's counter-chances are based around exploiting his superior development.

4 ♕c2 0-0
Black has several other options here, such as 4...c5, 4...d5 and 4...♘c6. Nonetheless, the text-move is currently the most popular choice.

5 a3 ♗xc3+ 6 ♕xc3 b6 7 ♗g5 *(D)*

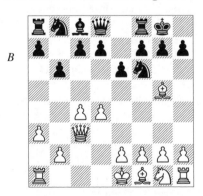

Black has continued to develop rapidly. White's last move is his most ambitious plan in this position. He intends to follow up with f3 and later e4, using his central pawns to take control of the central squares (notably e4), and also to blunt the effect of Black's bishop on the long diagonal. The drawback to the plan is the same as that in many 4 ♕c2 lines, namely that White is making a lot of moves with his queen and his pawns, and neglecting the development of the remainder of his pieces. If he can maintain his strong centre and catch up in development, he will usually have a clear advantage, so Black needs to take some energetic action to disrupt White's smooth build-up.

7...♗b7 8 f3 h6 9 ♗h4 d5
Black stops the move e4, and stakes his own claim in the centre.

10 e3 ♘bd7 11 cxd5 ♘xd5
This initiates a forcing sequence, whereby Black simplifies the position, but allows an endgame where White's bishop-pair gives him a small but clear edge. The alternative is to recapture 11...exd5, but experience has shown that this tends to give White the advantage in the middlegame, thanks to his bishops and strong pawn-centre. Most strong players agree that the endgame is a preferable choice for Black, although as this game shows, such a position can be rather thankless to defend.

12 ♗xd8 ♘xc3 13 ♗h4
White's only hope of an advantage is to keep his two bishops, so he would have nothing after 13 bxc3 ♖fxd8. Similarly, 13 ♗xc7 would also bring few dividends, since after 13...♘d5, the only way to keep the pawn is 14 ♗f4. Then after 14...♘xf4 15 exf4 ♖ac8, White has an extra pawn, but it is doubled, and his weakness on d4, combined with his inferior development, means that he cannot count on any advantage.

13...♘d5 14 ♗f2 c5 15 e4 ♘e7 16 ♘e2 ♖ac8 17 ♘c3 cxd4 18 ♗xd4 ♘c5 *(D)*
This is a typical position for this variation, and in many ways, for the Nimzo-Indian as a

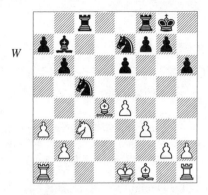

whole. White has retained the advantage of the bishop-pair, and managed to keep his pawn-structure intact. However, Black has completed his development, simplified the position, and himself has no weaknesses. Black is close to equality, but White can still count on a small edge. The question is whether he can increase it to more meaningful proportions. With accurate defence, Black should be able to draw, but this game shows that it does not take too many inaccuracies on his part for things to become serious.

19 ♖d1 ♖fd8

An important aspect of such positions is that in general, two bishops vs bishop and knight is a greater advantage than one bishop vs one knight. The reason is that even on an open board, a bishop has one significant weakness – it can only operate on squares of one colour. Consequently, as seen in the previous game, a knight can sometimes outplay a bishop, if the key points and weaknesses are on squares of the opposite colour to that on which the bishop operates. Two bishops, on the other hand, can between them control every square on the board, which means that they are usually stronger than the bishop and knight combination. Effectively, the whole is more than the sum of the parts.

It follows from the above that one of the main defensive techniques for the defender, if he has bishop and knight versus two bishops, is to exchange off his remaining bishop for its opposite number. Thus, in the present position, Black would like to play the move ...♗a6 at some point, and this idea is an important part of the subtext of what is going on in the position over the next few moves. At present, 19...♗a6? is tactically impossible, because of 20 ♗xc5, winning a piece.

20 ♗e3 ♖xd1+ 21 ♔xd1 e5

This move starts an important defensive idea for Black. When knights oppose bishops in a fairly open position, the knights are usually inferior, unless they can find a secure outpost in the centre, from which they cannot be easily dislodged. If they can do so, knights can often be at least as good as bishops, even in open positions. Leko's last move aims to secure the d4-square for his knights. Note that 21...♗a6 still fails to 22 ♗xc5.

22 b4 ♘e6 23 ♔c2 ♘c6 24 ♔b2 ♔f8 25 ♗c4 ♘cd4 *(D)*

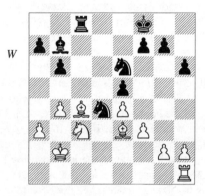

26 ♗xe6!

After reading the note to Black's 19th move, you may be confused as to why Kramnik played this exchange. Doesn't it contradict what I wrote above? Well, yes and no. The truth is that White would prefer not to make this exchange, but Black's excellent play over the last few moves leaves him with little choice. The bishop is under attack, and has no convenient retreat. If 26 ♗a2, Black can activate his bishop by 26...♗a6, whilst 26 ♗d3 is met by 26...♘f4 (this last line illustrates why Black carefully delayed his decision about which knight to put on d4, until he saw where White was going to place his king's bishop). Kramnik therefore decided that he had nothing better than to exchange on e6. Although his two-bishop advantage is then gone, he still has the chance to attack Black's queenside pawns, using his remaining bishop on e3 as part of the assault force.

This is a typical example of the transformation of an advantage. Instead of clinging on for dear life to a certain positional advantage, it often pays to transform it into an advantage of a different kind.

26...♘xe6 27 ♘b5

The point. Now Black's rook is forced into a passive position, since 27...a6? 28 ♘d6 would lose the b6-pawn.

27...♖a8 28 a4! ♗a6 29 ♘a3 *(D)*

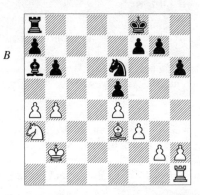

Now White is ready to drive the bishop back by 30 b5, also fixing the a7- and b6-pawns on dark squares, where they are vulnerable to attack from White's bishop.

29...♖c8?

Black fails to meet the threat. After the game, both players agreed that Black should keep his bishop active by 29...♗d3. This looks risky, but after 30 ♖d1 ♖d8 31 ♔c3 ♗e2 32 ♖xd8+ ♘xd8 Black should be able to draw, although he is still not out of the woods.

30 b5 ♗b7 31 ♖c1!

In opposite-coloured bishop endings, the stronger side usually wishes to avoid exchanges, since the presence of other pieces tends to give better winning chances. Here, however, is an exception. The black rook is the only piece which can defend the a7-pawn, so it is in White's interest to exchange it off. Once it is gone, White can force a passed pawn on the queenside by playing a5.

31...♖xc1 32 ♔xc1 ♔e7 33 a5 bxa5 34 ♗xa7

Now White has a passed pawn on b5, and if Black plays passively, White will bring up his king and eventually win the a5-pawn. Leko therefore, quite correctly, goes for counterplay on the kingside, by means of a temporary pawn sacrifice.

34...f5! 35 exf5 ♘f4 36 g3 ♘h3

It looks odd to put the knight offside like this, but it is probably the best chance. After the more obvious 36...♘e2+ 37 ♔d2 ♘d4 38 ♗xd4 exd4 39 b6, White should be winning; e.g., 39...♗xf3

40 ♘b5 ♔f6 41 ♘xd4 ♗d5 42 ♔c3 ♔e5 43 g4, and his knight can stop the black a-pawn after 43...a4 44 ♘b5.

37 ♘c4 ♘g5 38 ♘xa5 *(D)*

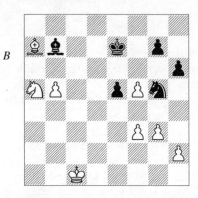

38...♗d5?

Black's last chance was 38...♗xf3. After the forced line 39 b6 ♔f6 40 ♔d2 ♗xf5 41 ♔e3 ♗a8 42 b7 ♗xb7 43 ♘xb7 ♔g4, Kramnik considered that Black has just enough counterplay to draw.

39 b6 ♘xf3 40 h3!

A nice final subtlety. Now 40...♘g1 loses to 41 b7 ♗xb7 42 ♗xg1.

40...♘g5 41 b7 ♗xb7 42 ♘xb7 ♘xh3 43 ♗b6 ♔d7?!

Tougher resistance could have been offered by 43...♔f6, but White is still winning. Although the variation is quite long, it is easy to understand. Black aims to win the g3-pawn with his king, and White, meanwhile, wins g7 with his bishop: 44 ♘d6 ♔g5 45 ♗d8+ ♔g4 46 ♗e7 ♔xg3 47 ♗f8 h5 48 ♗xg7 ♘g5 49 ♗xe5+ ♔g2 50 f6 h4. Now White uses the combined force of ♗+♘ to stop Black's passed h-pawn: 51 ♘f5 h3 52 ♘h4+ ♔f2 53 ♗f4 ♘f7. Now the h-pawn can go no further, since if Black plays ...♔g1 and ...h2, the pawn is lost after ♘f3+. White therefore continues 54 ♔d2, and marches his king up the board, to queen his f-pawn.

After the text-move, which loses an important tempo, White wins much more easily.

44 ♗e3 ♔e7 45 ♘c5 g6 46 fxg6 ♔f6 47 ♗xh6 ♔xg6 48 ♗e3 1-0

After 48...♔f5 49 ♔d2 ♔g4 50 ♘e4 ♔f5 51 ♔d3, White retains his last pawn and the black knight remains trapped on the edge of the board.

Game 47
Rune Djurhuus – Gabriel Sargissian
Turin Olympiad 2006
Ruy Lopez (Spanish), Berlin Defence

A cardinal principle of rook and pawn endings is to use one's rook as actively as possible. There is probably no other type of endgame where the difference in piece activity can make such a difference to the position. In this example, Black reaches a rook endgame with equal material, but the more active rook. This apparently small advantage proves enough for victory, without a clearly decisive error on White's part.

1 e4 e5 2 ♘f3 ♘c6 3 ♗b5 ♘f6 4 d3 *(D)*

This quiet continuation was a great favourite of Steinitz, the first official world champion. Nowadays, it is not considered to offer White any real advantage, and is mainly employed to avoid the so-called Berlin Wall endgame, which arises after 4 0-0 ♘xe4 5 d4 ♘d6 6 ♗xc6 dxc6 7 dxe5 ♘f5 8 ♕xd8+ ♔xd8 (see Game 31).

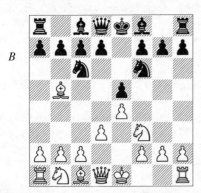

4...♗c5

An active deployment of the bishop. The older continuation 4...d6, followed by 5...g6, is also fine for Black. Putting the bishop on c5 in the Lopez usually runs into a later c3 and d4 by White, but with his pawn already committed to d3, this would involve the loss of a tempo, and is therefore less dangerous than usual.

5 0-0

5 c3 prevents Black's next move, and is perhaps a better try for the initiative.

5...♘d4 6 ♘xd4 ♗xd4 7 c3 ♗b6 8 ♘d2

That Black already has a very comfortable game is borne out by the fact that 8 d4 c6 9 ♗a4 d6 would leave him a whole tempo up on a line usually reached after 3...♗c5 4 0-0 ♘d4 5 ♘xd4 ♗xd4 6 c3 ♗b6 7 d4 c6 8 ♗a4 d6. The

latter variation is considered to give Black equal chances, and here Black would have the extra move ...♘f6.

8...c6 9 ♗a4 d6 10 h3 0-0 11 ♖e1 h6 12 ♘f3 *(D)*

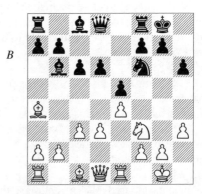

12...♘h5!

A typical move in such positions, especially when White has already played the move h3. Black intends ...♕f6 and ...♘f4, which White cannot stop by playing g3, since the h3-pawn would be hanging (in this position, so too would the g3-pawn). White also gains nothing from the tactic 13 ♘xe5?, which is refuted by 13...♕h4.

13 d4 ♕f6 14 ♘xe5

White understands that he has achieved nothing from the opening, and is in danger of ceding the initiative to Black, so he seeks refuge in simplification. In so far as White's ambitions in this game ever extended beyond half a point, it is clear that they do not do so from this point on.

14...dxe5 15 ♕xh5 exd4 16 e5

This is forced, since Black was threatening 16...dxc3, attacking f3, whilst 16 cxd4? would lose to 16...♕xd4, hitting both a4 and f2.

16...♕f5 17 ♕xf5 ♗xf5 18 ♗d2 ♖ad8 19 ♗b3 ♗e6 *(D)*

An interesting move. The bishop looks active on f5, but Sargissian decides that White's bishop on b3 is his most active piece, and therefore decides to exchange it off. Black could instead establish what looks like a dangerous advanced passed pawn with 19...d3, but in fact, the pawn would be securely blockaded and would not be at all easy to utilize effectively.

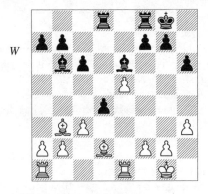

20 ♖ad1 ♖d7 21 ♗xe6

White's position is rather uncomfortable, and he seeks relief in exchanges, which proves a mistaken policy. 21 ♔f1 is probably better, although White still has problems to solve after 21...♖fd8.

21...fxe6 22 cxd4 ♗xd4 23 ♗e3 ♖fd8 24 ♗xd4 ♖xd4 25 ♖xd4 ♖xd4 *(D)*

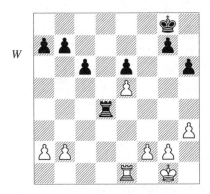

Although this position may look fairly level to the uninitiated, Black actually has a clear advantage. In the first place, his rook is much more active and controls the only open file. Secondly, he has a queenside pawn-majority, which can advance much more readily than White's majority on the other flank. And thirdly, the e5-pawn

is weak, and a potential target. Even so, it is hard to believe that White's position is already lost, but Sargissian wins in convincing style, without any obvious error from White.

26 ♖e2

White must prevent 26...♖d2.

26...♔f7 27 g4

This is also necessary, since otherwise, the black king will come to g6 and f5, attacking the e5-pawn. However, now the white pawn on h3 is weakened and is another potential target. In addition, when White later supports his e-pawn by playing f4, he must always reckon with the possibility of the pawn-chain being undermined by the counter-blow ...g5, since he can no longer defend f4 by playing g3. "Pawns don't move backwards!", as a wise man once pointed out.

27...c5 28 ♖e3?

In view of the variations given in the note to White's 30th move, this transfer of the rook to the third rank must be seen as a loss of time, probably White's only detectable error in this endgame. He should activate his king immediately by 28 ♔g2 and 29 ♔f3, although it is still not clear if this would be enough to draw.

28...a5! 29 ♖c3 b6 *(D)*

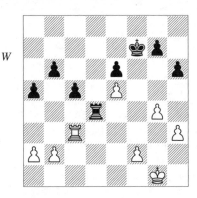

30 ♔f1!?

When playing his 28th move, Black had to take into account the obvious counter-attack 30 ♖b3. This would have to be answered by 30...♖b4!, when all depends on the pawn ending after 31 ♖xb4 axb4. Now White loses after 32 f4 g5! 33 f5 (or 33 fxg5 hxg5 and Black will bring his king round via c6 and d5, to win the e5-pawn) 33...exf5 34 gxf5 c4 35 ♔f2 h5, when his king cannot stop both of Black's passed pawns. 32 ♔g2 is a tougher defence, but Black is winning after 32...g5 33 ♔f3 c4 34 ♔e3 b5, followed by the transfer of Black's king to d5 via d7 and c6.

This is a good example of the importance of understanding pawn endings, and being able to calculate such endings deeply. In order to play the move 28...a5, Black had to see at least the variations given above, and understand that he can win the pawn ending. This is despite the fact that the game never actually reaches a pawn ending – as so often in chess, the threat proves stronger than its execution!

30...a4!

Now the counterattack by ♖b3 is ruled out.

31 a3 *(D)*

Once again, the pawn ending reached after 31 ♔e2 ♖e4+ 32 ♖e3 ♖xe3+ 33 ♔xe3 g5 appears lost for White.

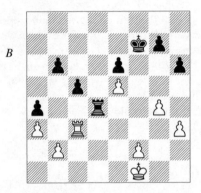

31...c4!

Do not hurry! It looks as though 31...♖e4 wins a pawn or forces a winning pawn ending after 32 ♖e3, but instead White can create counterplay by 32 b3!. After the text-move, the latter possibility is ruled out forever.

32 ♔e2 b5

Note that after Black's last move, the pawn ending after 32...♖e4+ 33 ♖e3 ♖xe3+?? 34 ♔xe3 would actually be winning for White, since Black's queenside pawns are crippled and will fall to the white king. Instead, Sargissian is playing for zugzwang in the rook ending.

33 ♔e3 ♖d5 34 f4 *(D)*

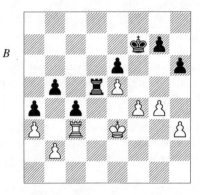

34...g5!

See the note to move 27. Now the white pawn on e5 is undermined. White is in zugzwang, since 35 ♔e4 loses to 35...♖d2.

35 ♖c2 ♖d3+ 36 ♔e4 ♖xh3

The h3-pawn, weakened by 27 g4, has duly dropped off.

37 f5 ♖g3

Now Black wins a second pawn, after which the remainder is fairly simple.

38 f6 ♖xg4+ 39 ♔e3 ♖g3+ 40 ♔e4 ♖d3 41 ♖h2 ♔g6 42 f7 ♔xf7 43 ♖xh6 g4 44 ♖h7+ ♔f8 45 ♖h6 g3 46 ♖xe6 g2 47 ♖g6 ♖d2 48 e6 *(D)*

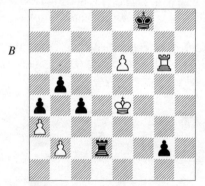

48...b4!

48...♖xb2 would also win, but Sargissian remembers one of the golden rules – do not forget tactics!

49 axb4 c3 50 bxc3 a3 0-1

White cannot stop both passed pawns.

Game 48
David Bronstein – Hugh Alexander
Hastings 1953/4
Dutch Defence, Staunton Gambit

Queen endings are amongst the most difficult endings to play in practice. The enormous power of the queen, and its scope for endless checks, means that even realizing a substantial material advantage can often be impossible. In the present game, one of the most famous in English chess history, Black succeeds in converting a two-pawn advantage into victory, but only after some 120 moves! The technical difficulties he faced, and the methodical way in which he overcame them, makes the ending highly instructive.

1 d4 f5 2 e4

This move, the Staunton Gambit, was regarded for many years as one of the most dangerous ways for White to counter the Dutch Defence, and many Dutch players preferred to adopt the move-order 1...e6 to avoid it (of course, in that case, Black must be ready to play the French Defence if White switches to 2 e4). Nowadays, fairly reliable responses have been worked out for Black against the Staunton, and moves such as 2 ♗g5 and 2 ♘c3 are considered more potent, if White is seeking an alternative to the main lines with c4 and g3.

2...fxe4 3 ♘c3 ♘f6 4 f3 exf3?!

But this acceptance of the pawn is really rather dangerous for Black. Modern theory recommends 4...d5.

5 ♘xf3 g6 6 ♗f4 ♗g7 7 ♕d2 0-0 *(D)*

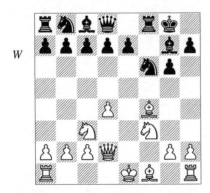

W

8 ♗h6

Very direct, but 8 ♗d3 may have been stronger, when a subsequent h4 will be hard to meet.

8...d5

Creating a nasty backward pawn and holes on the e-file, but Black needs to establish some

foothold in the centre, so as to develop his pieces. If he does not, he is liable to be slaughtered in his bed.

9 ♗xg7 ♔xg7 10 0-0-0?!

10 ♗d3 looks more natural, to discourage Black's next.

10...♗f5 11 ♗d3 ♗xd3 12 ♕xd3 ♘c6 *(D)*

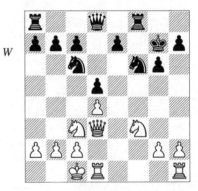

W

White has not played the opening very well, and although he has some compensation for the pawn, in the shape of pressure down the e-file, it is not clear that it is quite enough. The next stage of the battle centres around Black's attempts to free himself of his backward pawn by playing ...e5, and White's attempts to prevent this.

13 ♖de1 ♕d6 14 ♔b1 a6 15 ♖e2 ♖ae8 16 ♖he1 e6

It is already becoming clear that White will not be able to stop the advance ...e5 for much longer, as Black can prepare the move further with ...♘d7 and ...♖f5. Indeed, it is hard to find a constructive move for White, but his next move certainly does not help, and just donates two tempi to Black's cause. In view of what later happens, a move such as 17 h3 or 17 a3 would be slightly better. The first ensures that the pawn will not hang on h2 after the subsequent multiple exchanges on e5, whilst the second makes *luft* for the king and avoids later back-rank problems.

17 ♘e5?! ♘d7 18 ♘f3?

Having said A, White should say B as well, and at least exchange knights on d7.

18...♖f5 *(D)*

Black's play is admirably consistent. He now has every piece except his king controlling the e5-square, and can no longer be prevented from bursting his bonds with ...e5.

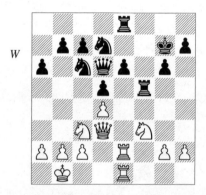

19 ♖e3 e5 20 dxe5 ♘dxe5 21 ♘xe5 ♖fxe5 22 ♖xe5 ♖xe5 23 ♖xe5 ♕xe5 24 ♕xd5 ♕xh2

See the note before move 17. If White had played 17 h3, Black's last move would not have been possible, and his ...e5 break would have required even further preparation.

25 ♕d7+ ♔h6 26 a3 ♕d6!

This is better than 26...♕xg2? 27 ♕xc7, when Black has problems defending his queenside pawns (note that the attempted counterattack against c2 with 27...♘d4?? loses a piece to 28 ♕f4+).

27 ♕c8 ♘d8 28 g4!? ♔g7 29 b3 c6 30 g5 *(D)*

This march of the g-pawn is a controversial decision by White. Placing the pawn on g5 certainly ties Black down for some time to come, and makes it hard for him to use his kingside pawn-majority in the near future. On the other hand, the further the g-pawn is from its base, the harder it is to defend, and Black eventually succeeds in winning the pawn. Passive defence at move 28 may objectively have been better, but it is always difficult psychologically to adopt such tactics.

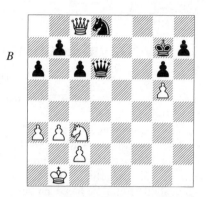

30...♕e7 31 ♕g4 ♘f7 32 ♘e4 ♕xa3

Black has won another pawn, but White has greatly activated his pieces, and Bronstein evidently felt that this offered better drawing chances than purely passive, waiting tactics.

33 ♕e6 ♕a5 34 ♘d6 ♘xd6!?

Black could snatch the g-pawn by 34...♘xg5, when White does not appear to have anything better than taking the b7-pawn in return. The resulting position should be winning for Black, but queen and knight are a potent attacking combination, and White would have many tactical resources. Instead, Alexander prefers to enter a pure queen ending, confident that he can gradually unravel his temporarily passive position, and eventually make his two-pawn advantage tell.

35 ♕f6+ ♔g8 36 ♕xd6 *(D)*

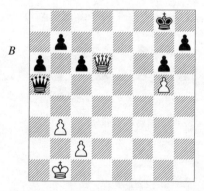

Thus we reach a pure queen ending, with Black having two extra pawns. With such a material advantage, one would expect the ending to be winning easily, but in fact, Black has a number of technical difficulties to overcome. In queen endings, material is often a less decisive factor than in some other types of ending. Instead, the two most important things are passed pawns and king protection. The powers of a queen often enable her to shepherd home a passed pawn unaided, in contrast to other pieces, such as rooks, which usually need the help of their king. Similarly, the queen's great mobility means that it can often give perpetual check to an exposed enemy king.

In the present case, Black has two extra pawns, but he does not have a passed pawn, nor is his king well protected. His task is therefore to improve his position gradually, and work towards the creation of a passed pawn. At every step of the way, he needs to take care to protect his king against perpetual check, and also to prevent White from establishing a passed pawn of his own on the queenside, which would provide him with counterplay.

36...♕e1+

36...♕xg5 would allow White to regain a pawn by 37 ♕b8+, followed by 38 ♕xb7+ and 39 ♕xc6. Admittedly, Black then has two connected passed pawns on the kingside, but there is no need to allow White any counterplay. The first step of Black's plan is to secure his queenside pawns against the white queen.

37 ♔a2 ♕e8

The next step in Black's plan is to transfer his king to a more secure position on the queenside, where it is less exposed to checks.

38 ♕c7 b5 39 ♔b1 ♕e1+ 40 ♔b2 ♕e6 41 b4!? *(D)*

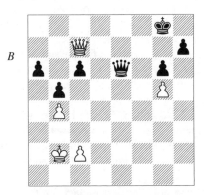

With this move, White hopes to hold up the advance of the enemy queenside pawn-majority, and fix the pawns on a6 and c6 as possible weaknesses. However, the move also exposes White's b-pawn to attack, which Alexander immediately exploits.

41...♕e4 42 ♕d8+ ♔f7 43 ♕f6+ ♔e8

The king sets off towards the queenside. White's next move attempts to prevent this, but Black evicts the enemy queen immediately. Instead, taking the h-pawn would result in Black establishing a passed pawn on the g-file after 44 ♕h8+ ♔d7 45 ♕xh7+ ♔d6 46 c3 (else the b-pawn drops) 46...♕g2+ and 47...♕xg5.

44 ♕d6 ♕d5 45 ♕f6 ♔d7 46 ♕g7+ ♔d6 47 ♕f6+

As before, there is no sense in White trading the g5-pawn for the h7-pawn, which would just give Black a passed pawn.

47...♔c7 48 ♕g7+ ♕d7 49 ♕e5+ ♕d6 50 ♕g7+ ♔b6 *(D)*

Black has achieved Stage 1 of his plan, and his king is now relatively safe from checks. Stage 2 is to achieve the advance ...a5 or ...c5, to get his queenside pawns moving.

51 ♕c3 ♕e7

The immediate 51...c5 52 ♕f6 is a little awkward.

52 ♕d4+ ♔b7 53 c3 ♕f7 54 ♕h8 ♔b6 55 ♕d4+ ♔b7 56 ♕h8 ♕d7 57 ♔a3 ♕e7 58 ♕f6 ♕c7 59 ♔b2 *(D)*

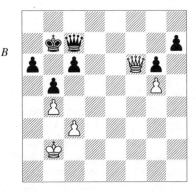

59...a5!

Mission accomplished. Now Stage 3 involves eliminating the white pawn on g5, so as to set up a passed pawn on the g-file. This is a relatively long process, since in order to do so, Black needs to return his king to f5, whilst at the same time defending his c6-pawn and preventing perpetual check. This is a typical scenario in queen and pawn endings. It is frequently impossible to win such endings without using one's king actively, even though this involves bringing it out of its shelter and exposing it to numerous checks from the enemy queen. The key technique is to place Black's queen in as powerful a central post as possible, after which it will usually be possible to bring out the king and find a way to avoid the checks.

60 bxa5 ♛xa5 61 ♛e6 ♛c7 62 ♔b3 ♛f4 63 ♛d7+ ♔b6 64 ♛d8+ ♔c5 65 ♛e7+ ♔b6

Note how throughout this ending, Black uses repetitions. As discussed in *50ECL*, this is a typical facet of endgame play. The repetitions gain time on the clock, as well as putting greater psychological pressure on the opponent, by emphasizing that it is Black who is master of the position. It never hurts to show the opponent who's boss!

66 ♛d8+ ♔c5 67 ♛e7+ ♔d5 68 ♛d7+ ♛d6 69 ♛g4 ♛c5 70 ♛d7+ ♔e5 71 ♛xh7 ♔f5 *(D)*

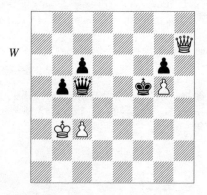

72 ♛d7+

White cannot hold the g-pawn by 72 ♛h4, because of 72...♛d5+ followed by 73...♛g2. Note, however, that Black cannot instead enter the pawn ending by 72...♛c4+??, since after 73 ♛xc4 bxc4+ 74 ♔xc4 ♔xg5 75 ♔c5, White will reach a theoretically drawn ending of king plus c-pawn on the 7th rank, versus king and queen. As ever, the transition into a pawn ending requires accurate calculation.

72...♔xg5

Stage 3 is thus completed. Black now has his passed pawn, and can move onto the fourth and final stage – advancing the pawn to queen. As always, he has to combine this with defending his king from the enemy checks, but judicious use of his queen on the central squares, plus threats of crosschecks (answering a check with a check, forcing off the queens) does the trick. Black needs only to remember the golden rule of almost all endings – do not hurry!

73 ♛d2+ ♔f6 74 ♛d8+ ♔f7 75 ♛c7+ ♔e7 76 ♛f4+ ♔g7 77 ♛d4+ ♛f6

Here we already see an example of a crosscheck – now White cannot play 78 ♛d7+ or 78 ♛a7+ because of 78...♛f7+, forcing the queens off. This technique is integral to queen endings.

78 ♛e4 ♔f7 *(D)*

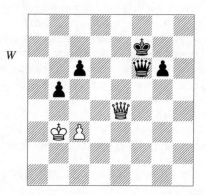

Black's plan is to return his king to the queenside, where the two black pawns provide better protection from checks. As noted earlier, the queen can force home the passed pawn by itself, and does not need its own king's assistance, unlike the situation in most other endings.

79 ♔b2 ♛d6 80 ♛f3+ ♛f6 81 ♛e4 g5

Whenever White has no particular threats, Black takes the chance to push his passed pawn.

82 ♛h7+ ♔e6 83 ♛e4+ ♔d6 84 ♛d3+ ♔c7 85 ♛h7+ ♔b6

The black king thereby completes yet another journey. It has so far gone from the kingside to the queenside, then out over to the kingside to win the g-pawn, and now back to safety on the queenside again. Such 'Long Marches' are characteristic of queen endings. Indeed, I cannot help suspecting that Mao Tse-Tung would have been quite a good player of such endings!

86 ♔c2 ♕f4 87 ♕e7 ♕f2+ 88 ♔b3 ♕d2 89 ♕e8 ♕d5+ 90 ♔b2 ♕d6 *(D)*

W

Black continually re-positions his queen, so as to prevent checks, and awaits the moment when the g-pawn can advance further.

91 ♕e3+ ♔c5 92 ♕e8 ♕f2+ 93 ♔b3 ♕f6 94 ♕d7

Or 94 ♕b8+ ♔c5 95 ♕a7+ ♔d6! 96 ♕b8+ ♔d5 and the checks run out.

94...♔c5 95 ♔c2 ♕e5!

This typical centralizing move is an essential part of technique in these endings. Black improves his queen's influence, and now prepares to put the queen on e4, to support the g-pawn's advance.

96 ♕d8 ♕e4+ 97 ♔b2 g4 98 ♕d7 ♔c4 99 ♕d1 ♕g2+ 100 ♔a1 c5 *(D)*

100...♔xc3 is simpler.

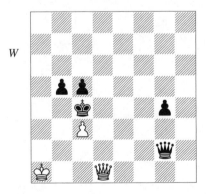

W

101 ♕c2!

A stalemate trick, typical of queen endings. Fortunately, Black need not take the queen.

101...♕f1+ 102 ♔b2 ♕d5 103 ♕d2+ ♔e4 104 ♕g5 ♕f5 105 ♕h4 ♔f3 106 ♕h1+ ♔e2 107 ♕g2+ ♔e1! *(D)*

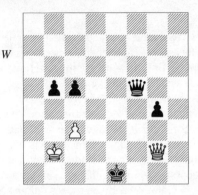

W

Note how the black king has penetrated into the very heart of White's position. This again is typical of queen endings. By placing his king on the same (or the adjacent) rank as the enemy king, Black sets up crosschecks. Thus, now 108 ♕g1+ is met by 108...♕f1, when capturing either pawn allows Black to force off the queens, with a winning pawn ending. The end is close.

108 c4 b4 109 ♕g1+ ♔e2!

Once again, care is needed. Now White would draw the pawn ending after 109...♕f1 110 ♕xc5 ♕f2+? 111 ♕xf2+ ♔xf2 112 c5.

110 ♕g2+ ♔e3 111 ♔b3 ♕d3+ 112 ♔a4 ♕xc4 113 ♕g3+ ♔d2 114 ♕f2+ ♔c3 115 ♕e3+ ♔b2

Once again, Black uses the technique of placing his king as close as possible to its opposite number.

116 ♕e5+ ♕c3 117 ♕g5 g3 118 ♕g4 g2 119 ♕g5 ♕c1 120 ♕xc5 ♕c2+

Avoiding White's last trap – 120...♕xc5?? is stalemate.

0-1

A monumental struggle, which reflects great credit on both players, as well as providing a great example of the essential techniques of queen and pawn endings.

7 Psychology in Action

Our final two games both deal with the subject of playing for a certain result. Very often in chess, a player faces a situation where he needs a win or a draw in one particular game, for example to win a tournament, or fulfil a title norm, etc. How should one best approach such games? Should one alter one's usual style of play, or openings, in a bid to improve one's chances of the desired result? The two games examined here involve one successful effort and one failure.

The main lessons to be learned from these two examples is to try to play the game 'normally', i.e. forget the particular circumstances, and try to play as if it were just another game. Of course, this is far easier said than done, but it is important to try. This is especially the case where a player needs only a draw. The temptation to play directly for the draw, eschewing complications, seeking every opportunity to simplify, etc., is very strong in such cases. However, the manner of Gurevich's demise in Game 49 is by no means unique, and many games have been lost as a result of a player mistakenly adopting such an approach. The best way to make a draw is to get a winning, or at least favourable position, and then offer a draw from a position of strength.

Game 49
Mikhail Gurevich – Nigel Short
Manila Interzonal 1990
French Defence, Exchange Variation

The most important thing about this game is the circumstances in which it was played. It was in the final round of the interzonal, which was played as a Swiss tournament. At the start of the game, Gurevich was half a point ahead of Short, and needed only a draw to ensure qualification for the Candidates matches. Short, on the other hand, needed to win to reach the Candidates. The game provides a classic illustration of the psychological pluses and minuses of such a situation, with Short getting things right, whilst Gurevich commits the fatal psychological error of playing solely for a draw.

1 d4 e6 2 e4?!

Already one of the decisive moments of the game. Mikhail Gurevich is, and always has been, one of the most erudite opening theoreticians in the world, and has made many valuable contributions to opening theory (see Game 9 for a perfect example). He is also a player who has always had a relatively narrow, but extremely well worked-out opening repertoire, from which he rarely departs. He is very much a 1 d4 player, occasionally varying with 1 c4, but had never, to my knowledge, opened 1 e4. Yet here, playing possibly the most important game of his life, he transposes into the French Defence as White.

The reason was the psychological situation described above. Gurevich needed only a draw in this game, whereas only a win would do for Short. Seeing Short's first move, Gurevich doubtless suspected that his opponent was intending to meet 2 c4 with 2...f5, the aggressive Dutch Defence. Most grandmasters, Gurevich included, would usually be happy to play the white side of the Dutch, which is not generally regarded as entirely sound from a positional viewpoint. However, given that he needed only a draw from this game, Gurevich was obviously trying to avoid any kind of sharp fight, even if it may objectively be in his favour. Instead, it occurred to him that after 2 e4, Black would no doubt play 2...d5, and then White could adopt the notoriously drawish Exchange Variation. Rather than saying "Get thee behind me, Satan!", he fell into the psychological trap.

2...d5(!)

Unlike his opponent, Short does not allow the desire for a certain result to put him off playing what is objectively the best move. After

2 e4, he must have realized that Gurevich intended to exchange pawns on d5, and some players in Short's situation might have been tempted to try to avoid this drawish line, by 2...c5. This move is unusual, but also not terribly good. After 3 d5, White simply stands better. Instead, Short decides to play the best move, 2...d5, and play the resulting equal position. After all, as a Russian IM once sagely pointed out to me, it is easier to beat somebody from an equal position that one is familiar with, than from an inferior position that one knows nothing about!

3 exd5 exd5 *(D)*

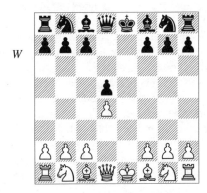

So here we have it, the Exchange Variation. The symmetrical pawn-formation, with only one open file, frequently presages a symmetrical build-up and multiple exchanges, just what Gurevich wanted. However, as many a grandmaster from Alekhine onwards has demonstrated, if Black is determined to fight for the full point, he can do so. Objectively, of course, the position is just equal, but equal is not the same as drawn. Most important of all, though,

naa26vigation">168   50 WAYS TO WIN AT CHESS26

is the psychological situation. By showing his hand so openly, White is already giving up the initiative psychologically, and many games have shown that it is very difficult to play one's best in such situations. This proves to be the case here too.

4 ♘f3 ♗g4

Short immediately breaks the symmetry, rather than copying White's set-up with 4...♘f6. Another, slightly more popular, way to do so is 4...♗d6.

5 h3 ♗h5 6 ♗e2

Garry Kasparov later showed that 6 ♕e2+! causes Black some slight inconvenience here, but Gurevich is not really thinking about making life difficult for Black – all he is concerned with is making a draw.

6...♗d6 7 ♘e5?!

Another move symptomatic of Gurevich's mood. He hurries to force more exchanges, but will soon find that he even stands slightly worse in the resulting position.

7...♗xe2 8 ♕xe2 ♘e7 9 0-0 0-0 10 ♗f4 ♖e8 11 ♕g4

The vis-à-vis of rook and queen on the e-file was dangerous, so Gurevich surrenders another tempo.

11...♗xe5!

A good exchange. As pointed out in the context of Game 45, a knight can often be stronger than a bishop, even in a position which is relatively open. A single bishop can only control squares of one colour, and so a knight, which can attack squares of both colours, can often outplay a lone bishop. In this position, the exchange of light-squared bishops, which Gurevich mistakenly forced on move 7, has left White with a slight weakness on the light squares, thanks to the fact that his d-pawn is fixed on a dark square. Short is therefore happy to exchange off one of White's knights, thus reducing the number of white minor pieces which can defend his light squares.

12 ♗xe5 ♘g6

Black is already a little better in this position. White's bishop is slightly bad, despite the relatively open position, and White's central light squares are weak. Most importantly of all, though, Gurevich must already have been feeling bad about the way things were going. He is an extremely strong player, and will already

have understood that he stands a bit worse. No doubt, he was already regretting the fact that he did not stick to his usual opening repertoire, in which case he would probably at this stage have had a position that was at least equal, if not better, and with which he was very familiar. Once such regrets and doubts creep into one's mind, it becomes progressively more difficult to play one's best.

13 ♗g3 ♘d7 14 ♘d2 ♘f6 15 ♕f3 c6 16 ♕b3 (D)

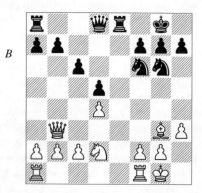

16...♕b6

Again, Short does not let the tournament situation affect his objectivity. Many players would avoid a queen exchange on principle in such a situation, on the vague grounds that simplification reduces their winning chances. Instead, Short appreciates that objectively, Black is happy to see the exchange on b6, because the resulting half-open a-file gives him play on the queenside. Even after the queens come off, there is lots of play left in the position, and Black retains a small advantage.

17 ♕xb6 axb6 18 a3?!

A further clear error, after which White's position becomes very difficult. It is well-known that in such structures, White must prevent his opponent from playing ...b5 and constantly threatening to break in with ...b4. A better move was therefore 18 a4, after which careful defence should enable White to hold without too much trouble. For example, 18...♖e2 can be met by 19 ♖fd1, followed by ♖ac1, ♔f1, ♘ moves and ♖e1, gradually repelling boarders. Although passive, White's position does not contain any real weaknesses, so Black has nothing special to do while White is untangling.

18...♘e4 19 ♘xe4 ♖xe4 20 ♖fd1 b5 (D)

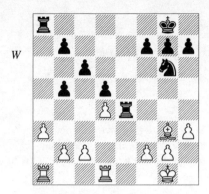

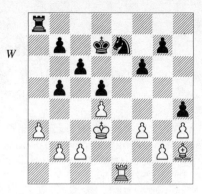

Now Black's advantage is clear. The exchange of the knights has accentuated the advantage of Black's remaining knight over the white bishop on g3, which has trouble finding anything effective to do. Black's rooks are more active than their opposite numbers, and there is the constant threat of ...b4, forcing a penetration down the a-file. White's position is prospectless, and despite stubborn resistance, Gurevich was unable to hold. One can imagine that he must by now have been feeling absolutely wretched.

21 &f1 f6 22 f3 &e6 23 &e1 &f7 24 &xe6 &xe6 25 &e1+

Short suggested that 25 &e1 was a better defence, with the idea of transferring the bishop to b4, where it prevents the breakthrough idea ...b4. In that case, Black would have switched his attack to the other flank, advancing his kingside pawns to squeeze White.

25...&d7 26 &e2

Here, too, we see another example of Gurevich's submissive mentality affecting his play. He is himself a master of such technical positions, and if he had been looking at the position objectively and with a clear head, he would have realized that Black wants to gain space on the kingside, and that White needs to fight against this. He could have done so with Short's suggestion of 26 &h2, planning to answer 26...h5 with 27 g4!. This would have given him better drawing chances than the rather routine text-move, which allows Black to fix the pawn on g2.

26...h5 27 &d3 h4

Now the g2-pawn is a permanent weakness, and the white bishop must always prevent the enemy knight from landing on f4.

28 &h2 &e7! (D)

Regrouping the knight to f5, from where it hits d4, and may later come to d6 and c4. Notice how the knight is able to operate with impunity on the light squares, safe from attack by the enemy bishop – a perfect illustration of the weakness of a lone bishop.

29 &f4 &f5 30 &d2 b6 31 &e2

Short points out that if 31 &b4, trying to prevent ...c5, Black simply plays 31...&c8 32 &e2 c5 33 &c3 and then returns his rook to a8 and thence, a4.

31...c5 32 &e3

32 c3 is no better. Another pawn would go to a dark square, thus worsening White's bishop, and Black would have a pleasant choice between exchanging pawns on d4, when White has an isolated d-pawn, or improving his position still further by ...&d6-c4.

32...b4!

The long-planned breakthrough smashes open the queenside.

33 axb4 c4+ 34 &c3 &d6

Black's pawn sacrifice is only temporary, since White cannot prevent ...&a4 and ...&b5+, winning the b4-pawn.

35 &e1 &a4 36 &d2 &xb4 37 &a1

Gurevich finally tires of passive defence, and seizes the chance to activate his rook. The alternative was 37 &c3 &a4, planning ...b5-b4+, when White's position is extremely difficult to hold.

37...&xb2 38 &a7+ &e6 39 &xg7 b5

Now ...b4-b3 is another threat.

40 &f2

Or 40 &a7 b4 41 &a6 b3! 42 &f4 &xc2+ 43 &d1 &xg2 44 &xd6+ &f5 and the black pawns are too strong.

40...b4 41 &c1 c3 42 &xh4 &f5 0-1

43 &g4 &e3 is curtains. Beautifully played by Short, but Gurevich's play was an object lesson in how **not** to play for a draw.

Game 50
Garry Kasparov – Anatoly Karpov
World Ch match (game 24), Seville 1987
Réti Opening

This game was one of the most dramatic in chess history. After blundering away the previous game of the match, Kasparov trailed by one point going into the 24th and final game. As defending champion, his only way to retain the world championship was to win the last game, thus saving his title by means of a 12-12 draw.

1 c4 e6 2 ♘f3 ♘f6 3 g3 d5 4 b3 *(D)*

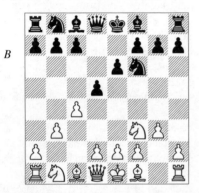

B

The opening needs some comment. Here we have Garry Kasparov, one of the most dynamic attacking players of all time, playing the most important, must-win game of his life, with the white pieces – and inside four moves, he is fianchettoing both bishops! I am sure that everybody watching the game expected to see Kasparov open 1 e4 and try to blow his opponent off the board. What is even more important is that Karpov himself almost certainly expected the same approach, and psychologically, that is what he was prepared for. Certainly, he would face some nervous moments, and would need to find some good defensive moves, but if he did so, he would defuse the attack and soon reach a position where he was safe.

Instead, Kasparov chooses a quiet opening, simply developing his pieces normally, and preparing for a slow manoeuvring middlegame. Objectively, this poses no threat to Black, but it also avoids any early simplification, or any early crisis. Instead, Karpov must just play chess for five hours. The brilliance of Kasparov's psychology lay in precisely this last fact. He understood that the one thing Karpov wanted was to

get the game over with – a short, sharp fight, neutralize the threats, and the world title was his. The very last thing he wanted was to have a long, slow game, where his opponent could maintain the tension over a prolonged period.

4...♗e7 5 ♗g2 0-0 6 0-0 b6 7 ♗b2 ♗b7 8 e3 ♘bd7 9 ♘c3 ♘e4 *(D)*

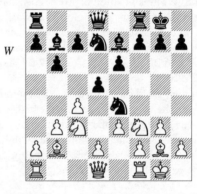

W

10 ♘e2!?
Both sides have developed their pieces in normal fashion, and objectively the position is equal. Black's last move aimed to exchange pieces by ...♘xc3 followed by ...♗f6. Given his must-win situation, Kasparov naturally prefers to avoid that, hence the text-move. His strategy is to keep pieces on the board, and maintain the tension for as long as possible, in the hope that his opponent's nerves will crack at some point.
10...a5
Now 10...♗f6 would be met by 11 d4, avoiding piece exchanges.
11 d3 ♗f6
Now that the pawn has been committed to d3, Karpov seizes the chance to exchange bishops.
12 ♕c2 ♗xb2 13 ♕xb2 ♘d6 14 cxd5 ♗xd5
The alternative recapture 14...exd5!? is also possible, but after 15 d4, Black would be almost

forced positionally to continue with 15...c5, since passive play would leave him standing somewhat worse because of his inactive bishop and White's play along the c-file. After 16 dxc5 bxc5, chances would be about equal, but the hanging pawns on c5 and d5 would require accurate, and active, play from Black. We discussed structures with hanging pawns in some detail in *50ECL*, and made the point that they can be strong when used dynamically, but are often a static target. Given the match situation, Karpov prefers to play quietly and not to have to seek active, dynamic play, and hence, it makes sense to avoid a structure with hanging pawns, whatever its objective merits.

15 d4 c5 16 ♖fd1 *(D)*

16...♖c8?!

The first small inaccuracy. Kasparov recommended 16...c4 as better. It is probably not a coincidence that Karpov's error involves shying away from a change in the pawn-structure. When a player is happy to draw, there is a natural tendency to avoid what appear to be unnecessary commitments. Given the relatively radical nature of many changes in the pawn-structure ("pawns don't move backwards", etc.), such changes will often appear to involve a commitment, which the player may find it psychologically difficult to accept.

17 ♘f4 ♗xf3

A small concession, but now forced because of tactical problems on the d-file. Thus, 17...♗b7? is bad in view of 18 dxc5 ♘xc5 19 ♕e5 ♘ce4 20 ♘h5, when Black must already surrender a pawn by 20...f6. Similarly, it is now too late for 17...c4?! since after 18 ♘xd5 exd5 19 bxc4 dxc4 (19...♘xc4 20 ♕b5 is also better for White, because of the weak d5-pawn) 20 a4!,

Black has a weakness on b6, whilst White's central pawn-majority threatens to advance with e4 and d5.

18 ♗xf3 ♕e7 19 ♖ac1 ♖fd8 20 dxc5 ♘xc5 *(D)*

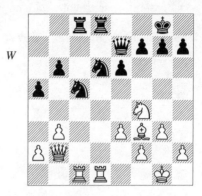

21 b4! axb4

After this exchange, the b6-pawn proves somewhat weaker than a2. However, 21...♘ce4 22 ♖xc8 ♖xc8 23 ♕d4 is also slightly better for White, since 23...e5? fails to 24 ♘d5.

22 ♕xb4 ♕a7 23 a3 ♘f5 24 ♖b1 ♖xd1+ 25 ♖xd1 ♕c7 26 ♘d3 *(D)*

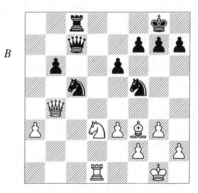

Despite Black's small inaccuracy at move 16, White has only a minuscule advantage, but the most important thing is that he has something with which to play on and torture his opponent. So long as he can keep the a- and b-pawns from being exchanged for one another, an exchange of queens will still leave him slightly better in the ending, because his rook and bishop will prove stronger than Black's rook and knight.

26...h6?!

Kasparov later recommended 26...g6 as a superior way to make *luft* for the king, although it was difficult to see at this stage that such would prove to be the case.

27 ♖c1 ♘e7?!

Again, 27...♘d6 may be slightly better, to prevent White's next move. The pressure, and the gradual onset of time-trouble, starts to tell on Black in this phase of the game.

28 ♕b5 ♘f5 29 a4 ♘d6 30 ♕b1 ♕a7 *(D)*

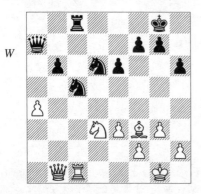

31 ♘e5!

The game is reaching a crisis, and after a couple of small inaccuracies, Karpov must now find a few good moves to prevent his position from fatally deteriorating. Kasparov's slow early play has brought about exactly the situation he wanted, with Black facing his crisis much later in the game than would have been the case, had White forced the pace earlier. With the destination of the world title at stake, one can only imagine how both players' nerves must have been jangling.

31...♘xa4?

This should have been the losing move. The other capture 31...♖xa4? is also bad, because after 32 ♕xb6, Black has real problems untangling his pieces. Kasparov then gives the line 32...♖a3! (the only move) 33 ♖d1 ♘f5 (the alternative 33...♘e8 34 ♖d8 ♖xd8 35 ♕xd8 ♕a1+ 36 ♔g2 ♕xe5 37 ♕xe8+ ♔h7 38 ♕xf7 is also good for White) 34 ♖d8+ ♖xd8 35 ♕xd8+ ♔h7 36 ♘xf7, when White has won a pawn. This line, incidentally, illustrates why Black should have preferred 26...g6, instead of 26...h6?!. In that case, his king would be on g7, defending the f7-pawn, in this last variation.

Instead of capturing on a4, Black should probably prefer 31...♘f5, with an unclear position. However, this is again a hard move to play from a psychological point of view. As

mentioned above, if Black can eliminate the queenside pawns, his drawing chances are enormously increased, since endings with all pawns on one side are notoriously drawish, especially when the defender has knights against bishops. Consequently, it is easy to understand that Karpov was desperate to make the capture on a4 work.

32 ♖xc8+ ♘xc8 *(D)*

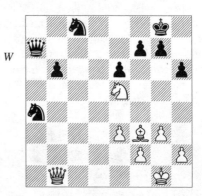

33 ♕d1??

But now it is Kasparov's turn to suffer from nerves. Having induced the decisive error from his opponent, he misses the winning continuation, which was 33 ♕b5!, threatening 34 ♕e8+. 33...♘d6 loses to 34 ♕c6 ♘f5 35 ♕e8+ ♔h7 36 ♘d7, and 33...♔f8 to 34 ♘c6 ♕a8 (other moves drop the a4-knight) 35 ♕d3! (threatening both 36 ♕d8# and 36 ♕h7) 35...g6 36 ♕d4!, when there is no defence to the queen penetrating to h8, as 36...♔g8 drops the queen after 37 ♘e7+. The toughest defence is 33...♔h7! but even then 34 ♘c6 ♕a8 35 ♕d3+! f5 (35...g6 36 ♕d7 ♔g7 37 ♘e5 wins for White) 36 ♕d8 wins, as the threats of ♘e7 or ♗h5 and ♕e8 are decisive.

Kasparov's move looks equally good, since it also threatens both the knight on a4 and a queen penetration to d8, but it allows a defence...

33...♘e7??

...which Karpov misses! He could have held by 33...♘c5! 34 ♕d8+ ♔h7 since after 35 ♕xc8, he can regain the piece by 35...♕a1+ and 36...♕xe5. White can make things a little more difficult for Black with 35 ♔g2, but then 35...f6! 36 ♘c6 ♕d7 holds.

34 ♕d8+ ♔h7 35 ♘xf7

White has regained his pawn and has several positional advantages. The e6-pawn is weak, as are the light squares around the black king, and the fact that queens are on the board allows White to create mating threats. Black's best hope is to exchange queens, even if it means surrendering the b6-pawn, because with all the remaining pawns on one side, he would have good drawing chances in such an ending. However, Kasparov is careful not to allow this.

35...♘g6 36 ♕e8 ♕e7

Forced, since 36...♘c5? 37 ♗h5 ♕a1+ 38 ♔g2 ♕f6 39 h4! wins for White, in view of the threat of 40 ♗xg6+ and 41 h5+.

37 ♕xa4 ♕xf7

Ordinarily, queen and knight cooperate very well together, and are often stronger than queen and bishop, but here, the weaknesses on the light squares around Black's king make the queen-and-bishop pairing especially potent.

38 ♗e4 ♔g8 39 ♕b5

Winning the b6-pawn.

39...♘f8 40 ♕xb6 ♕f6 41 ♕b5 ♕e7 42 ♔g2 g6 43 ♕a5 ♕g7 44 ♕c5 ♕f7 45 h4 *(D)*

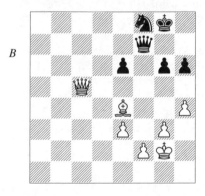

45...h5?

The final mistake, after which the position is definitely lost, thanks to the weakness of g6. 45...♔g7 offered better chances of survival, although the odds are still against Black.

46 ♕c6 ♕e7 47 ♗d3 ♕f7 48 ♕d6 ♔g7 49 e4 ♔g8 50 ♗c4 ♔g7 51 ♕e5+ ♔g8

The minor-piece ending after 51...♕f6 52 ♕xf6+ ♔xf6 53 f4 is also lost for Black, despite the pawns being on the same flank.

52 ♕d6 ♔g7 53 ♗b5 ♔g8 54 ♗c6 ♕a7 55 ♕b4!

Part of White's winning plan is to play e5, to fix further weaknesses in Black's position, but he needs to time it accurately. Thus, the immediate 55 e5? would allow 55...♕a5! 56 ♗e4 ♕e1, when it is still difficult to make progress.

55...♕c7 56 ♕b7! ♕d8 57 e5! *(D)*

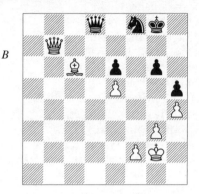

Now White's pieces are more actively placed, the time is ripe for this advance.

57...♕a5

57...♕d3 is answered by 58 ♗e8 ♕f5 59 ♕f3!, when White forces off the queens.

58 ♗e8 ♕c5 59 ♕f7+ ♔h8 60 ♗a4

Now that his queen has penetrated into the heart of Black's position, White only needs to arrange to attack the g6-pawn with the bishop. Black is able to prevent this only temporarily.

60...♕d5+ 61 ♔h2 ♕c5 62 ♗b3 ♕c8 63 ♗d1 ♕c5 64 ♔g2 1-0

At this point, seeing the writing on the wall, Karpov preferred to spare himself further agony, and resigned. If he had played on, Kasparov demonstrated the following winning variation: 64...♕b4 65 ♗f3 ♕c5 66 ♗e4 ♕b4 67 f3! (but not 67 ♗xg6?? ♘xg6 68 ♕xg6 ♕b7+ 69 ♔h2 ♕g2+!!, forcing stalemate, which would be an unfortunate way to lose the world championship!) 67...♕d2+ 68 ♔h3 ♕b4 (or 68...♕h6 69 f4 ♕g7 70 ♕xg7+ ♔xg7 71 ♗c6 and the ending is winning) 69 ♗xg6 ♘xg6 70 ♕xg6 ♕xh4+ 71 ♔g2!, and there is no stalemate.

Index of Players

Numbers refer to pages. When a player's name appears in **bold**, that player had White. Otherwise the FIRST-NAMED PLAYER had White.

ADAMS – Topalov 17
ALBURT – **Browne** 59
ALEXANDER – **Bronstein** 161
ANDERSSON – Seirawan 90
ANDREEV, N.P. – **Sokolsky** 79
ARONIAN – Sokolov, I. 39
BELIAVSKY – **Stanec** 82
BENNETT, T. – Keene 126
BOTVINNIK – **Lilienthal** 131
BRODSKY – **Mamedyarov** 123
BRONSTEIN – Alexander 161; **Dorfman** 120
BROWNE – Alburt 59
CARLSEN – Vescovi 140
CHEPARINOV – Stellwagen 67
CHERNIN – Van der Sterren 87
DJURHUUS – Sargissian 158
DORFMAN – Bronstein 120
EHLVEST – Novik 73
EMMS – **Wells** 20
FISCHER – Uhlmann 116
GELFAND – Short 26
GELLER – **Pilnik** 76
GEORGADZE, T. – **Kuzmin, G.** 55
GHEORGHIU – **Petrosian** 137; Watson, W. 11
GIDDINS – **Johansson, P.** 134
GLIGORIĆ – **Uhlmann** 101
GUREVICH, M. – **Salov** 36; Short 167
HEBDEN – **Hodgson** 8
HODGSON – Hebden 8
HORNER – **Littlewood, J.** 45
HOWELL, D. – Kramnik 104
JOHANSSON, P. – Giddins 134
KARPOV – **Kasparov** 170; **Ribli** 98
KASPAROV – Karpov 170; **Topalov** 23
KEENE – **Bennett, T.** 126
KHALIFMAN – **Sokolov, I.** 84
KOSTENIUK – Nielsen, P.H. 108
KRAMNIK – **Howell, D.** 104; Leko 155; Vaganian 128
KUZMIN, G. – Georgadze, T. 55
L'AMI – Mamedyarov 150
LARSEN – **Miles** 147
LEKO – **Kramnik** 155

LILIENTHAL – Botvinnik 131; Ragozin, V. 31
LITTLEWOOD, J. – Horner 45
MAMEDYAROV – Brodsky 123; **L'Ami** 150
MILES – Larsen 147
NIELSEN, P.H. – **Kosteniuk** 108
NIKOLIĆ – Paunović 94
NOVIK – **Ehlvest** 73
NOVIKOV, I. – **Sveshnikov** 112
NUNN – **Watson, I.** 49
O'KELLY, R. – Penrose 62
PAUNOVIĆ – **Nikolić** 94
PENROSE – **O'Kelly, R.** 62; Tal 52
PETROSIAN – Gheorghiu 137
PILNIK – Geller 76
POMAR – **Ribli** 43
RAGOZIN, V. – **Lilienthal** 31
RIBLI – Karpov 98; Pomar 43
SALOV – Gurevich, M. 36
SARGISSIAN – **Djurhuus** 158
SEIRAWAN – **Andersson** 90
SHORT – **Gelfand** 26; **Gurevich, M.** 167
SNAPE – **Summerscale** 64
SOKOLOV, I. – **Aronian** 39; Khalifman 84
SOKOLSKY – Andreev, N.P. 79
SPASSKY – **Stein** 143
STANEC – Beliavsky 82
STEIN – Spassky 143
STELLWAGEN – **Cheparinov** 67
SUMMERSCALE – Snape 64
SVESHNIKOV – Novikov, I. 112
TAL – **Penrose** 52; **Timman** 70
TIMMAN – Tal 70
TOPALOV – **Adams** 17; Kasparov 23
UHLMANN – **Fischer** 116; Gligorić 101
VAGANIAN – **Kramnik** 128
VAN DER STERREN – **Chernin** 87
VAN WELY – **Vasiukov** 14
VASIUKOV – Van Wely 14
VESCOVI – **Carlsen** 140
WATSON, I. – Nunn 49
WATSON, W. – **Gheorghiu** 11
WELLS – Emms 20

Index of Openings

Numbers refer to pages.

Benko Gambit 55, 59

Bogo-Indian Defence 134

Caro-Kann Defence
Classical Variation 108

Catalan Opening 98

Czech Benoni 62

Dutch Defence
Staunton Gambit 161

English Opening 20
Hedgehog System 90
Reversed Sicilian 87, 137

French Defence
Exchange Variation 167
Winawer Variation 116

King's Indian Attack 45

King's Indian Defence
Averbakh System 101
Classical Variation 64, 67
Gligorić Variation 73
Sämisch Variation 11

King's Indian/Benoni 70

Modern Benoni
♗d3 and ♘ge2 52
Taimanov Attack 49

Modern Defence
Classical Variation 126

Nimzo-Indian Defence
Classical Variation 155
Rubinstein System 36, 82
Sämisch Variation 31

Old Indian Defence 120

Queen's Gambit Declined
Exchange Variation 26
Semi-Slav Defence 84, 94
Slav Defence 39

Queen's Indian Defence
4 ♗f4 147
4 g3 ♗b7 131
Petrosian System 128

Queen's Pawn Opening 123

Réti Opening 43, 170

Ruy Lopez (Spanish)
Berlin Defence 104, 158
Exchange Variation 150
Smyslov Variation 143

Sicilian Defence
2 c3 112
4 ♛xd4 14
Boleslavsky Variation 76
Classical Scheveningen 17
English Attack 23
Taimanov Variation 140

Sokolsky Opening 79

Trompowsky Attack 8

Other Books from Gambit Publications

The Ultimate Chess Puzzle Book
John Emms
A great-value collection of 1001 chess puzzles with solutions. The book begins with some relatively easy positions suitable for novices, and ends with some extremely tough puzzles, which provide a mind-bending challenge even for top-class players. One of Gambit's most popular books.
240 pages, 248 x 172 mm; $24.95 / £16.99

How to Beat Your Dad at Chess
Murray Chandler
This fun tactics manual has been a favourite in clubs and schools. It teaches the 50 Deadly Checkmates – basic attacking patterns that occur repeatedly in games between players of all standards. Each mating motif is carefully and simply explained.
128 pages, 230 x 178 mm, hardback
$14.95 / £9.99

50 Essential Chess Lessons
Steve Giddins
"One of those books I wish I had 30-40 years ago. I would've become a master (if I had taken the time to study it)." – Bob Long, ChessCo
160 pages, 248 x 172 mm; $24.95 / £14.99

Winning Chess Explained
Zenon Franco
This book will improve your all-round chess strength. Topics include: Pawn Sacrifice, the Art of Manoeuvring, the Second Weakness, Permanent vs Temporary Advantages, Regrouping, Denying the Opponent Squares, and the Central Breakthrough.
192 pages, 248 x 172 mm; $26.95 / £15.99

Secrets of Modern Chess Strategy
John Watson
In a profound but thoroughly practical manner, this classic work explores how chess concepts have evolved over the past 70 years. Acclaimed double-winner of the 1999 British Chess Federation and 1999 United States Chess Federation 'Book of the Year' awards.
272 pages, 248 x 172 mm; $24.95 / £19.99

Creative Chess Opening Preparation
Viacheslav Eingorn
Grandmaster Eingorn is an chess opening trend-setter. Here he reveals the methods by which he prepares his openings, and shows the reader how new systems can be pioneered from scratch.
160 pages, 248 x 172 mm; $26.95 / £15.99

How to Play Dynamic Chess
Valeri Beim
"...an incredible work, simply the best I have ever read on this topic. I suspect even some players of the first rank will find something to think about, and the rest of us will have our games adjusted forever" – Don Aldrich, CHESS TODAY
176 pages, 248 x 172 mm; $27.50 / £15.99

Garry Kasparov's Greatest Chess Games, Volume 2
Igor Stohl
The final instalment of Grandmaster Stohl's classic work. The game annotations explain the reasoning behind Kasparov's decisions, and the principles and concepts embodied by his moves.
352 pages, 248 x 172 mm, hardback
$35.00 / £22.50

"John Nunn, Murray Chandler and Graham Burgess deserve a vote of thanks from the chess world for founding Gambit Publishing. Their books are well produced, with attractive covers, high quality paper and a clear layout. More importantly, they are well researched and accurate, utilizing computers to help authors make books which are as free of error as possible." – John Donaldson, International Master

www.gambitbooks.com